Jewish Tradition
and the
Nontraditional Jew

Jewish Tradition
and the
Nontraditional Jew

edited by Jacob J. Schacter

The Orthodox Forum Series
A Project of the Rabbi Isaac Elchanan Theological Seminary
An Affiliate of Yeshiva University

JASON ARONSON INC.
Northvale, New Jersey
London

This book was set in 11 point Goudy by Lind Graphics of Upper Saddle River, New Jersey, and printed by Haddon Craftsmen of Scranton, Pennsylvania.

Library of Congress Cataloging-in-Publication Data

Jewish tradition and the nontraditional jew / editor's introduction
    Jacob J. Schacter.
        p.   cm.
    Includes bibliographical references and index.
    ISBN 0-87668-479-7
    Series ISBN 0-87668-512-2
    1. Orthodox Judaism—Relations—Nontraditional Jews—Congresses.
    2. Jews in rabbinical literature—Congresses. 3. Orthodox Judaism-
    -Germany—History—Congresses.   I. Schacter, Jacob J.
    BM30.J49 1992
    296.8'32—dc20   91-32615

Manufactured in the United States of America. Jason Aronson Inc. offers books and cassettes. For information and catalog write to Jason Aronson Inc., 230 Livingston Street, Northvale, New Jersey 07647.

THE ORTHODOX FORUM

The Orthodox Forum, convened by Dr. Norman Lamm, President of Yeshiva University, meets each year to consider major issues of concern to the Jewish community. Forum participants from throughout the world, including academicians in both Jewish and secular fields, rabbis, *rashei yeshiva*, Jewish educators, and Jewish communal professionals, gather in conference as a think tank to discuss and critique each other's original papers, examining different aspects of a central theme. The purpose of the Forum is to create and disseminate a new and vibrant Torah literature addressing the critical issues facing Jewry today.

THE ORTHODOX FORUM:
Second Conference

May 20–21, 1990, 25–26 *Iyyar* 5750
The Spanish-Portuguese Synagogue, New York City

PARTICIPANTS

Dr. Norman Lamm, Yeshiva University
Rabbi William Altshul, Hebrew Academy of Greater
 Washington
Rabbi Yehuda Amital, Yeshivat Har Etzion, Israel
Rabbi Marc D. Angel, Spanish-Portuguese Synagogue, New York
Prof. David Berger, Brooklyn College and Yeshiva University
Rabbi Saul Berman, Yeshiva University
Dr. Moshe Bernstein, Yeshiva University
Rabbi Yosef Blau, RIETS/Yeshiva University
Dr. Judith Bleich, Touro College
Dr. Jay Braverman, Yeshivah of Flatbush
Dr. Elisheva Carlebach, Queens College
Rabbi Shalom Carmy, Yeshiva University
Rabbi Zevulun Charlop, RIETS/Yeshiva University
Dr. Yaakov Elman, Yeshiva University
Dr. Marvin Fox, Brandeis University
Rabbi Robert S. Hirt, RIETS/Yeshiva University
Dr. Ephraim Kanarfogel, RIETS/Yeshiva University
Dr. Lawrence Kaplan, McGill University
Rabbi Yaakov Neuburger, RIETS/Yeshiva University
Rabbi Nachum L. Rabinovitch, Yeshivat Birkat Moshe, Israel

Rabbi Michael Rosensweig, RIETS/Yeshiva University
Rabbi Yonason Sacks, Yeshiva University High Schools
Dr. Jacob J. Schacter, The Jewish Center, New York
Dr. Alvin Schiff, Board of Jewish Education, New York
Mr. Carmi Schwartz, Council of Jewish Federations
Dr. David Shatz, Yeshiva University
Dr. Moshe Sokol, Touro College
Dr. Haym Soloveitchik, Yeshiva University
Rabbi Moshe D. Tendler, RIETS/Yeshiva University
Dr. Chaim Waxman, Rutgers University, Yeshiva University
Rabbi Mordechai Willig, RIETS/Yeshiva University
Dr. Joel Wolowelsky, Yeshivah of Flatbush High School
Rabbi Walter Wurzburger, Yeshiva University and Congregation
    Shaarey Tefilah, New York

To my parents

Rabbi Herschel and Pnina Schacter

whose devotion to *Ahavat Yisrael*,
in ways both large and small,
has profoundly influenced my life

Contents

Preface

Jacob J. Schacter

One of the central problems facing the contemporary American Jewish community is the progressively deteriorating relationship between the various denominations within Judaism. In claiming that it alone is best equipped to meet the challenges of twentieth-century Jewish life, each one often presents its position with a lack of regard or respect for any alternate point of view. Most problematic is the fact that this deterioration is taking place at a time when the vast majority of American Jews are not formally affiliated with any religious movement at all and are in the process of being lost to the terrible scourges of intermarriage, assimilation, apathy, and indifference.

Orthodox Jews, in particular, face a very difficult dilemma. On the one hand, they are committed to the notion that the *halakhah* is normative and binding not only for themselves but for all Jews. They believe that it is God's will that every member of *kelal Yisrael* observe Jewish law as presented in the Bible and the

Talmud, as codified in the *Shulhan Arukh*, and as applied to contemporary times by authoritative religious decisors or *posekim*. It is this belief in the centrality of *halakhah* and in the absolute requirement to adhere to its dictates that, they believe, sets the Jews apart from the rest of the world, constituting the uniqueness and individuality of this "chosen people" among the community of nations. No deviation from this fundamental commitment on either ideological or practical grounds can be tolerated, they claim, for it would undermine and deny the very essence of a divinely revealed Judaism. Consequently, in the words of the prominent Reform Jewish theologian Eugene Borowitz,

> Theologically, Orthodoxy cannot recognize the teaching of Progressive Judaism as valid. The basic, authoritative Jewish texts of Jewish law clearly classify our modernist re-interpretation of Judaism as our tradition's equivalent of heresy, *apikorsut*. Ideally, it can never be condoned. . . . We cannot ask Orthodoxy to violate its own faith and accept Progressive Judaism, *de jure*, as a fully equivalent, if alternative, interpretation of Judaism.[1]

And if they cannot accept any other interpretation of Judaism as valid, then clearly Orthodox Jews will have serious problems with those Jews who do accept those interpretations as legitimate expressions of Judaism and certainly with those who propagate them as a matter of religious principle and personal prerogative.

Yet, many contemporary Orthodox Jews find it very difficult to accept the practical implications of this position. The classic manner of dealing with an *apikorus*—"one is required to actively destroy them and to bring them down to the nethermost pit"[2]—and the obligation to hate the wicked (*Pesahim* 113b) sound very harsh

---

[1] Eugene B. Borowitz, "Co-existing with Orthodox Jews," *Journal of Reform Judaism* 34:3 (Summer 1987): 55.

[2] Rambam, *Hilkhot Avodah Zarah* 10:1 and the relevant talmudic passages. Cf. Psalms 55:24.

to the ears of many who are unprepared to adopt such a policy toward neighbors, co-workers and, very often, close relatives. In the minds of many Orthodox Jews, a fundamental sense of *ahavat Yisrael*, a basic feeling of closeness toward a fellow Jew *(vu men shlokt a yid tut mir vay)* and a deep rooted fealty toward that mystical unit known as *kelal Yisrael* strongly militate against adopting, in any practical sense, such a strict, exclusionary attitude. R. Yehiel Mikhel Epstein, the nineteenth century author of the *Arukh ha-Shulhan*, enjoyed a warm relationship with one of the *maskilim* of his town. When asked how he could be close to a Jew who commits major violations of the Torah when the tradition mandates that we hate him, he responded, "Yes, it may be that I am obligated by law to hate him, but what can I do? I cannot hate a Jew." When the late first Chief Rabbi of Palestine, R. Avraham Yitzhak Hakohen Kook, was asked how he could love all those secular Jews who violate so much of Torah law, he replied, "Better that I err in engaging in groundless love than in groundless hatred."[3]

But the issue goes beyond mere sentiment. Strong arguments are also made on purely halakhic grounds against the more strict, extreme position. For example, in a famous, oft quoted passage, R. Isaiah Karelitz, known as the Hazon Ish, ruled that the laws of "downing" a heretic no longer apply in a time when God's presence is not directly evident and palpable in the world.[4] And, R. Yisrael Meir Hakohen, known as the Hafetz Hayyim, cited an opinion that the prohibition against hating another Jew (Leviticus 19:17) applies today even to a totally wicked person *("rasha gamur")*. His reasoning is based on the fact that since there is no one in our times who is capable of properly rebuking him, he cannot be held responsible for his actions.[5] While some continue to argue that halakhah today

---

[3]Both of these stories are cited in Aharon Yaakov Greenberg, *Iturei Torah*, vol. 2 (Tel Aviv: Yavneh, 1976), 325.

[4]*Sefer Hazon Ish: Yoreh De'ah* (Bnei Brak, 1962), *Hilkhot Shehitah* 2:16.

[5]R. Yisrael Meir Hakohen, *Sefer Ahavat Hesed* (Warsaw, 1888), 55b, no. 17. This is cited by the Hazon Ish, ibid., 2:28. See also Yisrael Hess, "Le-Mitzvat Ahavat Yisrael bi-Yamenu," *Morashah* 1(1971): 48–49; Moshe

indeed mandates hating other Jews,[6] others find such a conclusion to be indefensible and untenable.[7]

This volume seeks to address this issue from the perspectives of Jewish history, Jewish law *(halakhah)*, and Jewish thought *(hashkafah)*. The first two essays present the historical background to the current situation, clearly demonstrating how the problem we face today is not a new one, and presenting some of the approaches taken in medieval and modern times to deal with it. But the historical reality of Jewish nonobservance differed greatly during these two periods. During the middle ages, nonobservance was clearly an individual phenomenon. To be sure, neglect of various positive and negative commandments could be found in the medieval Jewish community to a greater or lesser extent, but these were only isolated instances in a society which, on the whole, was committed to the observance of Torah law. In Chapter 1, Dr. Ephraim Kanarfogel deals primarily with the neglect of *tefillin*, *tzitzit*, *mezuzah*, the desecration of the Sabbath, sexual promiscuity, and gambling, and attempts to formulate some criteria to account for the difference in the attitude toward such religious deviance in the Ashkenazic and Sephardic communities.

The problem became much more acute with the advent of Enlightenment and Emancipation in the second half of the eighteenth century, and the conscious attack on rabbinic authority and rejection of the binding nature of *halakhah* which developed in their wake. With the rise of the Reform movement at the beginning

Tzuriel, "Ha-Mitzvah shel 'Sinah le-Resha'im,' " *Ha-Maayan* 17:4 (1977): 2; Yaakov Neuman, "Ahavat Yisrael mul Sinat Yisrael," *Shanah bi-Shanah* (1984): 288; Shlomoh Halevi Wahrman, "Hovatenu Kelapei ha-Hilonim bi-Zemanenu," *Ha-Maor* 44:3 (1991): 13.

Both the prohibition against hating Jews and the obligation to rebuke transgressors appear in the same biblical verse (Leviticus 19:17).

[6]See, for example, David Ben-Zion Klein, "Bi-Inyan Mitzvat Sinah le-Resha'im," *Ha-Maayan* 18:1 (1977): 71–73.

[7]See the articles cited in the first section of Nathaniel Helfgot's bibliography at the end of this volume.

of the nineteenth century, deviance from *halakhah* became institutionalized and conceptually justified, and it moved from being a
minor phenomenon on the periphery of Jewish life to becoming the
dominant religious expression of the vast majority of Jews. Those
who still retained their allegiance to traditional Judaism found
themselves vastly outnumbered and they struggled to maintain
their values and beliefs, which included very definite feelings about
the religious posture of *all* Jews, against the onslaught of modernity.
It is one thing to deal with isolated cases of ignorant or religiously
weak individuals within an essentially committed and traditional
community; it is quite another to deal with fully developed ideolo-
gies represented by movements which rejected and claimed to
supplant traditional Judaism. Dr. Judith Bleich traces the range of
Orthodox reactions to the first hundred years of the Reform
movement from the founding of the Hamburg Temple in 1819
through the beginning of the twentieth century.

We decided to dispense with a separate analysis of this issue in
premedieval times because the ancient talmudic categories of *mumar*,
apikorus, *min*, *anus*, *tinok she-nishbah*, and others are relevant today
only to the extent that they have been defined and applied by medieval and modern *posekim*. For the purpose of formulating current
policy, a focus on these two later time periods would be sufficient.

The second half of the volume deals with a number of
practical legal and conceptual issues. Rabbi Yehuda Amital discusses the current obligation of individual Jews and rabbis to
rebuke a coreligionist who is not observant, the halakhic problems
related to *kiruv* (outreach), such as inviting a guest for Shabbat
knowing that he or she will drive a car on that day, and the matter
of permitting a minor infraction in order to prevent the committing
of a greater sin. Dr. Norman Lamm addresses the nature and
parameters of the obligation of *ahavat Yisrael* and analyzes whether
one is ever obligated to hate another Jew or consider him or her to
be outside the fellowship of *kelal Yisrael*. Rabbi Nachum L. Rabinovitch deals with the obligation and implications of *kol Yisrael
arevin zeh ba-zeh* (all Jews are responsible for one another), the

requirement to attract nonobservant Jews to Torah and religious observance, and the place of Sabbath desecrators, if any, in religious ritual, such as *minyan* and *zimmun*. The volume concludes with a useful bibliography of previously published articles on these issues, prepared by Rabbi Nathaniel Helfgot.

It is my pleasant task to express my *hakarat ha-tov* to those who played an important role in the publication of this volume. The papers printed here were first presented at a meeting of the Orthodox Forum, a think tank on issues facing contemporary Orthodoxy convened by Yeshiva University, which took place in New York City in May 1990, and which I chaired. I am pleased to express my thanks to Dr. Norman Lamm, President of Yeshiva University, for his overall support and encouragement of this project; to Rabbi Robert S. Hirt, Vice President for Administration and Professional Education at the Rabbi Isaac Elchanan Theological Seminary, an affiliate of Yeshiva University, for his constant involvement and dedication; and to Mr. Daniel Ehrlich of Yeshiva's Max Stern Division of Communal Services for his very competent technical assistance and helpful staff support.

I would also like to express my personal gratitude to Dr. Joel B. Wolowelsky for his general suggestions as well as his very useful assistance in helping prepare Rabbi Amital's and Rabbi Rabinovitch's original Hebrew papers for translation into English; to Rabbi Michael Berger for providing the first draft of these translations; to Dr. Moshe Sokol and Rabbi Kenneth Hain for their valuable advice; to the other members of the Orthodox Forum Steering Committee for their helpful input; to Arthur Kurzweil, Muriel Jorgensen, and the staff of Jason Aronson Inc. for all their efforts on behalf of this work. They are responsible for the handsomeness of the volume as well as the system of transliteration utilized throughout it.

Finally, my thanks to the scholars whose work we publish here. It was a great pleasure working with these highly capable individuals, all of whom have made significant contributions to contemporary Jewish life.

I hope that this volume will be of great practical benefit to rabbis, educators, and interested laypersons as they struggle with what is surely one of the most vexing and difficult Jewish problems of our time.

In History

1

Rabbinic Attitudes toward Nonobservance in the Medieval Period

Ephraim Kanarfogel

Medieval rabbinic authorities encountered several different modes of nonobservance. Perhaps the most vexing consisted of Jews who were converted, either willingly or forcibly, to Christianity or Islam. Halakhists had to consider the intention and possible intimidation of the apostate, as well as the extent to which he or she upheld Jewish practices and beliefs after conversion. They had to rule on the apostate's status as a Jew in regard to issues ranging from divorce to the status of the wine he touched. In addition, they had to set the conditions for his possible return and to define the posture toward him to be adopted by members of the Jewish community.[1]

---

[1] Obviously, conversion to Islam did not pose precisely the same halakhic problems as did conversion to Christianity. See, for example, J. Katz, "Sheloshah Mishpatim Appologetiyyim be-Gilguleihem," in his *Halakhah ve-Kabbalah* (Jerusalem: Magnes, 1984), 277–90; H. Soloveit-

It would be fair to say that in both Franco-Germany and Spain, medieval halakhists attempted to keep the door wide open for those who wished to return. They stressed the ultimate Jewishness of those who had converted as a result of the Crusades or the threats of violence in late medieval Spain, and eagerly welcomed their repentance. Only those who had willfully abandoned the practice of Judaism, as a result of greed or studied rejection, were considered beyond hope.[2] To be sure, it was necessary to protect the community from individuals or groups who flirted with the possibility of return over a long period of time only to remain entrenched in their apostasy, while wives and families who had remained true to their Jewish faith despaired of their own personal and economic well-being.[3] Nonetheless, medieval rabbinic leadership attempted to smooth the road back as much as possible. The re-adoption of Jewish practices and beliefs was often all that was required to remove any stigma.[4]

---

chik, "Maimonides' Iggeret Ha-Shemad: Law and Rhetoric," *Rabbi Joseph H. Lookstein Memorial Volume*, ed. L. Landman (New York: Ktav, 1980), 281–96, 310–19; and I. Twersky, *Introduction to the Code of Maimonides* (New Haven: Yale University Press, 1980), 452–53.

[2]See J. Katz, "Af al Pi she-Hata Yisrael Hu," *Halakhah ve-Kabbalah*, 255–67, and *idem*, *Exclusiveness and Tolerance* (New York: Schocken, 1961), 67–76; B. Netanyahu, "The Marranos According to the Hebrew Sources of the Fifteenth and Early Sixteenth Centuries," *Proceedings of the American Academy for Jewish Research* 31 (1963): 81–164. A shift in attitude may have occurred in the eighteenth century. See Katz, "Af al Pi she-Hata," 268–69, and cf. H. H. Ben-Sasson, "Musaggim u-Metziut be-Historiyyah ha-Yehudit be-Shilhei Yemei ha-Benayim," *Tarbiz* 29 (1960): 306–08.

[3]See G. Cohen's review of Netanyahu's *The Marranos of Spain from the late XIVth to the Early XVIth Century According to Contemporary Hebrew Sources* (New York, 1966) in *Jewish Social Studies* 29 (1967): 178–81. Cf. H. Soloveitchik (above, n. 1), 305–08.

[4]The nature and content of separate acts of repentance that may also have been required differed between Ashkenaz and Sefarad. See Netanyahu, above, n. 2.

The notion of recognizing a Jew's inherent Jewishness, irrespective of his commitment to *halakhah*, could also be applied to other individuals or groups who were outside the normative medieval Jewish community even if they were not associated with another religion. Maimonides' multifaceted evaluation of Karaism may be understood in this manner. It was necessary for Rambam to point out to his community, in sharp fashion, that which was objectionable about Karaite doctrine. But those Karaites who had been born into the doctrines promulgated by Karaism should not be classified halakhically as dangerous rebels but as *tinokot she-nishbu.*[5] Similarly, several *Rishonim* stressed that even inveterate

---

[5]This represents a plausible resolution of the seemingly contradictory statements concerning the status of Karaites within the Maimonidean corpus. See I. Twersky, *Code of Maimonides,* 84–86; G. Blidstein, "Ha-Gishah la-Kara'im be-Mishnat ha-Rambam," *Tehumin* 8 (1987): 501–10; D. Lasker, "Hashpaat ha-Qara'ut al ha-Rambam," *Sefunot* 20(1991): 145–61. (Professor Lasker was kind enough to provide me with a typescript of his article prior to its publication.) R. Yosef Haviva (*Nimmukei Yosef*) argued that the status of *tinokot she-nishbu* applied only to those who had literally been taken captive and were thus completely unaware of their religious obligations as Jews. In his view, even those Karaites who were simply following what they had been taught ought not be considered *tinokot she-nishbu.* See *Bet Yosef, Yoreh De'ah* 159, s.v. *ule-inyan ha-Kara'im. Shakh, Yoreh De'ah* 159:6, cited additional late medieval and early modern halakhists who concurred with the view of *Nimmukei Yosef.* The implications of this controversy for the modern period were discussed by R. Yaakov Ettlinger (d. 1871) in a well-known responsum on the status of transgressors in his day (*She'elot u-Teshuvot Binyan Tzion ha-Hadashot,* no. 23). R. Ettlinger concluded that the transgressors of his day were not to be compared to the Karaites who, in his opinion, had completely separated themselves from the normative halakhic process even with regard to such basic issues as marriage and divorce and circumcision. For an application of these sources to contemporary Jewry, see K. Auman, "The Halakhic Status of the Non-Observant Jew," *The Annual Volume of Torah Studies of the Council of Young Israel Rabbis in Israel,* ed. E. B. Quint and H. Luban, vol. 2 (Jerusalem, 1988), 31–35.

sinners *(mumarim)* who had not been exposed to proper rebuke or instruction had to be loved and could not be rejected.[6]

The different types of nonobservance in the Middle Ages described thus far would probably characterize or mirror the vast majority of nonobservant Jews today. It would be instructive to study in detail how *Rishonim* dealt with *mumarim*, *meshummadim*, and *tinokot she-nishbu*, both in theory and in practice.[7] A more significant contribution to the contemporary scene could be made, however, by studying topics such as the limits of *ahavat Yisrael* and the requirements of *tokhahah* in medieval rabbinic literature.

Since these areas have been covered in some of the other chapters in this volume,[8] I should like to turn to yet another mode of nonobservance that medieval rabbinic scholarship confronted.

---

[6]See N. Lamm, "Loving and Hating Jews as Halakhic Categories," *Tradition* 24 (1989): 113.

[7]For a thorough survey of medieval rabbinic sources dealing with *mumarim* and *meshummadim*, see Netanyahu above (n. 2). See also *Mafteah ha-She'elot u-Teshuvot shel Hakhmei Sefarad u-Tzefon Afrika*, ed. M. Elon, vol. 1 (Jerusalem: Magnes, 1981), 5, 12–13, 47–48, 63–64, 111, 115, 138–39, 176–79; vol. 2 (Jerusalem: Magnes, 1987), 23–24, 103–09; *Teshuvot u-Pesakim Me'et Hakhmei Ashkenaz ve-Tzarefat*, ed. E. Kupfer (Jerusalem: Mekitze Nirdamim, 1973), 282–97; E. E. Urbach, *Baalei ha-Tosafot* (Jerusalem: Mosad Bialik, 1980), 81–83, 242–44; M. Higger, *Halakhot va-Aggadot* (New York: Devei Rabbanan, 1933), 24–31; B. Rosensweig, *Ashkenazic Jewry in Transition* (Ontario: Laurier University Press, 1975), 26–31; A. Siev, "The Strange Path of an Apostate Jew," *Samuel K. Mirsky Memorial Volume*, ed. G. Churgin (New York: Sura Institute, 1960), 263–70; and the sources cited in *Tehumin* 1 (n. 8), 318. [On the difference between the terms *mumar* and *meshummad* and their use in rabbinic literature, see J. Katz, "Af al Pi she-Hata" (above, n. 2), and S. Zeitlin, "Mummar and Meshumad," *Jewish Quarterly Review* 54 (1963): 84–86.]

[8]See also A. Sherman, "Yahas ha-Halakhah Kelappei Ahenu she-Pershu mi-Derekh ha-Torah ve-ha-Mitzvot," *Tehumin* 1 (1980): 311–18; N. Lamm, "Hokheah Tokhiah et Amitekha," *Gesher* 9 (1985): 170–76; Y. Henkin, "Mutav she-Yihyu Shogegin ve-al Yihyu Mezidin bi-Zeman ha-Zeh," *Tehumin* 2 (1981): 272–80; G. Blidstein (above, n. 5).

This category too has relevance for contemporary religious life. Within the normative Jewish communities of medieval Europe, scholars, simple people, and sinners lived side by side. Rabbinic leaders and theoreticians had to develop strategies for dealing with common religious abuses and malfeasances that appeared within their communities. Rather than presenting a broad survey of these manifestations of nonobservance, I will describe how medieval rabbinic scholars and leaders dealt with patterns of nonobservance in three somewhat diverse areas of *halakhah*. I shall argue that rabbinic attitudes toward nonobservance in the medieval period were shaped, in large measure, by the religious character of the communities that they were dealing with and that they, in turn, helped to inform. The areas to be analyzed are the neglect of *mitzvot aseh* and *lo taaseh*—specifically, *tefillin/tzitzit/mezuzah* and *hilkhot Shabbat*; sexual promiscuity and deviation; and gambling.[9]

NONFEASANCE OF *TEFILLIN, TZITZIT,* AND *MEZUZOT*

The degree of malfeasance concerning *tefillin* varied. Several Ashkenazic sources focused on the fact that people had stopped wearing

---

[9] I have refrained from analyzing rabbinic responses to crimes such as murder and informing, which were committed in both Sefarad and Ashkenaz [see, e.g., H. J. Zimmels, *Ashkenazim and Sephardim* (London: Oxford University Press, 1958), 253; A. A. Neuman, *The Jews in Spain*, vol. 1 (Philadelphia: Jewish Publication Society, 1962), 13, 131–38] since the heinousness of these acts often merited unique punishments. I have likewise not dealt with detached Jewish communities in the late Middle Ages, such as those in Italy and Crete, whose overall level of observance lagged far behind the norm. See, e.g., M. Güdemann, *Ha-Torah ve-ha-Hayyim* (Warsaw: Ahi-Assaf, 1898), 3:186–97; I. Barzilay, *The Italian Enlightenment and the Jews* (New York: E. J. Brill, 1965), 206–09; and M. Benayahu, *R. Eliyahu Kapsali Ish Candia* (Jerusalem: Tel Aviv University, 1983), 42–44, 106–17.

tefillin for the entire day, which had been the preferred practice.[10]
The limiting of *tefillin* to the morning prayer service or slightly
beyond was due mainly to the fear of becoming unclean or the
professed inability of individuals to concentrate properly on the
tefillin for a lengthy period of time. There are, however, other
sources that reflect pervasive, outright neglect (i.e., that *tefillin* were
not being worn at all).[11] In the words of one *Tosafot:* "*Amai samkhu
ha-olam she-lo nahagu le-haniah tefillin?*" ["On what do those who do
not put on phylacteries rely?"][12]

As the passage just cited intimates, Ashkenazic halakhists attempted to mitigate or partially justify even the more severe forms
of neglect. *Tosafot* texts maintained that the problems concerning
tefillin in their day flowed from an inherent weakness in the
fulfillment of this precept that dated back to the talmudic era and
even beyond. Neglect was the "fate" of this precept, whether due to
the genuine need for enhanced bodily cleanliness when wearing
tefillin or simply because of indolence.[13] Moreover, the complexities
and numerous opinions within *hilkhot tefillin* generally, and espe-

---

[10]See *Tosafot Berakhot* 44b, s.v. *ve-livnei maarava; Pesahim* 113b, s.v.
ve-ein; Halakhot Ketanot le-R. Asher b. Yehiel, Hilkhot Tefillin, sec. 27.

[11]*Tosafot, Shabbat* 49a, s.v. *ke-Elisha; Tosafot, Rosh ha-Shanah* 17a, s.v.
karkafta; Shibbolei ha-Leket, ed. S. K. Mirsky (New York: Sura Institute,
1966), 88–89. Cf. N. S. Grünspan, "Le-Korot Mitzvat Tefillin ve-
Haznahatah," *Otzar Ha-Hayyim* 4 (1928): 159–64, and Z. D. Grünburger's
response in *Otzar Ha-Hayyim* 5 (1929): 71–72. There is much evidence
from the Geonic period for the neglect of *tefillin.* Here, too, some sources
reflect outright neglect, to the extent that questioners asked whether it
was *yuhara* to put on *tefillin* altogether, while others described the problem
as one of degree. See *Shibbolei ha-Leket,* 86–87, 91; M. M. Kasher, *Torah
Shelemah* 12:260–62, 265–66; *Otzar ha-Geonim,* ed. B. M. Lewin, *Berakhot,*
30 (no. 87), 41 (nos. 89–90); *Rosh ha-Shanah,* 27 (no. 17), 28 (no. 18), 29 (no.
22). Cf. Shakh, *Hoshen Mishpat* 87:41.

[12]*Tosafot R. Yehudah Sir Leon,* cited in *Teshuvot Maharik* (Venice, 1519),
no. 174.

[13]See above, n. 11.

cially the major controversy between Rashi and Rabbenu Tam (whose views were mutually exclusive), caused some to abandon the *mitzvah* out of ignorance, confusion, or perhaps, concern for *berak-hah le-vattalah*. As *Shibbolei ha-Leket* concludes: *"Mihu ikkar taama delo nahagu velo heheziku bahem [bi-tefillin] ha-olam mishum she-nehleku be-hilkhotehen Rashi ve-Rabbenu Tam. Hilkakh, lo yadinan le-me'ebad ke-hilkheta."* ["The main reason, however, that many do not maintain the precept is due to the halakhic controversies of Rashi and Rabbenu Tam. Thus, they do not know how to properly perform it."][14] Ashkenazic sources offered excuses for the poor performance by some, satisfied that the abuses were understandable and not wholly unexpected. To improve the situation, rabbinic writers stressed the importance of this *mitzvah* in light of its neglect, and issued halakhic compendia or handbooks devoted to it in order to clarify misunderstandings and stimulate proper performance.[15]

A different path was taken, however, by the Tosafist R. Moses of Coucy, author of *Sefer Mitzvot Gadol*. R. Moses preached about the neglect of *tefillin* in Spain, and apparently in Ashkenazic locales as well.[16] He did not offer any justification. Rather, in focused ser-

---

[14]*Shibbolei ha-Leket*, 89. See also Samson b. Eliezer, *Sefer Barukh She'amar* (Warsaw, 1880), 2–3, citing R. Abraham of Sinzheim, a student of R. Meir of Rothenburg; *Sefer Mitzvot Gadol* (Venice, 1546), *aseh* 22 (fol. 104b); R. Barukh of Worms, *Sefer ha-Terumah* (Warsaw, 1897), 110; and *Teshuvot Maharik* (above, n. 12). Cf. *Sefer Hasidim*, ed. J. Wistinetski (Frankfurt, 1924), sec. 1031.

[15]See, e.g., R. Isaac b. Moses, *Sefer Or Zarua*, nos. 531, 594; I. Ta-Shema, "Kavvim le-Ofyah shel Sifrut ha-Halakhah be-Ashkenaz ba-Meot ha-Yod Gimel/Yod Daled," *Alei Sefer* 4 (1977): 24–28, 37–41.

[16]Rabbi Moses of Coucy, *Sefer Mitzvot Gadol, aseh* 3: *"Kakh darashti mitzvah zu be-galuyyot Yisrael le-hokhiah she-kol ehad ve-ehad hayyav bi-tefillin u-ve-mezuzot."* At the end of this passage, R. Moses noted that he was able to convince thousands of Jews in Spain to accept these precepts (as well as *tzitzit*) while preaching there during the year 1236. *"Ve-khen bishe'ar aratzot hayiti ahar kakh ve-nitkablu devarai. . . ."* Other descriptions of the locales in which he preached refer specifically to lands other than

mons and words of rebuke, he forcefully urged the fulfillment of the *mitzvah* in practice. R. Moses' presentations regarding *tefillin* (and *mezuzah* as well) were occasioned by an additional impetus for neglect that was more troubling than those mentioned above. A number of normative and nonnormative commentaries and texts could be read or misunderstood as maintaining that *tefillin* represented a metaphysical concept rather than a ritual requirement. This (mis)reading made an impression in Ashkenaz,[17] but it was far more prevalent in medieval Spain and Provence where the tenets of philosophical rationalism were openly taught. No matter what his source may have been, R. Moses was undoubtedly aware of it.[18]

Other rabbinic figures in Spain also reacted to the neglect of *tefillin.* Another well-known preacher, Rabbenu Yonah of Gerona, stressed the importance of this precept as well as the consequences

---

Spain that were within *galuyyot Edom* (Christian Europe). Moreover, the phrase *galuyyot Yisrael* usually refers to Spain as well as these other communities. See below, n. 62. At least some of the other locales were in northern France or Germany. [Note the use of *eretz Edom* in *aseh* 22.] See E. E. Urbach, *Baalei Ha-Tosafot* 1:466–67; J. Katz, *Ben Yehudim le-Goyim* (Jerusalem: Merkaz Shazar, 1984), 106–07; M. Schloessinger, "Moses b. Jacob of Coucy," *The Jewish Encyclopedia* 9:70; and *Kitvei R. Avraham Epstein*, ed. A. M. Habermann, vol. 1 (Jerusalem: Mossad ha-Rav Kook, 1950), 219–20. Indeed, what we know about the state of observance of *mitzvat tefillin* (and *mezuzah* and *tzitzit*) in Ashkenaz serves to confirm the fact that R. Moses preached there as well.

[17]See the commentary of R. Yosef Bekhor Shor to *Devarim* 6:8, *Bamidbar* 12:8 (and *Vayikra* 17:11); the commentary of Rashbam to *Shemot* 13:9; *She'elot u-Teshuvot Maharam b. Barukh* (Prague, 1895), no. 649; E. E. Urbach, *Baalei ha-Tosafot* 1:135–36; S. W. Baron, *A Social and Religious History of the Jews*, vol. 6 (New York: Columbia University Press, 1958), 295–96; S. Kamin, "Ha-Pulmus Neged ha-Allegoriyyah be-Ferusho shel R. Yosef Bekhor Shor," *Mehkerei Yerushalayim be-Mahshevet Yisrael* 3 (1983–84): 367–92 and below, n. 33.

[18]See Y. Gilat, "Shetei Bakkashot le-R. Moshe mi-Coucy," *Tarbiz* 38 (1959): 55; and below, nn. 21–23.

of its neglect, and suggested that individuals press each other to fulfill it.[19] Spanish kabbalistic works with an eye toward socioreligious critique, such as the *Raaya Mehemna*, identified *ammei ha-aretz* as "wicked people, unmarked by symbols of purity, who do not have *tefillin* on their head and arm. . . ."[20] *Sefer ha-Rimmon* censured those who suggested that it was more effective to verbally remember the Creator than to wear *tefillin*.[21]

Spanish and Provençal sources noted that the custom to place ashes on the bridegroom's head, in the place which normally was the site of the *tefillin shel rosh*, had been abandoned in their areas due to the fact that many did not wear *tefillin*.[22] Yosef ben Zabara described at least one region in Provence in which *tefillin* and *mezuzot* were totally absent. In their place, the populace apparently substituted some form of divination that allegedly guided their actions.[23]

---

[19]See A. T. Shrock, *Rabbi Jonah ben Abraham of Gerona* (London: Edward Goldstein, 1948), 129.

[20]See the citations in Y. Tishby, *Mishnat ha-Zohar*, vol. 2 (Jerusalem: Mossad Bialik, 1961), 685–86.

[21]*The Book of the Pomegranate* (Moses De Leon's *Sefer ha-Rimmon*), ed. E. Wolfson (Atlanta: Scholars Press, 1988), 390–92. See also the passages from the writings of R. Yaakov bar Sheshet collected in B. Dinur, *Yisrael ba-Golah* 2:4, 284–85, and Dinur's note, 413 n. 6; Y. Baer, *A History of the Jews in Christian Spain*, vol. 1 (Philadelphia: Jewish Publication Society, 1961), 241.

[22]See *Sefer Ha-Mehktam* in *Ginzei Rishonim le-Massekhet Taanit*, ed. M. Hershler (Jerusalem, 1963), 278–79; *Sefer Avudraham ha-Shalem*, 361–62; Menahem Ibn Zerah, *Tzedah la-Derekh* 3:2:1; *Bet Yosef* to *Even ha-Ezer* 65, s.v. *uve-tokh ha-simhah*. See also Bahya b. Asher, *Kad ha-Kemah* in *Kitvei Rabbenu Bahya*, ed. C. Chavel (Jerusalem, 1970), 444–45; *She'elot u-Teshuvot Maharam b. Barukh* (Lemberg, 1860), no. 223; and *Sefer ha-Eshkol*, ed. A. Auerbach, 2:90.

[23]See Yosef b. Zabara, *Sefer Shaashuim*, ed. I. Davidson (Berlin, 1925), 142. See also Jacob of Marvège, *She'elot u-Teshuvot min ha-Shamayim*, ed. R. Margoliyot (Jerusalem: Mossad ha-Rav Kook), no. 26, 63–64 [on the Provencal origin of the author, see now I. Ta-Shema, "She'elot u-Teshuvot

Justifications were also offered by Ashkenazic halakhists for the many who did not don *tzitzit*. In response to a query from his son-in-law, R. Uri (*"Mai shena de-mekillin bah rov Yisrael she-ein mit'atfin bah bekhol yom"*), Raban noted that *tzitzit* were required only if one wore a four-cornered garment.[24] Tosafists recommended that one purposely wear a four-cornered garment (*tallit*), which would afford the wearer the opportunity to fulfill the precept of *tzitzit*.[25] It was apparent, however, that not everyone could or did purchase a *tallit*. Indeed, *Tosafot* formulations supported the Ashkenazic burial custom in which the *tallit* that the deceased was wrapped in had its *tzitzit* invalidated or removed. In their view, burying someone who had never fulfilled the precept of *tzitzit* during his lifetime constituted *lo'eg la-rash*, just as burying someone in invalid *tzitzit* had been considered *lo'eg la-rash* in the talmudic period.[26]

The absence of *tzitzit* in their day was attributed by some *Tosafot* texts to a change in clothing style. Four-cornered garments were no longer part of one's usual dress, as they were assumed to have been

---

min ha-Shamayim: Ha-Kovetz ve-Tosfotav," *Tarbiz* 57 (1988): 56–63]; Reuben b. Hayyim, *Sefer ha-Tamid*, ed. B. Toledano (*Otzar ha-Hayyim* 11, 1935), 10; *Sefer ha-Minhagot le-R. Asher b. Sha'ul mi-Lunel* in *Sifran shel Rishonim*, ed. S. Assaf (Jerusalem: Mekitzei Nirdamim, 1935), 129; and R. Menahem ha-Meiri, *Kiryat Sefer*, ed. M. Hershler (Jerusalem: Ha-Mesorah, 1956), author's introduction, 2. Cf. I. Twersky, *Rabad of Posquières* (Philadelphia: Jewish Publication Society, 1980), 23–24; C. Horowitz, *The Jewish Sermon in 14th Century Spain: The Derashot of R. Joshua Ibn Shu'eib* (Cambridge, MA: Harvard University Press, 1989), 11–14.

[24]*Sefer Raban*, ed. S. Z. Ehrenreich, sec. 40 (fol. 30c).

[25]*Tosafot R. Yehudah mi-Paris le-Massekhet Avodah Zarah (Shittat ha-Kadmonim al Massekhet Avodah Zarah)*, ed. M. Y. Blau (New York: Deutsch, 1969), 313; *Tosafot Pesahim* 113b, s.v. *ve-ein; Sefer Mitzvot Gadol*, aseh 26; *Perush R. Asher b. Yehiel le-Moed Katan* 3:80. Cf. my "The Aliyah of 'Three Hundred Rabbis': Tosafist Attitudes Toward Settling in the Land of Israel," *Jewish Quarterly Review* 76 (1986): 214–15.

[26]See, e.g., *Tosafot Berakhot* 18a, s.v. *le-mahar; Shabbat* 32b, s.v. *ba-avon tzitzit; Baba Batra* 74a, s.v. *piskei hada karna; Avodah Zarah* 65b, s.v. *aval osin oto; Niddah* 61b, s.v. *aval osin otam*.

in the talmudic period.[27] Other texts, however, identified the nonfeasance with religious laxity.[28] A formulation from the mid-thirteenth century asked, "So what if they will be embarrassed [at the time of burial]? They have denigrated the precept of *tzitzit* in their lifetime."[29] In any event, burial in a valid *tallit* was reserved only for singular scholars, thereby sparing those who did not wear *tzitzit* from the problem of *lo'eg la-rash.*[30]

---

[27]*Tosafot R. Yehudah mi-Paris* (above, n. 25); *Tosafot Berakhot, Shabbat, Baba Batra* in the above note; *Tosafot, Arakhin* 2b, s.v. *ha-kol hayyavin be-tzitzit.*

[28]*Tosafot Avodah Zarah, Niddah* (above, n. 26).

[29]*Perush R. Asher b. Yehiel* (above, n. 25); *Sefer Or Zarua, Hilkhot Avelut,* sec. 421 (fol. 86a). Cf. *Tosafot, Arakhin* (above, n. 27), and R. Meir b. Barukh mi-Rothenburg, *Teshuvot Pesakim u-Minhagim,* ed. I. Z. Kahana, vol. 3 (Jerusalem: Mossad ha-Rav Kook 1963), no. 7.

[30]See E. E. Urbach, *Baalei ha-Tosafot* 1:271. The distinctive *tallitot,* or fringed garments, worn by the German Pietists all day (in addition to their *tefillin*) were probably intended, among other reasons, to visibly remind the Ashkenazic communities of the importance of *tzitzit.* Cf. H. Soloveitchik, "Three Themes in the Sefer Hasidim," *AJS Review* 1 (1976): 329; I. Marcus, *Piety and Society* (Leiden: E. J. Brill, 1981), 98–99. It is possible that the *tallit katan,* which received approbation in Ashkenazic rabbinic literature of the late thirteenth century, was intended to address the *tzitzit* problem. See *Teshuvot R. Hayyim Or Zarua* (Leipzig, 1860), no. 4, and the practices of R. Meir of Rothenburg recorded in *Sefer ha-Agur,* ed. M. Hershler (Jerusalem: Pe'er, 1960), 21, secs. 28–29. Cf. *Sefer Mordekhai, Halakhot Ketanot,* sec. 943, *Sefer Or Zarua* (above, n. 29), and *Sefer ha-Agur,* sec. 26.

In the fifteenth century, however, those who wore the *tallit katan* outside or over their garments were considered to be exhibiting *yuhara.* See *Teshuvot R. Israel Bruna,* no. 96, and cf. *Magen Avraham, Orah Hayyim* 8:13. Interestingly, R. Meir of Rothenburg's student, and possibly R. Meir himself, was prepared to allow women to wear *tzitzit* (a *tallit?*) and pronounce the blessing over them. Maharil, however, considered this *yuhara.* See the sources and discussion in Y. Dinari, *Hakhmei Ashkenaz bi-Shilhei Yemei ha-Benayim* (Jerusalem: Mosad Bialik, 1984), 32–33. See also 215–16; cf. *Semag, aseh* 26.

Regarding the neglect of *mezuzot*, the rabbinic posture even in Ashkenaz tended more toward deep concern and less toward proposing possible justifications. Rabbenu Tam noted that "less than ten years have passed since there were no *mezuzot* in our entire realm."[31] R. Meir of Rothenburg added that "had they known how salutary *mezuzah* is for them, perhaps they would not have transgressed."[32] Perhaps the allegorical interpretation of *mezuzah* had gained currency in Ashkenaz.[33] Nevertheless, Maharam implicitly (and Maharil explicitly) suggested that questions and halakhic debates about which rooms and structures required *mezuzot* may have again played a role in the absence of *mezuzot* in Ashkenaz.[34]

NONOBSERVANCE OF THE SABBATH

Outright desecration of the Sabbath was not tolerated within any medieval Jewish community. Transgression of a *mitzvat lo taaseh*, and a severe one at that, could not be viewed in the same manner as the neglect of a *mitzvat aseh*. A comprehensive comparison of Sabbath observance is beyond the scope of this study. Nonetheless, we can readily discern a significant policy difference between Ashkenaz and Sefarad in regard to the violation of rabbinic or other lesser prohibitions on the Sabbath that were usually related to personal or business needs. Rabbenu Gershom was asked about the appropriate punishment for one who agreed upon the price of a horse and also took possession of it on *Shabbat*. He ruled that the appropriate punishment was lashes. In addition, if the place where

---

[31]R. Tam, cited in *She'elot u-Teshuvot R. Meir mi-Rothenburg* (Cremona, 1557), no. 108.

[32]Ibid. Cf. E. E. Urbach, *Baalei ha-Tosafot* 1:82.

[33]Cf. *Sefer Maharil* (reprinted New York, 1973), *Likkutim* (fol. 86b); Y. Y. Yuval, *Hakhamim be-Doram* (Jerusalem: Magnes, 1989), 317–18; *Sefer Mitzvot Katan*, sec. 154, and *Haggahot R. Peretz*, ad loc.; A. Ravitzky, *Al Daat ha-Makom* (Jerusalem: Keter, 1991), 38–39.

[34]See Maharam (above, n. 31) and *Teshuvot Maharil*, no. 94. Cf. Dinari, *Hakhmei Ashkenaz*, op. cit., 32, 217; I. Ta-Shema (above, n. 15).

this occurred was felt to be lax in regard to Sabbath observance, the rabbinical court should exercise its right to give additional lashes or punishments *(bet din makkin ve-onshin shelo min ha-Torah . . . laasot seyag la-Torah).*[35]

R. Isaac Or Zarua witnessed Rabiah administering lashes to those who ate bread that was baked by a non-Jew on the Sabbath, even though there was some debate in medieval Ashkenaz about what food a non-Jew could prepare for a Jew.[36] An Ashkenazic responsum from the eleventh century recorded the case of a boat with Jews on it that landed in a particular locale on the Sabbath. The local Jews boarded the boat and ate from the food of the Jews on the boat that had obviously been brought from afar on the Sabbath. Unnamed legal decisors forbade this action "but did not administer lashes since it was unintentional *(shogegin hayu)."* Had the transgression been purposeful, it would not have been more than an *issur shevut,* which apparently would have warranted lashes nevertheless.[37]

Shibbolei ha-Leket records the case of merchants whose wagon had broken down outside a town on *erev Shabbat.*[38] Their goods were being transported by hired non-Jewish workers as well as by Jews, and most of them reached the town before the Sabbath. The owners remained with the broken wagon until it was fixed (by non-Jews?), arriving in the community when the *kahal* was already leaving the synagogue on the Sabbath eve. None of the community members extended even a word of greeting. The merchants were not permitted to enter the synagogue the next morning, lest others sense that their actions were appropriate and be led to violate the Sabbath willfully. On Sunday, the community (communal court)

---

[35]*Teshuvot Rabbenu Gershom Me'or Ha-Golah,* ed. S. Eidelberg (New York: Yeshiva University, 1955), no. 9, 63–64.

[36]*Sefer Or Zarua,* sec. 358 (150, end). See also below, n. 42; cf. *Otzar ha-Geonim, Shabbat,* 114–15.

[37]See *Siddur Hasidei Ashkenaz,* ed. M. Hershler (Jerusalem: Hemed, 1972), 257–58, and n. 1; and E. Kupfer, *Teshuvot u-Pesakim,* 112–13.

[38]*Shibbolei ha-Leket,* ed. S. K. Mirsky, sec. 60, 276–77.

rendered its judgment, which included lashes and a fifty-day period of fasts, in addition to heavy charity donations. A second wave of fasting, for three days a month for an entire year, was also imposed. The text concludes that "if, God forbid, this had been done purposefully," they would have been even more stringent and imposed additional restrictions, including a severe ban for thirty days.[39]

Geonic literature mandated corporal punishment for *hillul Shabbat*, even in regard to *dinim de-rabbanan*.[40] This approach, however, was adopted only in Ashkenaz.[41] While lashes were administered in Spain for a number of serious crimes, there is no report of lashes for any form of *hillul Shabbat*.[42] Even more surprising is the fact that

---

[39]The twelfth-century Tosafist R. Hayyim Kohen called upon communal religious leaders *(shoftei Yisrael)* to be more aggressive in curtailing violations that involved *amirah la-akkum*. See J. Katz, *Goy shel Shabbat*, 55.

[40]See the text in S. Assaf, *Ha-Onshin Aharei Hatimat ha-Talmud* (Jerusalem: Ha-Poel Ha-Tzair, 1922), nos. 20, 26, 34. See also J. Mann, "The Responsa of the Babylonian Geonim as a Source of Jewish History," *Jewish Quarterly Review* 10 (1919–20): 342–45, 354–55.

[41]Ashkenazic sources openly referred to Geonic precedent in this matter. See *Shibbolei ha-Leket* (above, n. 38), 276; *Siddur Hasidei Ashkenaz*, 269, sec. 33. Cf. *She'elot u-Teshuvot R. Yaakov Weil* (reprinted Jerusalem, 1959), *Dinim va-Halakhot*, sec. 58.

[42]S. Assaf records instances of *malkot* being administered for various crimes in Sefarad (*Ha-Onshin, op. cit.*, 61–63, 70–71), but none were for cases of *hillul Shabbat*. See also *Mafteah ha-She'elot u-Teshuvot shel Hakhmei Sefarad* (above, n. 7) 1:166–67; 2:84–85, 104–05. Cf. Judah b. Barzillai, *Sefer ha-Ittim* (Cracow, 1903), sec. 30, 46–47. For the more restrained reaction in Spain to cases similar to that of Rabiah (above, n. 36), see Rashba, *Responsa* 1:709, 808. There is evidence for *issurei shevut* being punished in Spain by monetary fine. See Y. Baer, *History of the Jews in Christian Spain* 1:234–35. [On severe abuses of Sabbath observance in medieval Spain, see Shrock, *Rabbi Jonah*, 126–27; C. Horowitz, *The Jewish Sermon in 14th Century Spain*, 47–48; Judah b. Asher, *Zikhron Yehudah* (Berlin, 1846), no. 91 (fol. 44a–b).] Of course, as J. Katz has noted [*Goy shel Shabbat*, 56], not all Tosafists would have agreed with the position taken by Rabiah. What

Ashkenazic halakhists, who proposed suggestions for circum-venting certain rabbinic prohibitions, responded so harshly when an *issur de-rabbanan* was violated. Spanish halakhists, on the other hand, were less creative in terms of *heterim*, but also less vigorous in the punishment of deviations.[43]

SEXUAL PROMISCUITY

Sexual promiscuity and even adultery were never absent from any region in the medieval Jewish world. The rabbinic reactions in Ashkenaz and Sefarad, however, reflected different patterns of abuse. Jewish men commonly kept Jewish and non-Jewish concu-bines in Moslem Spain and later in Christian Spain.[44] The chal-lenges that these relationships posed to the rabbinic leadership were complex. Prolonged affairs, even with Gentile women, were reli-giously and morally reprehensible. At the same time, the wide-spread nature of these relationships, and the presence of even more

---

is significant is that Rabiah resorted to lashes where he felt they were necessary, based on an established tradition in Ashkenaz to administer lashes even for minor Sabbath violations.

[43]All of the attempts to reconcile halakhic guidelines with actual practices in medieval Europe that were analyzed by Prof. Katz in his *Goy shel Shabbat* emanated from Ashkenaz. See *Goy shel Shabbat*, 36, 167–72, 175–80. This pattern was also noted by Prof. Katz in regard to setting the time for *tefillat maariv*. See his "Maariv bi-Zemano u-Shelo bi-Zemano – Dugma le-Zikah ben Minhag, Halakhah, ve-Hevrah," *Zion* 35 (1970): 35–60. In regard to pawnbroking, see H. Soloveitchik, *Halakhah, Kalkalah ve-Dimmui Atzmi* (Jerusalem: Magnes, 1985), 111–14, 118–19. See also his "Religious Law and Change: The Medieval Jewish Example," *AJS Review* 12 (1987): 205–22.

[44]Perhaps due to their proliferation, Jewish and non-Jewish *pilagshim* were sometimes referred to interchangeably in medieval Sefardic rabbinic literature, despite the different halakhic problems engendered by each type. See, e.g., M. A. Friedman, *Ribbui Nashim be-Yisrael* (Jerusalem: Tel Aviv University, 1986), 296–98, and below, n. 50.

objectionable possibilities (i.e., relations with married Jewish women) also had to be considered.

R. Moses of Coucy preached at length in Spain during 1236 about the sinfulness of sexual relations with Gentile women. His audiences responded by "sending away many women *(hotzi'u nashim rabbot).*"[45] Rashba roundly condemned the actions of one man who had bought a maidservant to live with him and his Jewish wife following the birth of their daughter. After the maid conceived, the husband had her converted (as a *shifhah kenaanit*), and subsequently had yet another child with her, all to the chagrin and humiliation of his first wife and child. Rashba recommended to his questioner, a communal (rabbinic) leader, that the community in some way limit this practice and reconcile the husband with the first wife, lest others begin to deal flippantly with Jewish women.[46]

A *herem* was issued in Toledo in 1281 against sexual promiscuity in general, and the keeping of non-Jewish concubines in particular. Those who did not abide by the ban were threatened by R. Todros ben Yosef ha-Levi Abulafia with severe punishment.[47] Nonetheless, many who had vowed to honor the ban could not restrain themselves and either openly flouted the ban or attempted to circumvent it. Rashba advised the rabbinical leadership in Toledo to proceed cautiously and gradually in eliminating communal vices. "Patience and consensus will cause the masses to return to the

---

[45]*Sefer Mitzvot Gadol, lo taaseh* 112 (end). See also the letter of Ramban to his son concerning non-Jewish women, below, n. 54.

[46]Rashba, *Responsa* 1:1205. See S. Z. Havlin (below, n. 50), 237–40.

[47]See *Zikhron Yehudah*, no. 91 (esp. fol. 45a–b); H. Schirmann, *Ha-Shirah ha-Ivrit bi-Sefarad u-vi-Provence* 2 (Jerusalem: Mosad Bialik, 1960): 433–35; Y. Baer, "Todros b. Yehudah ha-Levi u-Zemano," *Zion* 2 (1937): 33–44; *idem, History of the Jews in Christian Spain* 1:257–61; M. Oron, "Derashato shel R. Todros b. Yosef ha-Levi Abulafia le-Tikkun ha-Middot ve-ha-Mussar," *Daat* 11 (1983): 47–51; Y. T. Assis, "Sexual Behavior in Medieval Hispano-Jewish Society," *Jewish History: Essays in Honor of Ch. Abramsky*, ed. A. Rapoport-Albeck and S. T. Zipperstein (London: Halban, 1988), 38–40.

proper path." For individuals, however, whose evil nature was well known, and who persisted in flouting the law, all forms of corporal punishment were to be considered.[48]

Specifically in regard to concubinage, Rashba was asked to deal with the situation of one man who had acquired a Moslem concubine and had then converted her to Judaism and married her without giving her a *ketubah*. He claimed that he was exempt from the *herem*, which required the sending away of Moslem concubines (as well as single Jewish sexual partners) in the absence of a valid marriage *with ketubah*, because he was now legally married to this woman and had, in any event, announced in the presence of witnesses that he did not accept the *herem*.

Rashba responded that this individual was clearly in violation of the Toledo *herem*, which was promulgated to promote Torah observance and eliminate sinful behavior. He had no right to exclude himself unilaterally from such a *herem*. Inter alia, however, Rashba noted that while the behavior of the individual in converting and marrying the woman could not have been sanctioned a priori, she could have remained with him as a *pilegesh* had it not been for the Toledo *herem*.[49] Given the gravity of the situation, and his sense that more moderate means had to be found to persuade people to change, Rashba considered a bona fide *pilegesh* relationship preferable to cohabitation with a non-Jewish woman and would have been willing to allow this relationship.[50]

---

[48]Rashba, *Responsa* 5:238. Cf. *Zikhron Yehudah*, no. 63.

[49]Rashba, *Responsa* 5:242.

[50]Rashba's major concern in this case, as in the responsum discussed above (n. 46), was how the presence and treatment of a *pilegesh* might negatively affect the structure and integrity of the family. The *pilegesh* relationship per se was never criticized. In responsum 4:314, however, Rashba writes, "I do not wish to show that it is permitted to marry a Jewish girl as a *pilegesh*, especially over and above his lawfully married Jewish wife." Perhaps the backing away from *pilegesh* in this situation was due to the fact that the husband in question had made a Jewess by birth (as opposed to a Moslem woman) into a *pilegesh* in order to damage his

There can be little doubt that these kinds of considerations were a factor in the famous responsum of Ramban on the applicability and permissibility of *pilagshut*. In writing to Rabbenu Yonah, Ramban held that *pilagshut* could be sanctioned within Jewish society at large, provided that the halakhic conventions designed to insure that the relationship would not be a promiscuous one (e.g., that she be *meyuhedet lo*) were observed. At the very end of his responsum, however, Ramban adds a postscript: "And you, our teacher may God keep you, in your locale warn them from [taking a] *pilegesh* — because if they know that it is permitted, they will act wantonly and have relations with them [even] when they are in a state of *niddut*."[51]

This responsum has been understood by some to mean that Ramban approved of *pilagshut* in theory only.[52] Others have argued that the content of the body of the responsum strongly suggests

---

relationship with his wife. Given these particular circumstances, *pilagshut* became an unacceptable option. This responsum also cites Rambam's negative view of *pilagshut*, which is not found in any of Rashba's other responsa on this topic. The heavy reliance upon Rambam alone in formulating the ruling, as well as other stylistic anomalies, has led S. Z. Havlin to question the attribution of this responsum to Rashba. As we have seen, Havlin's skepticism is rewarded if the contents of the other responsa of Rashba concerning *pilagshut* are taken into account. See S. Z. Havlin, "Takkanot Rabbenu Gershom Me'or ha-Golah be-Inyanei Ishut bi-Tehumei Sefarad u-Provence," *Shenaton ha-Mishpat ha-Ivri* 2 (1975): 209, 212, 237. Cf. Y. Baer, *History of the Jews in Christian Spain* 1:254–56 (and 434–36, n. 13) and E. G. Ellinson, *Nissu'in shelo ke-Dat Moshe ve-Yisrael* (Tel Aviv, 1975), 55–57. See also Rashba, *Responsa* 1:610, 628, 1187, 1249–50.

[51]*Teshuvot ha-Rashba ha-Meyuhasot la-Ramban*, no. 284. The text is annotated in *Kitvei ha-Ramban*, ed. C. Chavel, 1:381–82. Rabbenu Yonah was opposed to concubinage. See his *Shaarei Teshuvah* 3:94–95, 131–33 (reprinted Bnei Brak, 1970), 193–95, 212–14.

[52]See L. M. Epstein, *Marriage Laws in the Bible and Talmud* (Cambridge, MA: Harvard University Press, 1942), 75–76; Y. Baer, *History of the Jews in Christian Spain* 1:436, n. 14; Neuman, *The Jews in Spain* 2:40–41.

that the postscript did not issue from Ramban's pen.[53] In light of the common attitudes toward selecting sexual partners in medieval Spain, I believe that Ramban should be included among those who were prepared to accept properly monitored *pilagshut* as an alternative to random promiscuity. He did not want it to be suggested publicly because of the pitfalls that were inherent in it, but he made it available nevertheless, either to cover those who had already gotten involved or to accommodate those who were involved in less halakhically acceptable relationships. It must be recalled that Ramban felt it necessary to warn his son, who was at the Castilian court, of the grave sins incurred by engaging in sexual relations with non-Jewish women.[54]

Nahmanides' position becomes clearer if we compare his formulation with a responsum of R. Asher b. Yehiel. Rosh was asked if the family of a man who was having relations with a single Jewish woman, a servant in their home, may demand that the girl be ejected since the fact that she is his *pilegesh* is an embarrassment to them. Rosh responded that the rabbinical court should force him to remove her from the home since "it is well-known that she is embarrassed to immerse [herself] and he is thereby having relations with a *niddah*."[55] Rosh is much more strident than Ramban in expressing his concern about the possible violation of *hilkhot niddah*, but that may perhaps be explained by the fact that he was

<hr>

[53]See Ellinson, *Nissu'in shelo ke-Dat*, 72–79; R. Yaakov Emden, *She'elat Yavetz*, vol. 2, no. 15. See also the responsum of Ramban in *Sifran shel Rishonim*, ed. S. Assaf, 56, no. 1.

[54]See *Kitvei ha-Ramban*, 369–70. See also *Zohar* 2:3a–b (and Y. Baer, *History of the Jews in Christian Spain*, 437 n. 19); *Zohar* 2:87b; *Raaya Mehmna* 4:124b–125a; C. Horowitz, *The Jewish Sermon in 14th Century Spain*, 45–47.

[55]*She'elot u-Teshuvot le-R. Asher b. Yehiel* (reprinted Jerusalem, 1971), 32:13. The questioner had noted that "in this land [= Spain], men were often alone [*le-hityahed*] with single women [who served] in their homes." Cf. *Teshuvot ha-Rosh* 32:16, 54:8; *Teshuvot ha-Ritva*, ed. Y. Kafah (Jerusalem: Mossad ha-Rav Kook, 1959), no. 68.

responding to a specific case in which a disruption in the lives of the family members was in fact occurring. Even Rosh leaves open, albeit to a lesser extent than Ramban, the possibility that if the laws of *niddah* were observed, the *pilegesh* option could be considered.[56] R. Nissim Gerondi also countenanced *pilagshut*.[57]

As the formulations of Ran, Rashba, and Ramban indicate, the fact that a *pilegesh* was required to have the status of *meyuhedet lo* made this option preferable to the alternatives, since the possibilities of more objectionable sexual unions were thereby diminished. This notion was found most explicitly in the writings of R. Menahem Ibn Zerah who, noting that "many people in this land [Spain] take concubines," openly approved of these relationships and sought to insure that they would, in fact, minimize promiscuity.[58]

---

[56]Cf. *Teshuvot ha-Rosh* 36:1; and Ellinson, *Nissu'in shelo ke-Dat*, 68. Neuman's analysis of the opposing views of Rashba and Rosh regarding the overall level of morality in Spanish Jewish society (in his *The Jews in Spain* 2:3–11), could perhaps be supported by the difference in their positions concerning *pilegesh*. Neuman's hypothesis, that their views were affected most heavily by their personalities and the regions in which they lived, strikes me as artificial.

[57]*She'elot u-Teshuvot Rabbenu Nissim b. Reuben Gerondi*, ed. L. Feldman (Jerusalem: Moznaim, 1984), 306–07, no. 68.

[58]*Tzedah la-Derekh* 3:1:2 (reprinted Jerusalem, 1977), 136. There was a high incidence of *pilagshut*, sexual relations with maidservants, and other problems associated with *bo'alei niddot* throughout the Sefardic/Moslem world. See M. A. Friedman, *Ribbui Nashim be-Yisrael*, 291–339, 352–54; "Social Realities in Egypt and Maimonides' Rulings on Family Law," *Maimonides as Codifier of Jewish Law*, ed. N. Rakover (Jerusalem: Library of Jewish Law, 1987), 225–36; and "Harhakat ha-Niddah ve-ha-Minut etzel ha-Geonim, ha-Rambam u-veno R. Avraham al pi Kitvei Genizat Kahir," *Maimonidean Studies*, ed. A. Hyman, vol. 1 (New York: Yeshiva University, 1990) [Hebrew Section], 1–21; S. Shtober, "Al Shetei Bakkashot she-Hufnu el Rabbenu Avraham ben ha-Rambam (be-Inyan Shifhah/Pilegesh)," *Shenaton ha-Mishpat ha-Ivri* 6–7 (1979–80): 399–403;

There was a public controversy in at least one Spanish community in the early fourteenth century about whether it was better to try to remove promiscuous Jewish women from the town, since they did not immerse themselves ritually in addition to constantly violating the prohibition of *lo tihyeh kedeshah*, or whether it was better to allow them to remain. Banishing the Jewish prostitutes raised the spector of mixing "holy Jewish seed with foreign daughters." Moreover, there might be political risks or concerns about physical retaliation if Christian women were involved. R. Yehudah b. ha-Rosh responded cryptically to his nephew, Asher b. Shelomoh, that non-Jewish women were to be preferred, despite the physical risks, because relations with the Jewish women carried the penalties of both a *lav* and *karet*.[59]

None of the accommodations described above were ever suggested in Ashkenaz. At first blush, it would seem that this could be attributed to the fact that manifestations of sexual promiscuity were not as pervasive there as they were in Spain. Scholars have readily assumed, on the basis of a variety of sources, that the level of sexual promiscuity and adultery was quantitatively much higher in Sefarad than in Ashkenaz, even though the precise number of incidents is impossible to determine. Moreover, Spanish Jewish society as a whole appeared to have a much more permissive attitude toward certain types of sexual behavior.[60] These behaviors often threatened to become widespread. As a result, Spanish rabbis

---

Teshuvot ha-Rambam, ed. J. Blau, nos. 3, 189, 233, 242, 321, 353, 368–71; *Teshuvot ha-Rosh* 29:1.

[59]See *Zikhron Yehudah le-R. Yehudah b. ha-Rosh*, no. 17, and Y. T. Assis, "Sexual Behavior in Hispano-Jewish Society," 44–45.

[60]See Y. Baer, *A History of the Jews in Christian Spain* 1:236–42, 250–61; H. J. Zimmels, *Ashkenazim and Sephardim*, 253–59; C. Horowitz, *The Jewish Sermon in 14th Century Spain*, 41–49; Y. T. Assis, "Sexual Behavior in Medieval Hispano-Jewish Society," 25–51. Cf. A. A. Neuman, *The Jews in Spain* 2:8–12, and H. Soloveitchik, "Religious Law and Change: The Medieval Example," 221.

had to view sexual transgressions not merely with regard to the
individuals involved but to their larger implications as well.

At no time in the High Middle Ages were there waves of sexual
violations in Ashkenaz.[61] Illicit sexual encounters were considered
in Ashkenazic rabbinic literature as lapses on the part of individuals
rather than as a larger societal problem. It should be noted that R.
Moses of Coucy's major addresses on the evils of sexual relations
with non-Jews were delivered exclusively in Spain.[62] Only in the

---

[61]For evidence of sexual promiscuity in Ashkenaz, see, e.g., H. J.
Zimmels, *Ashkenazim and Sephardim*, 253; Y. Dinari, *Hakhmei Ashkenaz*,
88; B. Rosensweig, *Ashkenazic Jewry in Transition*, 33–34; Y. Y. Yuval,
Hakhamim be-Doram, 43, 186, 329–30.

[62]R. Moses addressed an introductory passage that he subsequently
included in his *Sefer Mitzvot Gadol*, "*le-galut Yerushalayim ve-li-she'ar
galuyyot Edom*," meaning Spain as well as other areas (countries) in
Christian Europe. See the end of his introduction to the *mitzvot aseh*. So,
too, his introduction to the negative commandments notes that he had
occasion to preach widely: "*She-asabev ba-aratzot le-hokhiah galuyyot Yisrael*." His preachings concerning *tefillin* were offered "*be-galuyyot Yisrael*."
These words then made an impact "*bi-Sefarad* [during his mission there in
1236; see above, n. 16] . . . *ve-khen bi-she'ar aratzot*" [*aseh* 3]. His exhorta-
tions concerning the need for increased Torah study were also "*le-galuyyot
Yisrael*" [*aseh* 16]. The need for Jews to deal honestly with fellow Jews and
Gentiles alike, owing to the length and severity of the exile, was preached
by R. Moses "*le-galut Yerushalayim asher bi-Sefarad ve-li-she'ar galuyyot
Edom*" [*aseh* 74]. On the other hand, his preaching concerning *yein nesekh*
was rendered only in Sefarad [*lo taaseh* 148], where there was a problem
that did not exist in Ashkenaz [cf. H. Soloveitchik, "Religious Law and
Change" (above, n. 43), 218] as was his advice concerning the construction
of *mikvaot* [*aseh* 248]. R. Moses' detailed assessment of the evils entailed in
sexual relations with non-Jewish women was made repeatedly, but only in
Spain: "*Ve-he'erakhti bi-derashot ka-elu be-galut Yerushalayim asher bi-
Sefarad ve-hotzi'u nashim nokhriyyot rabbot bishnat* 996 (= 1236 C.E.) . . ." [*lo
taaseh* 112]. R. Moses' designation of particular *derashot* for each area
appears to be quite precise. General remarks, standard problem areas
(Torah study, honesty), and widespread problems such as *tefillin* were

fifteenth century did German and Austrian rabbinic scholars (such as R. Israel Isserlein) begin to preach publicly against these sexual liaisons.[63]

On the other hand, the penitential literature of the German Pietists is replete with penances for those who had engaged in sexual relations with non-Jewish women, and for more severe indiscretions as well.[64] To be sure, given the hypersensitivity of *Hasidut Ashkenaz* to transgression,[65] the use of this literature as a historical

---

addressed to all locales that he covered. Problems endemic to Spain (*yein nesekh*, proper *mikvaot* [see above, n. 58]), as well as sexual relations with non-Jews, were spoken about only in Spanish communities. Cf. J. Katz, *Ben Yehudim le-Goyim*, 106–07.

[63]See S. Eidelberg, *Jewish Life in Austria in the XVth Century* (Philadelphia: Dropsie College, 1962), 84–86. On the increase in sexual crimes in late medieval Ashkenaz, see also Dinari, Yuval, and Rosensweig, above, n. 61. In the second half of the fifteenth century, R. Judah Mintz of Padua, [*She'elot u-Teshuvot* (Cracow, 1882), no. 5] acknowledged that there were those in the Jewish community who approved the presence of prostitutes as a means of preventing men from committing adultery with married women. Cf. above, n. 59. R. Judah Mintz did not himself condone this policy, but could do nothing to dislodge it. Cf. Maharam Padua, *Responsa*, no. 19; and R. Shelomoh Luria, *Yam shel Shelomoh*, *Yevamot* 2:11.

[64]See I. Marcus, "Hasidei Ashkenaz Private Penitentials," *Studies in Jewish Mysticism*, ed. J. Dan and F. Talmage (Cambridge: Association for Jewish Studies, 1982), 57–83; idem, "Hibburei ha-Teshuvah shel Hasidei Ashkenaz," *Mehkarim be-Kabbalah, be-Filosofyah Yehudit, u-ve-Sifrut ha-Musar ve-he-Hagut (Mukdashim li-Yeshayah Tishby)* (Jerusalem: Magnes, 1986), 369–84; idem, *Piety and Society*, 42–52, 79. In addition to the so-called sage-penitentials and private penitentials, Marcus has noted the existence of "responsa" authored by R. Yehudah *he-Hasid* to queries about which penances should be prescribed for particular sins. Even if these texts were inspired by actual questions, and were not merely a literary device, there is no evidence to suggest that the questions came from outside the small circle of the German Pietists.

[65]See H. Soloveitchik, "Three Themes in the Sefer Hasidim," *AJS Review* 1 (1976): 311–57.

source requires caution.[66] In any event, the penances themselves were meant to be utilized by wayward individuals and represented, quite obviously, the antithesis of accommodation.[67]

---

[66]The prominent place given to sexual transgressions in the penitentials, and the frequency with which they were mentioned, probably meant that the German Pietists believed there was cause for serious concern in Ashkenaz. The Pietists were not merely attempting to cover different theoretical possibilities, as was perhaps the case regarding penances for *yein nesekh*; see H. Soloveitchik, above n. 62. Still, the issue requires further study. Shaving with a razor, which became a problem in a number of European communities during the modern period [see, e.g., *Teshuvot R. Akiva Eiger*, vol. 1, no. 96; R. Samson Morpurgo, *Shemesh Tzedakah* no. 61; and R. Ovadyah Yosef, *Yehavveh Daat*, vol. 2, no. 16], does not appear to have been prevalent in medieval Ashkenaz. See, e.g., *Sefer Rabiah (Teshuvot)*, ed. D. Deblitzky (Bnei Brak, 1989), sec. 947 (123–25), and *Shibbolei ha-Leket*, ed. Y. Hasidah, vol. 2 (Jerusalem, 1989), 140. Yet, this prohibition leads off a category of penances in R. Eleazar Roqeah's *Hilkhot Teshuvah* [see I. Marcus, "Private Penitentials," above, n. 64], and its practitioners were censured by R. Eleazar in his *Sodei Razayya*. See Nathan Nata Spira, *Megalleh Ammukot* (Lemberg, 1882), fol. 39b [Leviticus 19:2]. See also *Sefer Hasidim*, ed. Wistinetski, sec. 1664. [Note that the exempla sections, which constitute a significant part of *Sefer Hasidim*, refer only sparingly to manifestations of sexual promiscuity. See H. Soloveitchik (above note), 330–35; I. Marcus, *Piety and Society*, 59–65; and Y. Baer, "Ha-Megammah ha-Datit ha-Hevratit shel Sefer Hasidim," *Zion* 3 (1937): 42 n. 56.] In consonance with their disdain for many aspects of the intellectual and communal leadership in Ashkenaz, the German Pietists may have taken a harsher view toward (potential) nonobservance in Ashkenaz than did normative (non-Pietist) halakhists. Cf. ms. Vatican Ebr. 183, fol. 173v, and below, n. 84. We have seen the strong position taken by Spanish Kabbalists against sinners in their realm. See above, nn. 20–21, 54.

[67]Note that both R. Moshe mi-Coucy and R. Yonah Gerondi, the two major *Rishonim* who actually functioned as public *mokhihim*, had affinities for *Hasidut Ashkenaz*. [See I. Ta-Shema, "Hasidut Ashkenaz bi-Sefarad: Rabbenu Yonah Gerondi—ha-Ish u-Fo'alo," *Galut Ahar Golah (Mehkarim*

GAMBLING

A final area of religious malfeasance that we shall note was the proliferation of gambling. Gambling was permitted, based on a cogent reading of the relevant talmudic sources, provided that it was not the gambler's sole source of livelihood and that the money being wagered was clearly acknowledged by all participants. It is therefore unlikely that the many *Rishonim* who ruled that gambling was permissible did so because of external considerations per se. Those who ruled that even casual gambling was improper could have reached this conclusion on the basis of an alternative analysis of the underlying Talmudic sources.[68] Sometimes, however, a

---

Muggashim li-Prof. Hayyim Beinart), ed. A. Mirsky et al. (Jerusalem, 1988), 165–73, and the literature cited in nn. 19–20; my *Jewish Education and Society in the High Middle Ages* (Detroit: Wayne State University Press, 1992), 74–79; and cf. C. Horowitz, *The Jewish Sermon in the 14th Century*, 25–26.] It is therefore not surprising that both were against *pilagshut* in Spain (above, nn. 45, 51), and that R. Moses was not prepared to justify the neglect of *mitzvot aseh* in Ashkenaz as other Tosafists were (above, n. 16).

S. Z. Havlin (above, n. 50), 205–13, has demonstrated that Jewish communal policy in Christian Spain was conducted in accordance with the *Takkanat Rabbenu Gershom* prohibiting polygamy, of which Spanish Jewry was aware, although the force of this policy was independent custom rather than the *takkanah* itself. A less formal policy in this matter could undoubtedly have facilitated the allowance of *pilagshut*. Cf. Y. T. Assis, "Herem de-Rabbenu Gershom ve-Nisu'ei Kefel bi-Sefarad," *Zion* 46 (1981): 251–77. It should be noted, however, that Ashkenazic halakhists made no attempt to *bypass* the *takkanah*. Moreover, they did not consider permitting *pilagshut* even for unmarried men. Cf. *Yam shel Shelomoh* (above, n. 63).

[68]See *Sefer Mordekhai le-Massekhet Sanhedrin*, sec. 689–91; *Mishneh Torah, Hilkhot Edut* 10:4, and *Haggahot Maimuniyyot*, ad loc. (sec. 5); *Perush R. Asher b. Yehiel le-Massekhet Sanhedrin* 3:3; *Tosafot, Eruvin* 82a, s.v. *amar R. Yehudah*.

Rishon does intimate in the course of a ruling or responsum that his negative ruling was occasioned by the fact that gambling had gotten out of hand or had become a potentially dangerous activity.[69]

The excessive gambling that appeared throughout the Jewish communities of Christian Europe spawned different types of reactions. Several Ashkenazic communities, including the joint *Kehillot Shum*, enacted legislation or passed restrictions designed either to curtail gambling by limiting it to certain holidays and nonmonetary forms, or to stop their members from gambling entirely.[70] In Spain, where the domestic and economic stresses that excessive gambling created were described in a number of responsa, the gamblers were excluded from participation in communal affairs and even given lashes.[71]

For their part, individuals who were trapped by this vice often took oaths promising that they would stop gambling. But the gambler frequently could not keep his oath and asked for a rabbinic release from it. A passage in the Talmud Yerushalmi proscribed release from an oath in circumstances where the one who had taken the oath could then continue to do something that was prohibited according to rabbinic law.[72] The applicability of this principle to gamblers' oaths was initially a matter of Talmudic interpretation. Ultimately, however, the possibility of temporal concerns playing a

---

[69]See, e.g., the responsum of R. Yosef Tob Elem in *Haggahot Mordekhai le-Massekhet Sanhedrin,* 722–23.

[70]See L. Finkelstein, *Jewish Self Government in the Middle Ages* (reprinted New York: Jewish Theological Seminary, 1964), 60, 228, 242; *Sefer Mordekhai le-Massekhet Sanhedrin,* sec. 695, and cf. *Sefer Raban,* ed. S. Z. Ehrenreich, fol. 224b. See also *Tosafot, Eruvin* 104a, s.v. *hakhi garis,* and *Sefer Mitzvot Gadol, lo taaseh* 65 (fol. 22a).

[71]See Rashba, *Responsa* 2:35, 286; 7:244, 270, 445, 501; Rosh, *Responsa* 11:10; 72:1; 82:2.

[72]*Yerushalmi Nedarim* 5:4. Cf. *Tosafot, Gittin* 35b, s.v. *kasavar.*

role in a *Rishon's* ruling becomes more likely.[73] Some of the halakhists who concluded that the vow could be nullified were inclined to
do so because it was very difficult for people to control their urge to
gamble. Indeed, even Ashkenazic halakhists were prepared to
accommodate the inveterate gamblers by allowing them to be
released from their ill-fated vows. The Tosafist R. Tuvyah of
Vienne ruled: "Now, in this era, the vow of [abstention from]
gambling should be nullified, for it is almost an involuntary act,
since they cannot control themselves."[74] R. Samuel of Evreux wrote
that "if it is certain that [the gambler] will not be able to restrain
himself and will violate his oath, it is better to release him from it."[75]

---

[73]See Rashba, *Responsa* 1:755, 3:305; 7:4, 537; *Meyuhasot la-Ramban*,
nos. 252, 286; Rosh, *Responsa* 12:5–6; *Zikhron Yehudah*, no. 71; Ran,
Responsa, no. 51.

[74]*Sefer Mordekhai le-Massekhet Shavuot*, sec. 787. Cf. *She'elot u-Teshuvot
ha-Rama*, ed. A. Siev (Jerusalem: Hemed, 1971), 440, no. 103.

[75]See *Sefer Orhot Hayyim le-R. Aharon ha-Kohen mi-Lunel*, ed. M.
Schlesinger, vol. 3 (Berlin, 1899), 495; *Mordekhai Shavuot*, 787; and L.
Landman, "Jewish Attitudes Toward Gambling: The Professional and
Compulsive Gambler," *Jewish Quarterly Review* 57 (1967): 302. The *Mordekhai* text reports that some boors *(rekim)* would wager their own bodies
and then have to be redeemed. R. Meir of Rothenburg was prepared to
nullify all vows taken by nonprofessional gamblers. See R. Meir b. Barukh
me-Rothenburg, *Teshuvot, Pesakim, u-Minhagim*, ed. I. Z. Kahana, vol. 2
(Jerusalem: Mossad ha-Rav Kook 1960), 247–48, sec. 178–79. Nonprofessional gambling, however, was technically not included in the proscribed
category of *mesahek be-kuvya*. Maharam's responsa also reveal the practice
of some gamblers to vow that if they continued to gamble, they would give
sums of money to charity. See Cremona, nos. 299–300; Lemberg, nos.
211–12; Prague, nos. 493, 500. [Note the harsh stance of *Sefer Hasidim*
toward those who gambled (ed. Wistinetski, sec. 853, 1236).] For the
deteriorating situation in late medieval Ashkenaz, see S. Eidelberg (above,
n. 63), 83–84, and B. Rosensweig (above, n. 61), 34. Cf. *Teshuvot ha-Rama*
(above note), 439–41.

COMMUNITY, HALAKHIC PROCESS, AND DECISOR

When evaluating the data that has been gathered in order to ascertain rabbinic attitudes toward nonobservance, we ought not succumb to temptation and conclude simply that medieval Ashkenazic society was more observant than Hispano-Jewish society. It is true that Spanish society alone had a courtier class, whose life-style was especially conducive to religious malfeasance,[76] and that the scholarly class in Spain was smaller and more detached from the rest of the population compared to its Ashkenazic counterpart.[77] In addition, the role that the study of philosophy played in undermining religious observance must also be considered.[78] At the same time, Ashkenazic society was far from utopian. The heinous crimes of murder, informing, and adultery were not unknown there.[79] Many Ashkenazic Jews who under difficult circumstances were challenged to accept Christianity did not choose martyrdom.[80] Contrary to a popular misconception, many Ashkenazic Jews were not scholars[81] and, as we have seen, many had difficulty in fulfilling

---

[76]See C. Horowitz, *The Jewish Sermon in 14th Century Spain*, 41–49.

[77]See I. Ta-Shema, "Shipput Ivri u-Mishpat Ivri ba-Me'ot ha-Yod Alef/Yod Bet bi-Sefarad," *Shenaton ha-Mishpat ha-Ivri* 1 (1974): 353–72, and Horowitz, 49–54.

[78]See, e.g., B. Septimus, "Narboni and Shem Tov on Martyrdom," in *Studies in Medieval Jewish History and Literature*, ed. I. Twersky, vol. 2 (Cambridge, MA: Harvard University Press, 1984), 447 n. 1.

[79]See above nn. 9, 61, 63.

[80]See H. Soloveitchik, "Religious Law and Change" (above, n. 43), 214–16.

[81]See, e.g., A. Grossman, *Hakhmei Ashkenaz ha-Rishonim* (Jerusalem, 1981), 21–23, and "Avaryanim va-Allamim ba-Hevrah ha-Yehudit be-Ashkenaz ha-Kedumah ve-Hashpaatah al Sidrei ha-Din," *Shenaton ha-Mishpat ha-Ivri* 8 (1981): 135–52; E. E. Urbach, *Baalei ha-Tosafot* 2:529; I. Ta-Shema, "Mitzvat Talmud Torah ki-Ve'ayah Hevratit/Datit be-Sefer Hasidim," *Sefer Bar Ilan* 14–15 (1977): 98–113.

some of the most basic religious precepts. Clearly, a more nuanced interpretation of the data is called for.

Medieval Ashkenazic society, due to its relatively insular nature, had a high level of what Jacob Katz has termed *kefifah la-samkhut*. Laymen in Ashkenaz were likely to follow what was prescribed by rabbinic decisors. As a result, Tosafists felt free to apply their dialectical methodology to categories such as *goy shel Shabbat*, and develop patterns of leniency that were often beneficial to Ashkenazic society.[82] When an unacceptable overextension or misguided malfeasance on the part of laymen did occur, however, the rabbinic response was swift and harsh. Such was the reaction in the *hilkhot Shabbat* cases that we have presented.

Ritva cites an Ashkenazic formulation, which perhaps captured the essence of this approach:

> A venerable Ashkenazic rabbi pointed out in the name of his French teachers, including Ri and R. Meir of Rothenburg,[83] that these words (*mutav she-yihyu shogegin*) were said only for their generation [of the talmudic period]. But in this generation, when they are lenient in a number of things, it is appropriate to make a *seyag la-Torah*, even in [matters that are] *de-rabbanan*, and to protest and to fine people so that they will not transgress, neither accidentally, nor willfully.[84]

To be sure, *mutav she-yihyu shogegin* was employed by Tosafists, and

---

[82]See J. Katz, *Goy shel Shabbat*, 55–56, 180–81.

[83]Maharam studied in northern France and is considered a student of the French Tosafists. See H. Soloveitchik, "Three Themes in the *Sefer Hasidim*," in *AJS Review* 1 (1976): 349; *idem*, "Can Halakhic Texts Talk History?" in *AJS Review* 3 (1979): 195.

[84]*Shittah Mekubbetzet, Asifat Zekenim le-Massekhet Betzah* (reprinted, New York, 1967), 30b, s.v. *ve-hiksheh* (fol. 23b). Ritva himself noted that in a situation where an attempt at rebuke would surely go unheeded, *mutav she-yihyu shogegin* would have to be retained. This confirms that the French formulation presumed a degree of *kefifah la-samkhut*.

the conditions of its use were discussed and refined.[85] Nonetheless, this statement may represent the belief of Ashkenazic halakhists that in order to provide the leniencies which were necessary in their era, it was necessary to inhibit any deviation from these guidelines, even those that occurred *be-shogeg*. The only vice-related act that was tolerated in Ashkenaz was the ubiquitous gambling oath.[86]

Professor Katz further maintained that because of the well-honed "ritual instinct" of even the common folk in Ashkenaz, halakhists were inclined to justify long-standing religious customs and practices that did not appear, at first blush, to be in accordance with Talmudic law.[87] It appears that the "ritual instinct" of Ashkenazic Jewry also allowed the malfeasance or nonfeasance regarding *tefillin*, *tallit* (and to a lesser extent *mezuzah*) to be explained away if not justified, by Tosafists. These precepts could not have been brazenly dismissed by members of a group that never strayed far from the directives of its rabbinic leadership. There must be a way to explain why some members behaved as they did. Indeed, it may have been the complexity of the *halakhah* itself which caused them to become confused or misguided. In any event, the response of Ashkenazic rabbinic leadership to common forms of nonobservance was linked

---

[85]See *Tosafot, Shabbat* 55a, s.v. *ve-af al gav* and parallels; *Sefer Mordekhai ha-Shalem al Massekhet Betzah* (Jerusalem: Makhon Yerushalayim, 1983), 103 (to *Betzah* 30a); *Sefer Raban, Massekhet Niddah*, ed. S. Z. Ehrenreich, sec. 336, fol. 141a; *Tosafot, Eruvin* (above, n. 68); and Y. Henkin (above, n. 8). The use of this principle does increase in the late thirteenth century and beyond. Maharam himself invoked it, followed by others, as a measure of rabbinic control over the religious life of the community was lost. See E. E. Urbach, *Baalei ha-Tosafot* 2:549–50; I. A. Agus, *Teshuvot Baalei ha-Tosafot* (New York: Yeshiva University, 1954), 175–76; and Y. Dinari, *Hakhmei Ashkenaz be-Shilhei Yemei ha-Benayim*, 61–63, 72.

[86]Cf. *Tosafot, Hagigah* 16a, s.v. *ve-yaaseh; Kiddushin* 40a, s.v. *ve-yaaseh;* so-called Rashi to *Moed Katan* 17a, s.v. *mah; Sefer Hasidim*, ed. J. Wistinetski, sec. 62; *Otzar ha-Geonim, Moed Katan*, ed. B. M. Levin, 20, 68; R. Naftali Zevi Yehudah Berlin, *She'elot u-Teshuvot Meshiv Davar*, no. 44; and Y. Dinari, *Hakhmei Ashkenaz*, 52–53.

[87]I. Katz, *Goy Shel Shabbat*, 176–79.

to their policy of using dialectic as a means of justifying existing societal practices as well as of fostering halakhic creativity.[88]

Spanish Jewish society, on the other hand, was clearly less devoted to its halakhic leadership.[89] Thus, Spanish halakhists, even those who had been trained by Tosafists and schooled in their methods of dialectical resolution, never felt the luxury of being able to expand the *halakhah*. They had to go mostly "by the book." Moreover, they made little attempt to justify societal practices that appeared to deviate from Talmudic law since the "ritual instinct" of the populace was not considered to be reliable.[90] In the same vein, they could not effectively explain away ritual malfeasance. Philosophical allegory and skepticism, rather than concern or confusion about proper performance, played a significant role in the neglect of certain *mitzvot maasiyyot*.[91]

---

[88]See J. Katz's review of E. E. Urbach's *Baalei ha-Tosafot* in *Kiryat Sefer* 31 (1956): 14.

[89]See M. Breuer, "Le-Heker ha-Tippologiyyah shel Yeshivot ha-Maarav Bimei ha-Benayim," *Perakim be-Toledot ha-Hevrah ha-Yehudit (Mukdashim li-Prof. Y. Katz)*, ed. E. Etkes et al. (Jerusalem: Magnes, 1980), 45–55; I. Ta-Shema, "Shipput Ivri u-Mishpat Ivri" (above, n. 77), and "Al Petur Talmidei Hakhamim me-Missim bi-Yemei ha-Benayim," *Iyyunim be-Sifrut Hazal, ba-Mikra, u-ve-Toledot Yisrael (Mukdash li-Khvod Prof. E. Z. Melammed)*, ed. Y. D. Gilat et al. (Ramat Gan: Bar Ilan University, 1982), 312–22; and J. Katz, "Rabbinical Authority and Authorization in the Middle Ages," *Studies in Medieval Jewish History and Literature*, ed. I. Twersky (Cambridge, MA: Harvard University Press, 1979), 48–51.

[90]See above, n. 43. H. Soloveitchik has recently argued (in "Religious Law and Change") that the difference between Ashkenaz and Spain in these matters had less to do with actual practices or reality and more to do with the self-perception or self-image that the rabbinic/halakhic leadership in Ashkenaz had developed. Cf. I. Ta-Shema, "Halakhah, Minhag u-Massoret be-Yahadut Ashkenaz ba-Me'ot ha-Yod Alef/Yod Bet," *Sidra* 3 (1987): 104–09, 138–47, 159–60. Ta-Shema stresses the role that *minhag* as an independent value played.

[91]For other *mitzvot aseh* that were neglected in Spain, see above, n. 21, and H. J. Zimmels, *Ashkenazim and Sephardim*, 256.

The gulf that separated laymen from the halakhic process in Spain necessitated that religious malfeasance be handled more delicately. As the material concerning sexual misconduct indicates, the issue of whether enforced restrictions would improve the situation always had to be considered. For this reason as well, Spanish halakhists could not possibly have prescribed lashes for violations of *issurei Shabbat de-rabbanan*.[92]

I am suggesting, in short, that rabbinic attitudes toward nonobservance in the Middle Ages were conditioned by the religious nature of the communities as well as by the fealty that the communities demonstrated toward the halakhic process and its decisors. Full validation of this thesis can be achieved only after a

---

[92] Another detail that accords with our interpretation of the differences between the Spanish and Ashkenazic communities, but requires further corroboration, should be noted. Members of the Ashkenazic communities themselves were involved in imposing restrictions on gambling (see above, n. 70) and in censuring those who violated *issurei Shabbat* (above, n. 38). Rashba, on the other hand, chastised a Spanish community in which a group of its members wished to repeal gambling restrictions already in force. See Rashba, *Responsa* 7:244, 270. Cf. 2:279, and *Teshuvot ha-Rashba ha-Meyuhasot la-Ramban*, no. 244. Moreover, Spanish communities, beginning with the mid-thirteenth century, appointed official *berurei averot* to monitor religious problems and enforce observances. The members of *Kehillot Ashkenaz* were apparently able to police themselves more informally. See Rashba, *Responsa* 3:304, 318; 4:311; *Meyuhasot*, no. 279; and Y. Baer, *A History of the Jews in Christian Spain* 1:231–25.

Professor Katz has noted, regarding Sabbath violations in eastern Europe during the sixteenth and seventeenth centuries, that as the *kefifah la-samkhut* decreased, rabbinic leadership curtailed its attempts to justify communal practices. The leaders appointed or acted themselves as *anshei tamid* or *memunim* (= *berurei averot*), to make sure that extant statutes were not being violated. See his *Goy shel Shabbat*, 70–83, 180–81, and H. H. Ben-Sasson, "Takkanot Issurei Shabbat Shel Polin u-Mashma'utan ha-Hevratit ve-ha-Kalkalit," *Zion* 21 (1956): 185–87.

comprehensive survey and analysis of all manifestations of religious nonobservance in the medieval period. Indeed, the fact that the results obtained thus far can be readily understood in light of established rabbinic and societal conventions and postures strongly suggests the value of undertaking the larger investigation.

2

Rabbinic Responses to Nonobservance in the Modern Era

Judith Bleich

"But if the watchman see the sword come and blow not the trumpet, and the people be not warned: if the sword come and take any person from among them, he is taken away in his iniquity, but his blood will I require at the watchman's hand. So you, O son of man, I have set you a watchman unto the House of Israel: therefore you shall hear the word at my mouth, and warn them from me" (Ezekiel 33:6–7). It was with these prophetic words that the Orthodox rabbis who appended their signatures to the manifesto *Shelomei Emunei Yisrael* opened their official document of protest in the wake of the Reform Rabbinical Conference that had taken place in Brunswick, Germany, in 1844. Similarly, when these same individuals resolved to publish a Hebrew-language journal "to raise the honor of Torah and to remove stumbling blocks from the path of faith," they gave the journal the title *Shomer Tzion ha-Ne'eman* (Faithful Guardian of Zion) and inscribed on the masthead of each issue the words: "founded by an association of rabbis and scholars standing in the breach and guarding the holy charge."

In seeking to analyze the various forms of response toward the nonobservant as gleaned from nineteenth- and twentieth-century rabbinic writings one must understand that, for the most part, the authors were responding, under pressure of events, to what they regarded as an organized, concerted attack upon the foundations of Judaism. Their responses, whether overly restrictive or (on rare occasions) surprisingly mild, were prompted by a conviction that, as the watchmen unto whom had been entrusted the preservation of the embattled fortress, they must safeguard against the breaches that might bring down even the outer walls and turrets and thereby leave the inner precincts exposed.

Nonobservant individuals were always to be found within the Jewish community. At times their numbers were few; at other times, many. Toward the end of the eighteenth century one finds increasingly frequent references to transgressors and a change in the tone of rabbinic homilies and admonitions in reaction to the rising incidence of nonobservance and the increasing severity of infractions. In the course of time, remonstrations concerning lack of meticulousness in observance, self-indulgence, pursuit of luxury, and even undue attention to changing fashions in attire gave way to rebuke of those who concern themselves with secular education rather than Torah study and of those who transgress Jewish law publicly and defiantly.[1]

These admonitions were usually addressed to anonymous individuals and apparently generated little, if any, opposing response. With the growing laxity of observance there came a new

---

[1]See, for example, the admonitions of R. Jacob Emden, *Siddur Bet Yaakov* (Lemberg, 1904), "Mussar Naeh, Halon ha-Shevi'i," 314–15; R. Jonathan Eibeschutz, *Yaarot Devash* (Lemberg, 1863), 1:11a–12a; 2:23a, 65a–66b; and R. Yehezkel Landau, *Derushei ha-Tzelah*, 47–38, 103–04. See also Azriel Shohet, *Im Hilufei Tekufot: Reshit ha-Haskalah be-Yahadut Germanyah* (Jerusalem: Bialik Institute, 1960), 35–42, 89–122, 139–73.

disregard for rabbinic authority. The issue was first joined in 1782 in the clash between traditional rabbinic leaders and Naphtali Hertz Wessely over the projected educational program advocated in the latter's *Divrei Shalom ve-Emet*.[2] But it was with the advent of an organized movement for religious reform in the early nineteenth century that the issue of nonobservance assumed an entirely new guise. From that point on, rabbinic reaction focused upon the fact that the nonobservant were no longer religiously weak or even recalcitrant individuals but were adherents of a movement that sought to supplant traditional Judaism. The Reform movement was regarded as posing such a threat because of four factors: (1) the public and communal nature of the transgressions of its adherents, (2) recognition of deviationist rabbinic authorities as mentors, (3) the open and avowed agenda for innovation, and (4) renunciation of fundamentals of faith. With the emergence of institutionalized Reform as a separate and distinct religious denomination, rabbinic responses differed radically from those of an earlier age.[3] The responses to this challenge were manifold and diverse and each merits separate examination and analysis.

---

[2]See the very pertinent discussion in Jacob Katz, *Out of the Ghetto: The Social Background of Jewish Emancipation 1770–1870* (New York: Schocken Books, 1978), 145–50.

[3]Much of the historical and bibliographical literature regarding this period of history has been written from a partisan point of view and reflects a pronounced bias, if not outright distortion of facts. Recent work in this field is far more objective and has done much to redress the balance. Significantly, the standard history of the Reform movement, David Philipson, *The Reform Movement in Judaism* (New York: Ktav, 1967) has been superseded by an excellent work, Michael Meyer's *Response to Modernity: A History of the Reform Movement in Judaism* (New York: Oxford University Press, 1988), which strives for the objectivity and evenhandedness that is notably absent in Philipson's writing. Nevertheless, even this outstanding work, at times, misses the mark in understanding and analyzing the reaction of the Orthodox and certainly does not even lay claim to detailing their response.

THE INITIAL RESPONSE: *ELEH DIVREI HA-BERIT*

The innovations of the Hamburg Temple prompted the first major response of the Orthodox in the form of a classic work of responsa, *Eleh Divrei ha-Berit* (Altona, Germany, 1819), a collection of twenty-two responsa signed by forty rabbis from Germany, Poland, France, Italy, Bohemia, Moravia, and Hungary. Appended to the Hebrew text are German excerpts in both Hebrew and Gothic characters. The material published in *Eleh Divrei ha-Berit* contains virtually all the substantive arguments offered in objection to Reform innovations. In subsequent polemics the sources and arguments set forth in that volume were cited over and over again.

Needless to say, publication of this work evoked a shrill response. The respondents in *Eleh Divrei ha-Berit* were berated by defenders of Reform on account of their excessive legalism, despite the fact that they were merely rebutting the purportedly halakhic arguments of Reform innovators. In much of the secondary literature, writers who have focused attention upon the liturgical controversies have found fault with this collection of responsa[4] while only a

---

[4]From Graetz (Heinrich Graetz, *Geschichte der Juden*, 2nd ed., rev. by M. Brann [Leipzig: O. Leiner, 1900], 396–97) to Plaut (W. Gunther Plaut, *The Rise of Reform Judaism* [New York: World Union for Progressive Judaism, 1963], 34–37) and Petuchowski (Jacob J. Petuchowski, *Prayerbook Reform in Europe: The Liturgy of European Liberal and Reform Judaism* [New York: World Union for Progressive Judaism, 1968], 90–97), writers who have focused on these liturgical controversies have maligned *Eleh Divrei ha-Berit* and its propositions as "mostly not valid and some of them downright childish" (Graetz, 396). Israel Bettan, writing in 1925 ("Early Reform in Contemporaneous Responsa," *Hebrew Union College Jubilee Volume* [Cincinnati, 1925], 425–43), in a somewhat patronizing and condescending tone, did recognize that some of these responsa reflected a different intellectual tradition as depicted by "the best products and truest exponents of a Jewish culture which though not wholly past is fast receding from the horizon of Jewish life" (423). But, even in 1990, when Bettan's predictions have proved false, few have conceded that *Eleh Divrei ha-Berit* reveals an eerie perspicacity and, sadly, a sound prophetic sense.

few have recognized that the rabbinic writers did forthrightly confront the wide spectrum of issues involved and that *Eleh Divrei ha-Berit* reveals an almost uncanny prescience. The respondents had realized that what appeared to be minor ritual innovations heralded a revolutionary approach to Jewish law. As they predicted, in the following decades Reform spokesmen abandoned all allegiance to *halakhah* and instituted full-fledged reforms in all areas of Jewish religious life.

Yet, at the outset, one of the striking features of the encounter between Orthodoxy and Reform was the focus on questions of Jewish law and the attempt of writers who favored Reform to prove that the new norms of conduct could be justified on the basis of halakhic sources. In the first decade the language of the debate was Hebrew and the style and content that of classic responsa literature.[5]

---

[5]Writing of this extended "battle of the proof texts," Petuchowski (ibid., 98) notes that it is of abiding interest that the early Reform writers sought to justify their actions in the arena of *halakhah*, for this underscores the fact that they assuredly had no intention of founding a new religion but wished to base their liturgical reform on a Judaism rooted in the Bible, Talmud, and Codes. His assessment is predicated upon the assumption of intellectual honesty on the part of these early writers, i.e., the assumption that they actually believed that the proof-texts and precedents cited served to support the conclusions they set forth.

In contradistinction, one of Rabbi Tzevi Hirsch Chajes's gravest accusations in refuting Reform halakhic arguments was the charge of intellectual dishonesty. See *Minhat Kenaot*, published in *Kol Sifrei Maharatz Hayes*, vol. 2 (Jerusalem: Divrei Hakhamim, 1958), 973–1036. Chajes claimed that many of the halakhic rulings of Reform writers were based on their finding a precedent in some totally obscure source, giving such precedent undue weight and, moreover, frequently, even citing the obscure leniency out of context in a manner that served to distort its original intention. Such distortion and citation out of context could lead the reader to the most bizarre conclusions:

> The rabbis at their forefront justify their actions, saying the law is on their side and they are acting in accordance with Torah . . . based on

Menahem Mendel Steinhardt of Hildesheim served as one of the three rabbis who were appointed to head the Jewish Consistory of Westphalia. While in that office, Steinhardt's erudition was enlisted in the attempt to give legitimacy to Israel Jacobson's earliest religious reforms. While Steinhardt's *Divrei Iggeret*, published in Rödelheim in 1812 with the addition of comments and notes by Wolf Heidenheim, certainly falls within the ambit of mainstream halakhic literature, in many significant respects it prefigures the style, motifs, and even insinuations, of later defenders of Reform practice.[6]

Continued opposition to the ritual innovations in Berlin prompted the Reform partisans to commission another halakhic defense of their innovations. In 1818, in Dessau, Germany, Eliezer Liebermann, a Hungarian Jew regarding whose credentials there is only uncertain information,[7] published a treatise of his own, *Or*

---

some isolated dicta that are found in the Talmud or Midrash with regard to other matters and they endow them with alien connotations . . . in order to lead the masses of the people astray. They base themselves on esoteric nonnormative opinions, which can, at times, be found in the writings of decisors or on an unclear expression that may be found in some verse that, at first glance, seems tangentially to have some relationship to the matter at hand, even if, after study of the source, one recognizes that they have not penetrated to the depth of its meaning. . . . And even if it were so . . . in any event there is not sufficient basis in isolated words and the statements of individuals to supersede all the other words of the Sages that are clear and explicit . . . [Ibid., 986–988]. They search as for treasures and precious jewels for these obscure sources that have not been found by any previous great Torah scholars. [Ibid., 988, note].

[6]See my "Menahem Mendel Steinhardt's *Divrei Iggeret*: Harbinger of Reform," in *Proceedings of the Tenth World Congress of Jewish Studies*, Division B, History of the Jewish People, vol. 2 (Jerusalem: World Union of Jewish Studies, 1990), 207–14.

[7]Regarding the somewhat mysterious Eliezer Liebermann, see Yekutiel Greenwald, *Korot ha-Torah ve-ha-Emunah be-Hungaryah* (Budapest: Kats-

Nogah, together with a collection of responsa of others, *Nogah ha-Tzedek*. The latter responsa were authored by Sephardic rabbis in Italy, Shem Tov Samum of Leghorn and Jacob Recanati of Verona, and two Hungarian rabbis, Aaron Chorin of Arad and Moses Kunin of Ofen. These responsa dealt with the earliest ritual innovations, in particular, use of the organ in the synagogue and prayer in the vernacular. Interestingly, while he maintained that daily prayer with a *minyan* is not an obligation, nor even a *mitzvah*, Aaron Chorin urged the Reform congregation to arrange for public prayer on weekdays. Chorin cited an opinion of Maharil that advises individuals to pray at home with proper devotion. For while the Talmud (*Berakhot* 6b) states that God is angry if He comes to the synagogue and does not find ten men there, this is not the case when the holiness of the synagogue is desecrated by individuals whose behavior is indecorous. However, noted Chorin, the criticism and conclusion of Maharil apply to the Orthodox whose communal prayers lack reverence and solemnity. Since Reform congregants do conduct themselves with decorum they, then, might indeed arouse God's ire if they fail to pray with a *minyan*.[8] Ironic was Liebermann's suggestion in *Or Nogah* that German Jews should pray in their vernacular but that Polish Jews should pray in Hebrew, not simply because their knowledge of the holy tongue was superior to that of their German coreligionists, but because they should not be encouraged to pray in "the corrupt German in which they are fluent as a patois."[9]

Much of the technical legal argumentation presented in *Eleh Divrei ha-Berit* represented an attempt on the part of the Orthodox to discredit *Or Nogah* and *Nogah ha-Tzedek*, both their content and the reliability and authoritativeness of the respondents.

---

burg, 1921), 41–43; *idem*, *Li-Flagot Yisrael be-Hungaryah* (Deva: Markovitch and Friedman, 1929), 8–9; Meyer, *Response to Modernity*, 50, 407 n. 151.

[8]"Kinat ha-Emet," *Nogah ha-Tzedek*, 25.

[9]*Or Nogah*, pt. 1, 8–9.

In their introductory comments to *Eleh Divrei ha-Berit* the members of the Hamburg *Bet Din* emphasized that these responsa were not the product of a predisposition to negativism or of a zeal to condemn.[10] They underscored the salient distinguishing characteristics of the social and religious problem posed by the innovations introduced by the members of the Hamburg Temple Society: The changes constituted the actions of a group that had separated itself from the traditional community for the express purpose of instituting changes in both custom and law. They represented a carefully designed agenda and were the product of a concerted, organized plan to establish alternative ecclesiastic authorities to rule on matters of religious ritual. Moreover, the innovations did not represent the private acts of individuals but were public in nature and involved an entire community. Sinners and backsliders were always to be found, and, sadly, more so in recent times, the rabbis averred, but "they did not separate themselves entirely from the community to constitute separate councils and to motivate the children of Israel publicly to change the customs of Israel and the laws of our holy Torah."[11] There was always reason to hope for the repentance and spiritual improvement of transgressors. In such individual cases, benign neglect might, in the long run, constitute a wiser policy than denunciation or punitive measures. But the public, communal, and divisive nature of the actions of the Hamburg Temple Society necessitated a reasoned and forceful response that might have been avoidable under other circumstances.

> [For] now, on account of our great sins, the disease has spread in the Jewish community, for some persons have begun to gather together to legislate laws of iniquity, to change the customs of Israel in contradiction of the words of our holy Sages. . . . The page is too short to include all their deleterious

---

[10]*Eleh Divrei ha-Berit*, Introduction, ii.
[11]Ibid., iii.

practices and customs in which they have chosen arrogantly to oppose the holy words of our Sages, the *Bet Din* of their city and the vast majority of our congregation who are faithful and observant of the divine laws.[12]

Moreover, the official community could not allow itself the option of silence in the face of such organized rebellion lest silence be mistaken for agreement: "Then we said that now is not the time to be silent or to place a hand over the mouth. If we are silent we will be found guilty for people will say, 'The rabbis have been silent and silence is acquiescence.' "[13]

The substantive portions of most of these responsa deal with technical, halakhic questions regarding changes in the liturgy, recitation of prayer in the vernacular, and use of the organ in the synagogue both on the Sabbath and on weekdays. Some respondents simply cited general dicta opposing abrogation of time-hallowed practice *(minhagan shel Yisrael Torah hu)*,[14] while others cited a host of halakhic sources and precedents to bolster their restrictive pronouncements.[15]

Apart from their particular arguments against abrogation of established practices, the writers protested the hubris of the innovators in relying upon little-known individuals whose scholarship and authority were, at best, dubious. A number of respondents explicitly cast aspersions upon the character and qualifications of the champions of Reform, Eliezer Liebermann and Aaron Chorin.[16] The recantation of Aaron Chorin and his renunciation of the innovations he had earlier espoused are of particular interest. Chorin's recantation is appended by Hatam Sofer to the latter's

---

[12]Ibid., iii–iv.

[13]Ibid., v.

[14]See, for example, ibid., 1–3, 70.

[15]See, for example, the discussion regarding the use of an organ, ibid., 30–32, 67, 74–79, 85–86.

[16]See, in particular, ibid., 21–22, 30ff., 77, 89.

third letter in *Eleh Divrei ha-Berit*. Even more remarkable is the fact that Chorin later retracted his recantation.[17]

Vituperation and invective were not wholly absent. The Reform clergy were characterized as evil and wicked men. It was imperative to combat such individuals for "the hands of the wicked" must be weakened and the "the house of the wicked" must be eradicated.[18] Some respondents urged representations to civil au-

---

[17]Ibid., 97–98. On Chorin and the recantation see Meyer, *Response to Modernity*, 158, 432 nn. 41, 42; Philipson, *The Reform Movement*, 442 n. 112.

[18]See, for example, *Eleh Divrei ha-Berit*, 24, 26, 53, 59, 64, 84. For the often-employed play on words *moreh horaah—moreh ha-raah*, see Solomon Schreiber, *Iggerot Soferim* (Vienna and Budapest: Joseph Schlesinger, 1933), sec. 1, 51. With respect to the language employed, one should be mindful of the style and idiom of rabbinic pronouncements in general and their penchant for hyperbole. Much of the polemical literature on both sides was couched in derogatory and derisive language. See Alexander Guttmann, *The Struggle over Reform in Rabbinic Literature During the Last Century and a Half* (New York: World Union for Progressive Judaism, 1977), 139–46. In *Eleh Divrei ha-Berit*, 21, 24, *Or Nogah* was referred to as *Divrei Aven*, Words of Iniquity (the term *Aven* was formed as an acrostic derived from the first two letters of the word *Or* and the initial letter of *Nogah*) and those who followed the prescriptions of the "Shining Light" (*Or Nogah*) were described as "walking in darkness, not light." The Reform writers employed a similar style. Eliezer Liebermann, *Or Nogah*, pt. 2, 4, wrote of the Orthodox that their eyes were blinded and therefore they could not see the truth. The Orthodox were branded as *"stillständler"* (inert) and mocked as backward and unenlightened. See Plaut, *The Rise of Reform Judaism*, xxiii. In the protracted debate concerning the question of delayed burial one finds, at times, particularly tasteless comments of Reform partisans regarding efforts on the part of the Orthodox to secure timely burial. A sensitive reader would certainly find sarcastic remarks concerning the bereaved and their sincere attempts to honor the dead to be offensive. See, for example, *Der Israelit des neunzehnten Jahrhunderts* (IdNJ) "Die Beerdigung der jüdischen Leichen in Altona," 6 (1845): 214–15.

thorities in order to gain their assistance in the repression of this dangerous movement.[19]

A variety of other motifs may also be found in *Eleh Divrei ha-Berit*. A staunch championship of the privileged position of Hebrew as the language of prayer and spiritual contemplation is found in the responsa of R. Mordecai Benet,[20] R. Jacob of Lissa,[21] R. Moses Sofer,[22] and R. Akiva Eger.[23] R. Akiva Eger associated a

---

[19]*Eleh Divrei ha-Berit*, 23, 26.

[20]Ibid., 15.

[21]Ibid., 79–81.

[22]Ibid., 10–11, 38. Cf., also, *Teshuvot Hatam Sofer, Hoshen Mishpat*, no. 192 and *Likkutim*, vol. 6, nos. 84, 86. On the use of Hebrew, see also *Eleh Divrei ha-Berit*, 49–50, 65–66, 73, 89. Cf., also, R. Yaakov Emden, *Siddur Bet Yaakov*, 314; and R. Jonathan Eibeschutz, *Yaarot Devash*, pt. 2, 18a, 78a.

[23]*Eleh Divrei ha-Berit*, 27–28. As early as September 5, 1815, R. Akiva Eger authored a brief responsum in which he explicitly opposed proposals that prayer services be conducted in the vernacular. This responsum is published in L. Wreschner, "Rabbi Akiba Eger's Leben und Wirken," in *Jahrbuch der juedischenliterarischen Gesellschaft (JJLG)* 3 (1905): 75–77 and in *Likkut Teshuvot ve-Hiddushim mi-Rabbi Akiva Eger* (Bnei Brak, 1968), 11–13. R. Akiva Eger's opinion on this matter was, in all likelihood, solicited by Rabbi Meir Weyl, then Associate Chief Rabbi of Berlin, who sought to stymie the religious reforms introduced into private synagogues in Berlin that very year by Israel Jacobson and advocated before the Prussian authorities by David Friedlander. As one of his most extensive correspondents, Weyl, at times, consulted Eger on matters of policy concerning negotiations with government officials and Reform partisans. See Wreschner, *JJLG* 2 (1904): 41, 60–62; 3:35. Cf. Ludwig Geiger, *Geschichte der Juden in Berlin*, vol. 2 (Berlin: J. Guttentag, 1871), 210–30. For the scholarly correspondence of Eger and Weyl, see *Teshuvot Rabbi Akiva Eger*, vol. 1 (Warsaw, 1834), nos. 23, 40, 64, 107, 112, 154, and *Teshuvot Rabbi Akiva Eger*, vol. 2 (Vienna, 1859), nos. 75, 82, 83, 85, 94, 118, 119; *Teshuvot Rabbi Akiva Eger mi-Ketav Yad* (Jerusalem, 1965), nos. 37, 39, 43, 71, 84; *Teshuvot Hadashot le-Rabbenu Akiva Eger* (Jerusalem, 1978), *Yoreh De'ah*, no. 2, and *Hoshen Mishpat*, nos. 2, 9. In his responsum,

sense of fierce national pride with advocacy of the use of Hebrew. R. Mordecai Benet voiced concern for the education of future generations in predicting that if the passages regarding the ingathering of exiles and the rebuilding of Jerusalem were to be eliminated from the prayers, future generations would lack an appreciation for these fundamentals of faith.[24]

In bemoaning the motives of the Reform leaders, many of the respondents underscored the desire of the innovators to ingratiate themselves with non-Jews and to assimilate. "Truthfully," wrote R. Eleazar Fleckles, "they are lacking in faith and all their intent is but

---

Eger expressed opposition to the use of the vernacular in the liturgy for reasons that were based entirely upon technical application of halakhic requirements. However, his negativism toward this innovation clearly extended beyond halakhic technicalities. More significant than the legal argumentation is his analysis of the motivation underlying this specific reform and the tenor of his concluding comments which constitute a call for self-pride and self-awareness: "He whose intent is for the sake of Heaven and whose desire is not specifically to preen himself in the eyes of the nations and to be similar unto them and to lower the language of splendor, the holy tongue, from its honor, will concede the truth" (Wreschner 3:37).

It is instructive to compare this responsum with what is perhaps the very earliest responsum regarding prayer in the vernacular. That responsum, dated March 20, 1809, and authored by Samuel Eger of Brunswick, a cousin and colleague of Akiva Eger, addressed itself to the introduction of prayer in the German language by Israel Jacobson in his school in Cassel. Unlike Akiva Eger, Samuel Eger readily concedes the halakhic argument but similarly focuses on the motivation of the innovators. Use of the vernacular, he asserts, will only give support to those who seek to undermine tradition and will eliminate all incentive for the study of Hebrew. Moreover, retention of Hebrew in prayer serves as a necessary link uniting Jews throughout the world. The responsum is published in B. H. Auerbach, *Geschichte der israelitischen Gemeinde Halberstadt* (Halberstadt: H. Meyer, 1866), 219–21.

[24]*Eleh Divrei ha-Berit*, 13.

to acquire a name among the nations . . . but in truth they are neither Jews nor Christians."[25] As R. Moses Sofer put it in his letter, "The intent of these individuals is to curry favor in the eyes of the nations and the officials."[26]

Turning aside from the intricacies of the halakhic disputations regarding the question of whether an organ might be used in the synagogue or whether the formulae of certain prayers might be changed at will, the respondents emphasized the significant theological and philosophical issues raised in the particular liturgical changes adopted in the Hamburg Temple Prayerbook. The innovators had tampered with the text of prayers concerning the Messiah, the rebuilding of Jerusalem, the ingathering of the exiles, and resurrection of the dead. The alterations introduced in the text of these prayers reflected a rejection of fundamental principles of faith. R. Mordecai Benet declared that one who questions these beliefs is, if not a heretic, at the very minimum, spiritually misguided. Eliminating such passages from the prayerbook would result, heaven forfend, in future generations being cut off from the historic traditions of *kelal Yisrael* and becoming "totally separated from the body of the entire congregation of Israel."[27]

The respondents certainly had a clear understanding of the theological chasm that existed between the exponents of Reform and the traditionalists. The Orthodox rabbis did not believe in the slightest that the controversy revolved upon merely minor cosmetic changes in the ritual. R. Akiva Eger wrote bluntly, "Is not this, heaven forfend, the overthrowal and uprooting of religion?" Changing minor details, he argued, would ultimately cause the unraveling of the entire fabric of religious life.[28]

In a succinct statement decrying any form of ritual innova-

---

[25]Ibid., 17.

[26]Ibid., 33. Cf. the language of R. Akiva Eger, in his 1815 responsum (cited in n. 23 above).

[27]*Eleh Divrei ha-Berit*, 13. Cf. ibid., 22, 67.

[28]Ibid., 27.

tion, Eger presented the ideological substratum upon which this viewpoint was based. He underscored the interrelationship and interdependence of the Oral and Written Law in declaring, "They are united and bound together and are inseparable," and asserted that without rabbinic interpretation as expressed in the Oral Law, biblical commandments are incomprehensible. For example, absent rabbinic exegesis, biblical terms describing *tefillin* are entirely unintelligible. The characteristics of acts labeled as "labor" and proscribed on the Sabbath are not delineated in Scripture.[29] Therefore, as he argued elsewhere, "without total faith in the words of the Talmud according to tradition the entire Torah would fall."[30]

The strongest criticism of the innovators was the charge that they had sundered the unity of the community. In sharpest language, R. Eliezer of Triesch, in his second letter, criticized the motives and actions of the Hamburg Temple leaders and accused them of destroying the solidarity of the Jewish people:

> And now let us judge together. . . . Why have you separated yourselves from the community? And why were you not concerned regarding [the prohibition of] "And you shall not make groups and groups" that our Sages have interpreted as you shall not create separate groups? . . . Why are you relying . . . on the decision of one rabbi (in the work called *"Nogah ha-Tzedek"*) and why did you not consult the scholars of your city, the great rabbis of your *Bet Din Tzedek* from whom goes forth Torah to the residents of your esteemed community? . . . What benefit will accrue to you if you separate from the community and from the entire body politic of the people? . . . It will be devastating for generations to come . . . if you be separated from Jews and not reckoned among the nations. . . . What will you answer on the Day of Judgment? What will you say on the Day of Reckoning? . . .

---

[29]Ibid., 27.

[30]*Iggerot Soferim*, sec. 1, 50. Cf. also *Drush ve-Hiddush mi-Ketav Yad*, 176.

People of the Lord of Abraham! Look to the Rock whence you are hewn. Are we not all sons of one man? Do we not all have one Father? . . . Who knows if you will not, heaven forfend, cause lamentation for generations and all the children of Israel shall weep for you?[31]

R. Jacob of Lissa pleaded, "We, too, call out to you with an entreaty of love. . . . What is the benefit of creating a split and separation of hearts in Israel?"[32]

Its many harsh comments notwithstanding, *Eleh Divrei ha-Berit* was not entirely strident in nature. A conciliatory note is sounded by R. Eliezer of Triesch in the same letter in which he berates adherents of Reform for sowing dissension in the Jewish community. He goes so far as to apologize in case he has inadvertently been too negative or stinging in expressing his opposition to the innovators:

If my pen has slipped . . . do not count it to me as a sin, for from my great pain and distress I have spoken thus and for the zeal of the Lord of Hosts . . . and what shall I do, my Father in Heaven has decreed . . . in an explicit commandment of the Torah, "You shall surely reprove your fellow and not bear sin on his account." I have shown you the good and correct way and far be it from me that I should cease to pray on your behalf.

I shall raise my hands to the Lord and pray to the God of heaven and earth and their hosts, forgive the transgressions of your servants for the entire people are unwitting and give them a new heart, and a correct spirit renew in them, and let them all form together one association to serve You with a perfect heart.[33]

---

[31]*Eleh Divrei ha-Berit*, 92.
[32]Ibid., 82.
[33]Ibid., 93.

Most striking is the self-critical note struck by R. Eliezer of Triesch and his positive suggestions for self-improvement in the practices of the Orthodox community. He draws attention to the rabbinic teaching that transgression breeds further transgression and that punishment is often encountered in the very area in which one has sinned. Surely the religious community must examine its own actions and practices with a critical eye. If contention and controversy have erupted in matters of synagogue ritual perhaps it is a reflection of negligence and contentiousness among the observant in precisely that area of divine service. It is for the leaders and rabbis of the community to seek, in the spirit of authentic Jewish tradition, to make synagogue services more edifying. It is for them to eradicate all manner of social inequity and to concentrate on enhancement of brotherly love and neighborliness in the community. Their own leadership must be free of moral flaws. Above all, they must strive to promote the ideals of harmony and love for fellow Jews, for no Jews—by implication, not even backsliders—are without redeeming qualities.[34] The dissidents must be approached with love and gentleness, "with a soft expression and intelligent ethical reproof," and brought back "to be one people with us as they were until now, all together in one accord to serve the great and awesome God."[35]

The issues raised by the writers in *Eleh Divrei ha-Berit* were amplified by rabbinic writers in the years that followed and, as we shall note, were the subject of ongoing rabbinic discussion.[36]

---

[34]Ibid., 94–96.

[35]Ibid., 96.

[36]Publication of *Eleh Divrei ha-Berit* engendered several replies, among which was a satire, *Herev Nokemet Nekom Berit*, published anonymously by Meyer Israel Bresselau in 1819. That work has been praised excessively for its unusual Hebrew satirical style. See Meyer, *Response to Modernity*, 60, 409 nn. 183, 184; Plaut, *Rise of Reform Judaism*, 37; and Petuchowski, *Prayerbook Reform*, 97. It is indeed a not too remarkable satire of the style

typically associated with Purim parodies. Notable are two sharp ripostes to comments in *Eleh Divrei ha-Berit*. Rabbi Moses Sofer had commented, *inter alia*, that a further reason for recitation of prayer in Hebrew is the fact that the holy tongue is the language of the King of kings. In appearances before royalty, subjects speak the language of the sovereign they address, even if he understands other tongues. Similarly, in addressing the King of kings it is seemly to use His language (*Eleh Divrei ha-Berit*, 10–11). Bresselau responded by asking, What has happened to the man Moses (i.e., Moses Sofer)? Is God to be likened to a human being? "And to whom shall you liken Me?" (Isaiah 40:25) (*Herev Nokemet*, 15). Turning to the responsum of R. Jacob of Lissa, Bresselau is more stinging. R. Jacob had cited Isaiah 6:9, "Hear you, but understand not," and argued that we must follow tradition even if we comprehend it not. We may not rely solely on the perceptions of our own intelligence for our intelligence is all too limited (*Eleh Divrei ha-Berit*, 79). Indeed, countered Bresselau, we may not follow "our own intelligence" for it is all too limited. R. Jacob has written well regarding himself! And, by implication, regarding all the Orthodox who are categorized by know-nothingism, following and understanding not (*Herev Nokemet*, 15).

The satiric style was continued in some of the pamphlets published on both sides of the debate, all too often in a form more puerile than witty. A curious example of this genre which surfaced in the United States is the brief pamphlet *Emek Refa'im* by M. E. Holzman, published in New York in 1865 and addressed to the "Doctors" (*Refa'im* a pun on the Hebrew *rofim*, doctors) of the Reform clergy and, in particular, to one "Doctor Lavan" (German *weiss*, white), Dr. Isaac Mayer Wise. Following dissemination of Wise's prayerbook, *Minhag America* (Cincinnati, 1857), the author undertook to warn Wise in a satiric manner that America is a "free country," but not free from divine retribution.

The satiric style continued to characterize the Reform-Orthodox debate at a much later time. In a letter regarding a pamphlet entitled *Kuntres le-Maan Ahai ve-Re'ai* attacking Reform, Rabbi A. I. Kook criticizes the use of satire in the course of polemic: "Satire is a medium that it is fitting to employ with caution and in a precise measure, both from the vantage point of propriety and, more so, from the vantage point of the law. . . ." See *Iggerot ha-Reiyah*, vol. 2 (Jerusalem: Mossad ha-Rav Kook, 1968), 144.

POSSIBLE SCHISM OR BAN?

As the Reform movement grew and established itself as a separate denomination, the policy to be adopted with regard to those who identified publicly with the movement became a major issue. Were they to be treated simply as transgressors or were stronger communal sanctions to be imposed?

As one of the staunchest advocates of Orthodoxy who countered fiercely any encroachment of Reform, Hatam Sofer coined the aphorism *hadash asur min ha-Torah* (that which is new is forbidden by the Torah) as a battle slogan in opposing all manner of Reform innovation.[37] As a champion of Orthodoxy, he inveighed against exponents of Reform "who have distanced themselves from God and His Torah, due to our many sins," and cautioned against any association with them: "Do not dwell in their vicinity and do not associate with them at all . . . and do not say, the times have changed. For we have an old Father, may his name be blessed, and He has not changed and will not change. . . ."[38] Nevertheless, even Hatam Sofer stopped short of issuing an outright interdict or ban. In one of his responsa Hatam Sofer comes close to endorsement of a ban, but even in that statement he takes note of possible repercussions at the hands of civil authorities and limits himself to the hypothetical declaration that "if their judgment were in our hands" he would rule that the status of adherents of Reform is identical to that of sectarians and heretics and would demand total separation from them. Those comments, published in his responsa collection, are quite emphatic:

> If their judgment were in our hands, it would be my opinion to separate them from our domain; our daughters not to be given to their sons, nor their sons [to be taken] for our daughters, so

---

[37]See, for example, *Teshuvot Hatam Sofer, Orah Hayyim*, no. 28.

[38]See Hatam Sofer's last will and testament printed in S. Schreiber, *Hut ha-Meshulash* (Tel Aviv: Mesorah Press, 1963), 152–53.

that we should not come to be drawn after them and that their congregation be like the congregation of Zadok and Boethus, Anan and Saul, they for themselves and we for ourselves. All this appears to me as *halakhah,* but not to be implemented in practice in the absence of permission and authorization of the government; in the absence of this [permission] my words should be void and considered as naught.[39]

Twenty odd years later, following the Reform rabbinical conferences, the possibility of ban *(herem)* or schism again loomed large on the horizon. It is instructive to examine several responses to these conferences in order to appreciate the tension in the Orthodox camp and the reluctance to take so final a step.

In Altona, Rabbi Jacob Ettlinger and his colleagues published a formal protest in the form of a written manifesto entitled *Shelomei Emunei Yisrael* (The Faithful Believers of Israel), encompassing both a Hebrew and German text and bearing the signatures of seventy-seven Orthodox rabbis. This manifesto came to be regarded as the official statement of the Orthodox and received much wider endorsement. In the years that followed, the number of signatories rose to over three hundred.[40]

It must be noted that references to the manifesto as a ban or anathema are simply misstatements of fact.[41] The document contains no anathema or imprecation, nor does it single out any individual for attack. Even its critics admitted that the manifesto

---

[39]*Teshuvot Hatam Sofer,* vol. 6, no. 89.

[40]The manifesto is dated 1845 but the pamphlet does not indicate the city of publication. The German text was republished in *Der Israelit* 10 (1869): 177–80. An English translation was published in the British *Voice of Jacob* 4 (1845): 136–37, 142–43 and in the American *Occident* 3 (1845–46), 146–49, 198–201. *Israelit* 10 (1869): 177, refers to 300 signatories. Cf. *Iggerot Soferim,* sec. 1, 85. On the reaction evoked by the protest, see Philipson, *The Reform Movement,* 159–62.

[41]"Die Beerdigung," *IdNJ* 6 (1845): 213.

was restrained in expression and did not strike the strident note they associated with many other Orthodox pronouncements.[42] The relative moderation of tone reflected in the manifesto was the product of the influence of R. Jacob Ettlinger.[43]

Although Ettlinger's influence was decisive with regard to the manifesto, his moderation was not always accepted with equanimity by the more extreme among his colleagues. Probably the best example of those disparate modes of reaction is to be found in an encounter that took place between Ettlinger and Rabbi Solomon Eger. Following the conferences in Brunswick and Frankfurt, R. Solomon Eger, son and successor of R. Akiva Eger and a renowned authority in his own right, resolved to issue a ban against Reform Jews declaring them to be outside the pale of the community of Israel. Eger informed Ettlinger of his intention whereupon the latter summoned Eger to Altona to discuss the matter in person. Eger undertook the journey and was received with great cordiality and honor by Ettlinger as well as by the rabbis and *Klaus* scholars of Hamburg and Altona. Eger anticipated Ettlinger's unreserved endorsement and cooperation in circulating the text of the proposal but was soon disenchanted. Ettlinger conceded that, in theory, Eger was justified in wishing to pronounce a ban; however, in practice, he refused to sanction such a course of action. This policy of restraint had other prominent advocates as well. R. Solomon Eger also describes a meeting with R. Nathan Adler of London who was visiting in Hanover at the time.[44] Eger wished to obtain the support of Adler, but his entreaties were deflected.

---

[42]Ibid., 100.

[43]On Ettlinger's role in organizing and publicizing this protest see Chajes, *Minhat Kenaot* 2:1019, note; *Iggerot Soferim*, sec. 3, 6–7; *IdNJ* 6:213; *Israelit* 10 (1869): 569; 12 (1871): 941; *Die jüdische Presse* 3 (1872): 343.

[44]*Iggerot Soferim*, sec. 1, 83. Adler had returned to Hanover from London for the celebration of his mother's eightieth birthday. The visit is described in *Der treue Zionswächter* 3 (1847): 230–31, 238–39, and in *Voice of Jacob* 6 (1847): 192.

In a private communication in which he discussed the incident and described his keen disappointment, Rabbi Solomon Eger interpreted the attitude of Ettlinger and his colleagues as the product of fear of untoward repercussions:

> Although they were forced to admit that the matter was halakhically correct, they were unwilling to act upon it. For the sage, the Chief Rabbi of Altona, despite all his piety and despite all that has been done through him to denigrate the deeds of these rebels in the pages of the *Guardian of Zion* through Dr. Enoch,[45] is yet afraid to do such a thing against the wicked who rule over him. For so do they honor and elevate him in accordance with the custom of the people of Germany . . . that he conducts his rabbinate in such a manner as [was customary] in the past and no small or big matter is changed in the synagogues of Altona and Hamburg without permission of the rabbinate. I was greatly impressed with their ancient customs. . . . The rabbis of Germany are afraid to quarrel publicly with the wealthy and to publicize a ruling such as this against the heretics lest these turn to evil ways in public and they [the rabbis] lose the good status they yet enjoy.[46]

Eger later observed that it would have been wiser to have approached the rabbis of Hungary for assistance in his campaign against Reform.[47] This assessment of the difference in approach on the part of the rabbis of the Hungarian school and that of Jacob Ettlinger and Nathan Adler is well founded. It is, however, incorrect to attribute the reaction of Ettlinger and Adler to cowardice or

---

[45]Rabbi Samuel Enoch, principal of the Jewish secondary school in Altona, served as editor of the Orthodox weekly *Der treue Zionswächter* until he became rabbi of Fulda in 1855.

[46]*Iggerot Soferim*, sec. 1, 84.

[47]*Iggerot Soferim*, sec. 1, 85.

self-serving motives. Their refusal to be party to a formal ban or interdiction was a reasoned decision consistent with a carefully formulated policy eschewing methods judged to be counter-productive.[48]

Even more restrained was the position of R. Eliyahu Ragoler of Kalisch, who not only cautioned against issuing a ban but even questioned the wisdom of publishing public protests lest such action fan the flames of controversy and only exacerbate the problem: "It is necessary to be very careful . . . in determining how to publish against them," wrote Ragoler, "for even from a contro-versy between great Sages of the land, both of whose intentions were for the sake of Heaven, there sprang many evils."[49]

In 1849 the prominent Galician rabbinic scholar, R. Tzevi Hirsch Chajes, published a Hebrew monograph entitled *Minhat Kenaot* written in response to the Brunswick and Frankfurt Reform Rabbinical Conferences of 1844 and 1845.[50] *Minhat Kenaot* presents one of the most comprehensive halakhic discussions of Reform innovations, ranging from details of synagogue ritual to

---

[48]Cf. Yonah Emanuel, "Perakim bi-Toledot ha-Rav Yaakov Ett-linger z"l," *Ha-Maayan* 12 (1971–1972): 32, on the opposition of R. Samson Raphael Hirsch and R. Azriel Hildesheimer to the issuance of bans.

[49]*Teshuvot Yad Eliyahu, Pesakim*, pt. 1, no. 25.

[50]The thrust of many of Chajes's previous scholarly writings, *Torat Nevi'im* (1836), *Darkei Horaah* (1842–43), and *Mevo ha-Talmud* (1845), had been directed to a defense of tradition and an attempt to discredit the work of innovators and critical scholars. The Reform Rabbinical Confer-ences gave further impetus to this apologetic and polemical bent. In the introduction to *Minhat Kenaot*, Chajes writes that he had prepared that monograph in response to the Frankfurt Rabbinical Conference and wished to publish it as a *davar be-itto*, a timely response in the proper time and place, while the influence of the conference was yet palpable, but his efforts had been stymied by official censors who prevented publication of the work at that time. See Chajes, *Minhat Kenaot*, 975, and Mayer Herskovics, *Maharatz Hayes: Toldot Rabbi Tzevi Hirsch Hayes u-Mishnatto* (Jerusalem: Mossad ha-Rav Kook, 1972), 196–97, 490–91.

questions of Sabbath observance, circumcision, and intermarriage. In *Minhat Kenaot* Chajes presents a historical and theological elucidation of sectarianism and of sects prevalent during the talmudic period. Chajes traces sectarianism from its earliest manifestations reflected, in his opinion, in the biblical account of the golden calf and of the adherents of Korach (following *Tanhuma* and *Midrash Yalkut*) and later in the worship of the devotees of the Shrine of Micah and of the shrines in Beth-el and Dan as well as the heresies of the Sadducees, the Essenes, the early Christians, and the Karaites.[51] His historical survey concludes with a discussion of the innovators of his own time whom he regards as having set themselves apart as a separate sect and as having utterly rejected the binding force of Torah as one discards old fashions in favor of new. Chajes endeavors to place the Reform movement in a historical perspective and to compare and contrast it to earlier deviations from normative Judaism. He concludes in no uncertain terms that, halakhically, the status of exponents of the Reform movement is in no way different from that of members of the sects of antiquity:

> There is no doubt whatsoever that all the rulings that our Sages of blessed memory decreed for the Sadducees and Karaites apply to them . . . i.e., to those who comport themselves according to the Rabbinical Conferences and separate from their brethren and join to choose for themselves innovations of which our forefathers could not conceive. . . . I frankly do not know whether they continue to have any relationship whatsoever with us . . . save for the fact that the majority of them yet circumcise their children. . . . Except for that, they have already separated from us in all matters of faith and practice.[52]

---

[51]Chajes, *Minhat Kenaot*, 981–85. See the lengthier discussion in *Darkei Mosheh*, in *Kol Sifrei* 1:442–53.

[52]Chajes, *Minhat Kenaot*, 1012.

Despite the strong and unequivocal nature of this statement, as well as of other statements couched in similar language elsewhere in *Minhat Kenaot* and his other writings, Chajes was ambivalent about implementing in practice what he deemed valid in theory:

> Behold I will not hide the truth. Greatly is my heart pained to pronounce my verdict against them in this manner, to estrange from us a large populace, particularly our brethren of German descent, who are accomplished in wisdom and knowledge, far superior to other members of our nation in other countries.[53]

Quite apart from his hesitation to alienate and estrange a large number of his coreligionists, Chajes was also wary lest internal dissension and rift within the Jewish community serve as ammunition for anti-Semites at the very time that Jews were under keen scrutiny as they fought to gain rights and privileges from European governments. He was extremely wary of adding fuel to possible anti-Semitic allegations at such a sensitive time. Above all, he sought to avoid an irreparable schism.

Drawing on a biblical precedent, Chajes cites the reaction of the Jewish people following the outrage at Gibeah (Judges 21:3). After taking an oath not to marry members of the tribe of Benjamin, all Israel lifted up their voices and wept sorely and they said, "Oh, Lord, God of Israel, why has this come to pass that there should be today one tribe lacking in Israel?" How can it have come to pass, writes Chajes, that we should ourselves cut off our own flesh and blood in our own day? What has become of the imperative to seek peace in one's own locale and pursue it elsewhere? As the Sages teach, he adds, even if Israel worships idols, if there be peace among them, punishment is mitigated.[54]

---

[53]Ibid., 1012–13.
[54]Ibid., 1013.

Accordingly, Chajes equivocated and put aside his theoretical ruling, noting that the Reform movement was losing some of its initial impetus. In Galicia, it had not secured a foothold. Even in Germany the conferences did not engender overwhelming popular support. Certainly, the Breslau Conference had not been a raging success. The initial glamor and attraction of change had already begun to pale. Hence, concludes Chajes, "since the danger is not so terrifying for us now, perhaps it is no longer so urgent on our part for us to battle to separate a great multitude from our community."[55]

But that was not Chajes's final word on the subject. He again vacillates and notes the various provisions of Jewish law applicable to those who lead the community astray. He further cites the talmudic judgment that an act of mercy toward those who seduce the innocent ultimately results in malevolence toward the rest of the world. Finally, Chajes concludes that the negative rulings pronounced against the Reform movement should be regarded as applying only to its leaders, not to their followers. He contends that the masses had been led astray by their leaders and that, accordingly, their seduction by skilled demagogues must be deemed a mitigating circumstance constituting quasi-duress.[56]

---

[55]Ibid., 1013.

[56]Ibid., 1014. The ambivalence inherent in this position did not pass without notice by Chajes's detractors. They did not understand, or wish to understand, his inner torment. One of the most virulent of these, the Galician scholar and satirist, Joshua Heschel Schorr of Brody, who criticized Chajes's stringencies mercilessly, cites *inter alia* the contradictory statements in *Minhat Kenaot*: "The generation is evil and licentious" and "The danger is great" as opposed to "Praise the Lord, in Galicia they have no foothold" and "The danger is not so pressing." In a biting satire and play on the well-known *piyyut* of the evening service of the Day of Atonement "As clay in the hands of the potter," he writes of Chajes: "Behold, as the curtain in the hands of the embroiderer, at will he makes it even; at will he makes it uneven. So is the truth in the hands of this sophist. At will he

During the following decades other rabbinic decisors appear to have followed the same pattern. They held up the specter of schism but threatened it as a last resort to be implemented only in the event that the Reform movement proceed to adopt drastic innovations in areas of marital law. Thus R. Hayyim Ozer Grodzinski, who maintained that secession from a unified community was a question of policy dependent on local conditions rather than a clear-cut matter of *halakhah*, wrote explicitly that should Reform leaders institute certain further innovations with regard to marriage and divorce it would become necessary for the entire community to separate itself totally from adherents of Reform. But at no time was this threat carried out in practice.[57]

ENLISTMENT OF CIVIL AUTHORITIES

Yet another form of response to the activities of the nascent Reform movement involved complaints to civil authorities and efforts to secure governmental intervention in the internal religious affairs of the Jewish community. Involvement of civil authorities became an extremely sensitive matter and an area of strife in the Reform–Orthodox struggle. Attempts to involve the civil authorities were possible because not only was there no separation of Church and State in nineteenth-century Germany but also because the *kehillah* was a quasi-governmental body subject to regulation by the State. Moreover, the civil authorities had reason to fear every liberal movement as a potential challenge to the authoritarian nature of the State and were also motivated by a desire to preserve the

---

makes his tongue smooth, and at will jagged." And he concludes bitingly: "A hypocrite and a chameleon is this rabbi!" See Herskovics, *Maharatz Hayes*, 325–26.

[57] *Ahi'ezer: Kovetz Iggerot*, ed. Aaron Suraski, vol. 1 (Bnei Brak: Netzach Press, 1970), 244–45. This "Letter Regarding the *Kehillot* in Germany" was also published in *Sefer ha-Zikaron le-Rav Weinberg*, ed. E. Hildesheimer and K. Kahana (Jerusalem: Philipp Feldheim, 1969), 9–12.

religious status quo on the assumption that State-supported established religious denominations would continue to promote loyalty
and submissiveness to the authority of the State.[58]

There is no gainsaying the fact that the Orthodox were prepared
to enlist the cooperation of government officials in their attempt to
stymie the advances of Reform. The Orthodox authorities in Berlin
had no compunctions in encouraging the suspicions of Prussian
government officials who, for reasons of their own, found Reform
innovations unwelcome.[59] Similarly, in Breslau, R. Solomon
Tiktin and his supporters did not hesitate to encourage the Prussian
authorities in their investigations into Geiger's purportedly radical
political activities.[60] In responsa included in *Eleh Divrei ha-Berit* one
finds the suggestion of R. Eliezer Triesch of Moravia that requests
be addressed to civil authorities to assist in suppression of these
dangerous Reform tendencies[61] and the even more aggressive advice of R. Abraham Eliezer ha-Levi of Trieste urging that Jews in
positions of influence press the authorities to harass leaders of the
Reform movement relentlessly.[62] Years later, in the manifesto
Shelomei Emunei Yisrael, the same tactics were again advocated:
"Embrace all means in your power, every legally permitted method,
to defeat their counsels and to frustrate their designs." Accompa-
nying that exhortation was the observation that the beneficent and

---

[58]Cf. Robert Liberles, *Religious Conflict in Social Context: The Resurgence
of Orthodox Judaism in Frankfurt am Main, 1838–1877* (Westport, CT:
Greenwood Press, 1985), 12, 15, 235 n. 23, on government support of
Reform in the 1830s and 1840s. See also Guttmann, *Struggle over Reform,*
97–104.

[59]Michael Meyer, *Response to Modernity,* 46; and idem, "The Religious
Reform Controversy in the Berlin Jewish Community, 1814–1823," *Leo
Baeck Institute Yearbook* 24 (1979): 139–55.

[60]Max Wiener, *Abraham Geiger and Liberal Judaism: The Challenge of
the Nineteenth Century,* trans. from the German by Ernst J. Schlochauer
(Cincinnati: Hebrew Union College Press, 1981), 18–19.

[61]*Eleh Divrei ha-Berit,* 22–24.

[62]Ibid., 26.

liberal governments under whose rule Jews found themselves favored a society firmly based upon sound and well-established
religious principles rather than upon the untested innovations of
exponents of Reform.[63] A contemporaneous communication of the
Jerusalem rabbinate was even more explicit: "Whoever has influence with the government, turn your attention to the capital in
order to strengthen the breaches of the perfect Torah."[64]

Reform writers have objected that "once religion became the
object of the struggle for power, those involved persuaded
themselves that the end justified the means."[65] However, in point
of fact, partisans of the Reform movement, when capable of doing
so, sought to involve government authorities in such controversies
no less so than did the Orthodox. This was the case in the election
of Rabbi Akiva Eger to the chief rabbinate of Posen which was
fraught with tension and conflict. Despite his unquestioned
position as the preeminent talmudist of the era—or, arguably,
precisely because of that status—his candidacy was vigorously
contested by a group of young intellectuals who did not hesitate to
make representations to government officials charging that Eger
was known to be "a fanatic . . . not in a position to teach pure
religion and true morality" and that he "diametrically opposes
the spirit of the times [and] promotes only bigotry and
prejudice. . . ."[66] In a deposition dated August 28, 1815, bearing
the signatures of twenty-two opponents, it was contended that not
only would Eger be unable to fulfil the functions of a preacher and

---

[63]Page 1 of the Hebrew text. *Voice of Jacob* 4 (1845): 136, contains an
inaccurate translation.

[64]*Shomer Tzion ha-Ne'eman*, no. 10.

[65]Wiener, *Abraham Geiger*, 19–20. Cf. Philipson, *The Reform Movement*,
24, 35.

[66]Wreschner, "Leben and Wirken," *JJLG* 3:9–10. See also Philipp
Bloch, "Die ersten Culturbestrebungen der jüdischen Gemeinde Posen
unter preussischer Herrschaft," *Jubelschrift zum 70. Geburtstage von H.
Graetz* (Breslau: S. Schottlaender, 1877), 200–01.

teacher of morality as demanded by the times, but that his very presence in Posen would serve to stifle intellectual progress. Revealing their deep-seated animosity, opponents of his candidacy declared, "He will deaden any disposition toward enlightenment and culture, while the number of [Talmud] students, augmented on account of him, will contribute to the unsettling of all intelligence, will muddle the senses of the youth and thwart the true development of their spiritual potential."[67]

Even more significant is the fact that the very earliest religious reforms instituted in Westphalia were imposed upon the populace without their consent by the Consistory headed by Jacobson who employed the coercive force of the secular authorities for that purpose. It is ironic that, although the Consistory specifically proscribed private services under penalty of fine and a threat that if obedience were not forthcoming "unpleasant measures of force would be necessary,"[68] when, after the dissolution of the Consistory, Jacobson's own private services in Berlin were banned, he was outraged.[69] Later, in Hamburg, both sides vied for government support to such an extent that Gabriel Riesser was prompted to

---

[67]Wreschner, "Leben Und Wirken," *JJLG* 3:9–10.

[68]*Sulamith*, vol. 4, pt. 1, 366–80 (see especially sec. 43). The royal edict of July 5, 1811, imposed financial penalties on those who worshiped other than at the official synagogues. *Sulamith*, vol. 3, pt. 2, 211–13. These efforts to promote standardized services evoked much resentment and the authorities were deluged with petitions for private services at least for the High Holy Days. Following repeated remonstrations, Jews in Hanover obtained the right for one private synagogue to continue to function. See Ludwig Horwitz, *Die Israeliten unter dem Königreich Westfalen* (Cassel: Calvary, 1900), 66–70. Cf., Auerbach, *Geschichte*, 140, 145–46.

[69]Jacob Rader Marcus, "Israel Jacobson," *Central Conference of American Rabbis Yearbook* 38 (1928): 456, notes that "the tolerance which he refused to accord, he demanded of others. Like all men passionately engrossed in a great idea he was blind to the other man's point of view. I suspect that Jacobson, although a very witty and genial man, completely lacked a sense of humor."

comment wryly: "The great majority of the members of our Congregation would much rather endure the displeasure of Almighty God than that of the Senate . . . in which noble sentiment the Orthodox party is fully their equal."[70]

COMMUNAL STRINGENCY

Because of the relatively rapid growth of the Reform movement, many rabbinic authorities—particularly Hungarian rabbis of the school of Hatam Sofer—were moved to adopt an even more stringent policy with regard to any ritual change than they might have advocated under other circumstances. The phenomenon of communities in which relatively minor aesthetic innovations were swiftly followed by the adoption of full scale programs of liturgical and ritual reform reinforced the opinion of these rabbinic leaders that the wisest policy was a stance of absolute conservatism. Resistance even to insignificant changes in synagogue practice that might have been sanctioned from the vantage point of *halakhah* was perceived as the prudent course of action. Accordingly, a form of siege mentality prevailed under which any accommodation in matters of synagogue and ritual affairs was eschewed. Specific issues—location of the *bimah* in the center of the synagogue, wearing of clerical robes, performance of weddings in the synagogue, and preaching in the vernacular, for example—regarding which there might have been legitimate differences of opinion, and with regard to which permissive as well as restrictive opinions were forthcoming in other times and other places, were all decided in a restrictive manner by the vast majority of these Hungarian rabbis in order to present a united Orthodox front against innovation.

These authorities were entirely candid in enunciating the considerations underlying this policy. In a discussion of the changes

---

[70]Cited in Moshe Rinott, "Gabriel Riesser," *Leo Baeck Institute Yearbook* 7 (1962): 22.

instituted in the *Chorshulen* (choral synagogues),[71] R. Yehudah
Aszod conceded that many of his interlocutors had noble intentions but warned that they erred nonetheless "as experience has
taught" because the new modes of behavior "that are known as
Reform" frequently began with minor matters, only for the true
agenda to be revealed later. The result was the eradication of the
unique characteristics of Jewish worship and the erosion of Jewish
law. Therefore, concluded Rabbi Aszod, "Anyone who changes is
at a disadvantage . . . and this has been our uniqueness . . . not to
change a thing in any matter of new practice."[72] Maharam Schick
similarly wrote, "Experience testifies unto us that as long as Israel
preserved their customs there was Torah and fear [of God] among
Israel and from the time that they have begun to make changes in
their customs, religion has been constantly deteriorating."[73] R.
Abraham Samuel Benjamin Sofer (known as Ketav Sofer) also
wrote that instigators of Reform initially introduced relatively
innocuous changes: "Not with big things did they begin, but with
minor customs and enactments." It is that experience, he asserted,
that evoked rabbinic resistance since the experiences of "these
communities are always before our eyes."[74]

---

[71]The *Chorshulen* were Orthodox synagogues that boasted male choirs
with no instrumental accompaniment. The choir was derided by some as
a modern innovation inconsistent with traditional practice. Advocates of
the *Chorshulen* favored adaptations designed to promote decorum and
aesthetically pleasing services.

[72]*Teshuvot Yehudah Yaaleh, Yoreh De'ah,* no. 39.

[73]*Teshuvot Maharam Shik, Even ha-Ezer,* no. 87.

[74]*Iggerot Soferim,* sec. 3, 10. See also R. Solomon Schreiber, "Ohel
Leah," published as the introduction to Rabbi Abraham Samuel Benjamin Sofer, *Sefer Ketav Sofer al ha-Torah* (Tel Aviv: Sinai Press, 1980),
27–28. R. Solomon Schreiber relates that his father, Ketav Sofer, declined
to join forces with R. Meir Eisenstadt, author of *Teshuvot Imrei Esh,* in an
organized protest against a group of radical Reform partisans. Ketav Sofer
stated that he was not concerned with opposing radical innovators since
their views would, in any event, not influence the broad masses of

Hatam Sofer, asked to rule on the permissibility of moving the *bimah* from its central position, issued an unequivocal negative ruling, voicing his oft-quoted aphorism: "Innovation is forbidden by the Torah."[75] Thereafter, the issue of the location of the *bimah* was elevated by the Orthodox in Hungary to a position of a fundamental principle and became symbolic of the entire struggle for and against Reform. Moving the *bimah* from the center of the synagogue came to be regarded by the Orthodox as the thin edge of the wedge of Reform. Some followers of Hatam Sofer went so far as to rule that it is preferable to pray privately than to pray in a synagogue without a central *bimah*.[76] In a responsum dealing with that very question, R. Azriel Hildesheimer emphasized that it was an issue that many rabbis had raised to the level of "an obligatory battle" and hence had come to represent the much broader issue of rabbinic authority. Moreover, he noted that he had never seen this innovation instituted in a community unless they had a "spark" of Reform and, as a result, he deemed it to be a matter with regard to which rabbis should not turn a blind eye.[77] Nevertheless, others did not view this ruling as absolute. At a much later date, Rabbi Moses Feinstein wrote that the stringent attitude of Hungarian rabbis who forbade prayer in an edifice in which the *bimah* was not located in the center of the synagogue was a *horaat shaah* – an *ad hoc* ruling promulgated as a means of stemming the tide of Reform and applicable only in that locale and at that time.[78]

Hungarian Jews. He was, however, far more distressed when the innovators accepted basic halakhic premises but "were permissive with regard to rabbinic enactments and customs of Israel."

[75]*Teshuvot Hatam Sofer, Orah Hayyim*, no. 28.

[76]See the discussion in R. Zalman Sorotzkin, "Be-Inyan Haamadat ha-Bimah be-Emtza Bet ha-Knesset," *No'am* 5 (1961): 55–57.

[77]*She'elot u-Teshuvot Rabbi Ezriel, Yoreh De'ah*, no. 20.

[78]*Iggerot Mosheh, Orah Hayyim*, vol. 2, nos. 41, 42. Elisha S. Ancselovits, in his unpublished paper "The Boundaries within which Traditional Judaism Faced Modernity: Part I, Opposition to the Relocation of the

Another area in which rabbis tended to extreme stringency because of these considerations was the issue of change in the nature of the *mehitzah*, or partition, between the men's and women's sections of the synagogue. Asked whether it would be permissible to accede to a request to change a partition fashioned of wide boards for one of narrow slats "permitting people to see and be seen," Maharam Schick, in a strongly worded negative reply, remarked that the matter is one of gravity "especially in our generation when it might be likened to the Jewish custom regarding the shoelace, for which one is obligated to sacrifice one's life if need be" (*Sanhedrin* 74b).[79] Responding to a similar query, Rabbi Hillel Lichtenstein extended the ruling in declaring that even if there is not a single woman present in the synagogue, one may not pray there since "on account of this willful violation it has become desecrated."[80] In a discussion of laws pertaining to synagogue construction, Rabbi Hayyim of Sanz stressed that with regard to the determination of this question local custom plays a decisive role and it is therefore forbidden "to vary and build a synagogue in a fashion other than in accordance with the custom that we have always followed in this country." R. Hayyim of Sanz also added the comment that this is a matter regarding which the talmudic ruling requiring martyrdom for violation of even the most minor of Jewish customs is applicable.[81]

In other countries and at a later date other halakhic issues became the rallying point in the struggle again sectarian practices. In the United States a major issue in the early part of the twentieth century was that of mixed pews. That, however, was an issue involving an unequivocal breach of *halakhah*. In his written comments on this matter—one of the rare occasions on which he

---

Bimah and Wedding Ceremony," examines several other sources relating to this topic.

[79]*Teshuvot Maharam Shik, Orah Hayyim*, no. 77.

[80]*Teshuvot Bet Hillel*, no. 104.

[81]*Teshuvot Divrei Hayyim, Orah Hayyim*, no. 18.

expressed his views in writing—Rabbi Joseph B. Soloveitchik declared that a synagogue that adopts mixed seating forfeits its sanctity and that one should forego *tefillah bi-tzibbur* even on the High Holy Days rather than pray in such a synagogue. He, too, ruled that organized hostility toward religious practices requires a "heroic stand" even in matters involving a minor custom:

> I know beforehand the reaction to my letter on the part of our apostles of religious "modernism" and "utilitarianism." They will certainly say that since a great majority of the recently constructed synagogues have abandoned mixed seating, we must be out of step with the masses. This type of reasoning could well be employed with regard to other religious precepts, such as the observance of Sabbath, or the dietary laws. However, we must remember that an ethical or Halachic principle decreed by God is not rendered void by the fact that the people refuse to abide by it. . . . The greater the difficulty, the more biting the ridicule and sarcasm, and the more numerous the opponent then the holier is the principle, and the more sacred is our duty to defend it. In my opinion, the Halachic dictum, *bishe'ath gezerath ha-malchuth afillu mitzvah kallah kegon le-shinuye arketha de-mesana, yehareg ve'al ya'abor* [at a time of religious persecution through governmental decree, even for a minor custom, such as involving changing a shoelace, let one suffer death sooner than transgress it] (Sanhedrin 74b), requiring of us a heroic stand in times of adversity, applies not only to political or religious persecution originated from some pagan ruler, but also to situations in which a small number of God-fearing and Torah-loyal people is confronted with a hostile attitude on the part of the majority dominated by a false philosophy.[82]

---

[82]"Message to a Rabbinic Convention," *The Sanctity of the Synagogue*, ed. Baruch Litvin (New York: The Spero Foundation, 1959), 110–11.

It is important to note that even those authorities who ruled permissively with regard to some of these matters were aware of the need for extreme caution because of the nature of the controversy with Reform. Thus, in his discussion of the relatively moderate innovations introduced in the *Chorshulen*, R. Tzevi Hirsch Chajes was careful to state that, in themselves, those changes did not, strictly speaking, constitute halakhic violations. Chajes clearly expressed his approval of sermons in the vernacular and the elimination of *piyyutim* as modifications that serve to enhance decorum during the services. He, however, cautioned against excessive expenditure for synagogue edifices and added the halakhic ruling that architectural designs that consciously simulate church architecture are forbidden by Jewish law. He included in that category the bells placed on several synagogues in Germany for the purpose of summoning worshippers to services—an innovation first instituted in the Temple of Jacob inaugurated by Israel Jacobson in Seesen in 1810.[83] However, elsewhere Chajes was careful to point out the manner in which even permissible innovations should be introduced, and cautioned that sensationalism and publicity must be avoided in order to prevent confusion on the part of the untutored masses. Enumerating customs that can and should be modified in synagogue practices—for example, sale of Torah honors and recitation of some of the *piyyutim*, which are essentially impermissible interpolations in the blessings of the *Shema*—he noted that such practices were abrogated by individual rabbis in certain areas of Poland and Russia and that quarrels or divisiveness had not ensued. Chajes attributed this to the fact that these changes were instituted without publicity, formal gatherings, or public announcements. He stated that with reference to innovations or changes in ritual, it is of paramount importance to recognize that gatherings and fanfare are generally harmful for a number of reasons but primarily because the untutored masses are unable to distinguish between customs that have the force of law and mere

---

[83]Chajes, *Minhat Kenaot*, 990–91.

folkways. If folkways are abrogated the ignorant may mistakenly conclude that the law can also be altered arbitrarily. For this reason, explained Chajes, the Sages counsel conservatism and caution with regard to changing any aspect of synagogue practice. He also contended that customs and practices pertaining to the synagogue and communal life have a certain spiritual power and serve to strengthen bonds of solidarity and feelings of national pride among the scattered Jewish people.[84] For that reason one must exercise exceeding caution with respect to their observance; vigilance is necessary lest divisiveness be created and "the people thereby become sundered in half."[85]

THE NONOBSERVANT AS INDIVIDUALS

Changing sociological realities prompted rabbinic authorities to undertake a fundamental reassessment of certain time-hallowed distinctions. Although rabbinic authorities reacted with stringency to ritual innovations even remotely akin to those advocated by exponents of Reform, their response to lapses in observance on the part of individuals was far more tolerant. There was even an underlying feeling of sympathy for the plight of those whose deficiencies in observance were motivated by economic hardship. Increasingly large numbers of individuals no longer conformed to Orthodox standards of religious and ritual observance.[86] Confronted with this fact, many authorities drew a crucial distinction between individuals whose deviation from religious practice was

---

[84]Tzevi Hirsch Chajes, *Darkei Horaah*, chaps. 6 and 7 in *Kol Sifrei* 1:238–42.

[85]Ibid., 242.

[86]See Salo W. Baron, "The Modern Age," in *Great Ages and Ideas of the Jewish People*, ed. Leo W. Schwartz (New York: Random House, 1956), 363–64. Baron notes that as early as 1770 an anonymous writer (Mordecai van Aron de Pinto) urged abolition of the Sabbath and holidays for economic considerations.

prompted by economic considerations, or was born of ignorance, and those whose nonobservance was the result of an ideological metamorphosis.

This distinction was enunciated and justified in halakhic categories in a seminal responsum authored by Rabbi Jacob Ettlinger.[87] In talmudic sources the status of a *"mumar* with regard to the entire Torah,"* a person who rejects the commandments of the Torah in their entirety, is tantamount to that of an apostate. The *Gemara* (*Hullin* 5a) declares that one who desecrates the Sabbath in public is to be regarded as a *"mumar* with regard to the entire Torah." Rashi, *ad locum*, elucidates this categorization by noting that public desecration of the Sabbath, *ipso facto*, constitutes denial of the divine role in creation of the universe. In publicly rejecting his obligation with regard to Sabbath observance the transgressor denies both God as Creator and the veracity of the biblical account of creation. Hence the Sabbath-desecrator is a *"mumar* with regard to the entire Torah."

The novel socioreligious phenomenon of otherwise devout and believing Sabbath-desecrators prompted Ettlinger to a reassessment of the implications of such desecration. Although he appended a caveat declaring that his discussion was only theoretical in nature and not intended as a normative ruling, Ettlinger noted that the Sabbath-desecrators of his day could hardly be categorized as heretics:

> However, as to Jewish sinners of our time I do not know how to consider them. . . . For because of the multitude of our sins the sore has spread greatly, to such an extent that for most of them the desecration of the Sabbath has become like a permissible act. . . . There are those among them who offer Sabbath prayers and recite the *kiddush* and then violate the Sabbath. . . . The Sabbath desecrator is considered a *mumar* only because, by denying the Sabbath, he denies the creation and

---

[87] *Binyan Tzion he-Hadashot*, no. 23.

the Creator. But this man acknowledges them by his prayer
and *kiddush*. And certainly their sons who arise in their places,
who neither know nor have heard of Sabbath ordinances, are
like . . . children taken captive. . . .

Ettlinger believed that the motives prompting many of his contemporaries to become lax in religious observance were economic
rather than ideological in nature. Yet, although he was not prepared to regard the masses as heretics, he nevertheless emphasized
that this liberal stance could not be extended to encompass those
individuals who flagrantly rejected fundamental dogmas of Judaism. Accordingly, he declared that his ruling could not be regarded
as applicable in instances in which "it is clear to us that [the
individual] is aware of the Sabbath laws and yet audaciously
desecrates the Sabbath in the presence of ten assembled Jews, for
such a person is comparable to an absolute *mumar*. . . ."[88]

The practical consequences of the ruling were significant.
Although Ettlinger presented this decision only as a theoretical
hypothesis (*she-lo le-halakhah la-maaseh*), it soon became standard
practice to count Sabbath-desecrators as members of the quorum
for public prayer and to accord them the privilege of being called to
the Reading of the Law. Neither practice could have been
permitted other than on the basis of a rationale similar to that
advanced by Ettlinger. To this day, when pressed for a defense
of such practices, rabbinic authorities invariably reply with a
citation to this responsum. Of particular interest are the permissive
rulings of R. David Tzevi Hoffman[89] and, more recently, of the

---

[88]In the United States, R. Abraham Rice affirmed the position that
Sabbath desecrators should not be called to the Torah and when his
opinion could no longer prevail he ruled that one should not answer
"Amen" to the blessings recited by a Sabbath desecrator. This unpopular
stance aroused much dissension. See Israel Tabak, "Rabbi Abraham Rice
of Baltimore," *Tradition* 7:2 (Summer 1965): 107–08.

[89]*Melamed le-Ho'il, Orah Hayyim*, no. 29.

late R. Moses Feinstein,[90] both of which cite Ettlinger as precedent.

The reasoning underlying this pivotal halakhic decision is also reflected in a basic theological distinction formulated by Ettlinger. In several passages in his homiletical-exegetical work, *Minhat Ani*, he draws a sharp distinction between individuals who have abandoned observance for pragmatic and financial reasons and those whose rejection of *mitzvot* is predicated upon ideological considerations. In his commentary on *Be-haalotkha* Ettlinger states:

> For there are two categories of transgressors, [There are] transgressors by virtue of [human] nature, those who do not overcome their passions but in their hearts believe in the Torah and the commandments and there are sinners . . . who sin not on account of desire, but because they do not believe in the Torah and deny its commandments. The distinction between these two [categories], in which there may be discerned the origin of their transgression, is if they only sin to transgress a negative commandment so that they do not put a rein on their passions to guard against forbidden pleasures, but they observe the positive commandments which are not contrary to their passions. In this it may be recognized that they believe in the Torah. However, if not only do they sin in transgressing negative commandments, but also do not observe the positive commandments of the Torah, this indicates that they deny the Torah.[91]

Individuals who desecrate the Sabbath for material gain, but nevertheless participate in rituals associated with Sabbath obser-

---

[90]*Iggerot Mosheh, Even ha-Ezer*, vol. 2, no. 20. Rabbi Feinstein disagrees with Ettlinger's line of reasoning but reaches the same conclusion on different grounds. See also ibid., *Orah Hayyim*, vol. 1, no. 33. Cf. the discussion of these responsa in Samuel Morrell, "The Halachic Status of non-Halachic Jews," *Judaism* 18 (June 1969): 455–57.

[91]Rabbi Jacob Ettlinger, *Minhat Ani* (Jerusalem, 1963), 91a.

vance (e.g., the recitation of *kiddush*) were, according to Ettlinger's analysis, to be regarded as "transgressors by virtue of [human] nature," but not as heretics. It is to the status of such individuals that Ettlinger's halakhic ruling was addressed.

It was Ettlinger's contention that a considerable number of those who were attracted to the Reform movement were individuals whose motivation was primarily economic or social in nature. Accordingly, they sought to disregard those commandments which might lead to financial hardship or create embarrassment in association with non-Jews. Ettlinger underscored the need to differentiate between individuals whose intent was merely "to ease the yoke of Torah according to the needs of the times" and individuals who denied the divinity of the Torah and rejected its basic doctrines.[92] Those whose transgression was motivated by passion could more readily be guided back to the path of Torah.[93]

While many who assimilated were indeed motivated by social or economic considerations and the desire for material success that appeared to them to be contingent upon acculturation and loss of ethnic distinctiveness, there were a growing number of individuals whose nonobservance was founded upon an intellectual rejection of the fundamentals of faith. It was this latter group to whom rabbinic figures found it much more difficult to relate. Although Ettlinger presumed that the vast majority of the nonobservant were motivated by materialistic concerns, he nevertheless cautioned that even those individuals who were motivated by heretical views and who must be deemed to be "total transgressors" were not to be written off as hopelessly lost to Judaism.[94] But, as will be shown, it was his disciples who were to turn their energies to that segment of the nonobservant population.

---

[92]Ibid., 39b.

[93]Ibid., 130b–131a. Cf. ibid., 110a–111a.

[94]Ibid., 91b.

NONOBSERVANT CLERGY

The celebrated Geiger–Tiktin controversy constituted one of the earliest clashes between proponents of the nascent Reform movement and the traditional establishment. With the election of Abraham Geiger in 1838 as a rabbinic colleague of the aged Solomon Tiktin, the Breslau *kehillah* became embroiled in a protracted and acrimonious dispute over rabbinic leadership. Although the conflict eventually culminated in an uneasy truce, by no means were its reverberations stilled. Over one hundred and fifty years later, the issues raised in that controversy still divide the Jewish community and are the basis of dissension and discord among the various factions and segments of our people in the Diaspora as well as in the State of Israel.

While champions of Geiger have portrayed the struggle as a battle on behalf of the principle of freedom of thought,[95] the crucial issue at stake was the question "Who is a rabbi?" Under dispute was not Geiger's scholarship, talents, or abilities, but whether or not he could properly claim the right to exercise rabbinic authority or, more accurately, whether the incumbent rabbi, Solomon Tiktin, was acting correctly in refusing to serve with Geiger lest he thereby legitimate Geiger's position as a "rabbi and teacher in Israel."

At the time, writing in defense of Geiger, David Einhorn declared that departure from observance of ceremonial laws when prompted by sincere conviction does not render an individual unfit to hold rabbinic office.[96] Not surprisingly, a diametrically opposite view had been enunciated earlier by Rabbi Akiva Eger in a letter to residents of Eisenach in which he declared categorically that the mantle of rabbinic authority may not be donned by any and all. There are clear limitations upon who may be recognized as a rabbinic decisor. Responding to a detailed query, Rabbi Akiva Eger stated unequivocally that the halakhic decisions of an individual

---

[95]Philipson, *The Reform Movement*, 60.
[96]Ibid., 70.

who does not himself abide by the strictures of both biblical and rabbinic law have no binding force whatsoever. Quite simply, Rabbi Akiva Eger argues, such an individual's conduct is governed by one of two motives; in either event he is unfit for rabbinic office. Either he lacks the requisite knowledge or he is knowledgeable but does not accept talmudic law as normative. If he is ignorant, how can he presume to issue legal rulings? If he is knowledgeable but knowingly repudiates talmudic law, how can he be regarded as a *rabbinic* decisor?[97] The view articulated by Rabbi Eger reflects the attitude of the Orthodox vis-à-vis sectarian clergy[98] that prevails to this very day.

CONCERN FOR UNITY

Contemporary attacks on the Orthodox community focus on Orthodox intransigence with regard to questions of personal status and call the Orthodox community to task for a lack of concern for the unity of *kelal Yisrael*. Ironically, in *Eleh Divrei ha-Berit* the strongest and most penetrating criticism of the Hamburg Reform leadership is couched in identical terms. They were taken to task for instituting innovations that effectively shattered the cohesiveness and unity of the Jewish community:

> Why have you separated yourselves from the community? . . .
> What benefit will accrue to you if you separate from the

---

[97]*Iggerot Soferim*, sec. 1, 51.

[98]On clergy who differ in their theological views or who, even if observant, identify with non-Orthodox denominations see R. Moses Feinstein, *Iggerot Mosheh, Even ha-Ezer*, vol. 1, no. 135; *Even ha-Ezer*, vol. 2, no. 17; *Even ha-Ezer*, vol. 3, no. 3; *Even ha-Ezer*, vol. 4, no. 13, sec. 3, and no. 78; *Yoreh De'ah*, vol. 1, no. 160; *Yoreh De'ah*, vol. 2, nos. 125, 128; *Yoreh De'ah*, vol. 3, no. 77; Rabbi Aaron Soloveichik, "Teshuvah be-Inyan Mikveh," *Ha-Darom* 55 (*Elul* 1986): 15–30; and *idem*, "Be-Inyan Kiddushei Shomranim," *Ha-Pardes* 61:2 (November 1986): 8–19.

community and from the entire body politic of the people? . . .
It will be devastating for generations to come. . . .[99]

A similar argument was formulated by an Orthodox rabbinic
writer in the United States. Writing in the *Occident* in 1845, Rabbi
Abraham Rice penned an eloquent plea for unity:

> The only and legitimate pride which the Jew bears in his heart
> is, that with us there are no sects, that the Jew in the East is
> like the one who lives in the West — that the religion in the
> South must be as it is in the North. This unity may be lost
> through a single ill-advised alteration; every ignorant man
> would daringly attempt to modify the religion according to
> the notions of his feeble intellect; and there would arise a
> multitude of sects without any parallel. But no! O God, Thy
> name is one and thy people Israel will remain one.[100]

Eugene Borowitz, a prominent contemporary Reform writer,
candidly concedes that classical exponents of Reform did not regard
unity as a paramount value:

> Had *Kelal Yisrael* been our most significant concern we could
> never have brought Progressive Judaism into being, for its
> creation seriously divided the Jewish community by defying
> the accepted community leadership and the established tradi-
> tions of our people.[101]

Yet, more often rabbinic writers were placed on the defensive
and were accused of being those who were responsible for rendering
Jewish unity a nullity since they would not compromise with regard
to issues of Jewish law that threatened to split the Jewish people

---

[99]*Eleh Divrei ha-Berit*, 92.

[100]Rabbi Abraham Rice, "Erroneous Doctrines," *Occident* 2 (1844–45):
471.

[101]Eugene Borowitz, "Co-existing with Orthodox Jews," *Journal of
Reform Judaism* 34:3 (Summer 1981): 57.

asunder. An incisive response to these frequently voiced accusations may be found in *Minhat Ani*, in comments on the scriptural portion of *Pinhas*. Ettlinger asserted that although unity is a fundamental value and a prerequisite for divine redemption, it is but one value among many:

> If you see that there are rebellious individuals who wish to destroy your Torah, then it is the time to act for the Lord, to wage the war of the Lord against them. . . . And he who wages the war of the Lord against the heretics should not restrain himself on account of a false argument that peace is great and it is better to grasp in friendship anyone who may be termed a Jew than to create a separation of hearts . . . and the reason for this is that although peace between man and man is great, nevertheless, even better is peace between Israel and their Father in Heaven. Therefore, he who avenges the vengeance of the Lord to strengthen the Torah, he is the one who desires peace and seeks it diligently.[102]

This principle is evidenced in the narrative of Phineas. In avenging the Lord, Phineas killed a prince of the tribe of Simeon and was nevertheless rewarded with the covenant of peace. Scripture states, "Behold, I give unto him my covenant of peace" (Numbers 25:12), and the Midrash adds, "it is indeed just *(be-din hu)* that he receive his reward . . . My covenant of peace."[103] Although Phineas' action seemingly fostered dissension and aroused the antagonism of an entire tribe, ultimately this very action brought peace between the Almighty and Israel. Therefore, *Minhat Ani* concludes, the Midrash uses the expression "it is indeed just *(be-din hu)*" with reference to Phineas' reward.[104]

Similarly, in his essay "Phineas–Eliyahu," Samson Raphael

---

[102]Ettlinger, *Minhat Ani*, 106a.

[103]*Bamidbar Rabbah* 21:1

[104]Ettlinger, *Minhat Ani*, 104b–105a.

Hirsch emphasized that the covenant of everlasting priesthood was granted to Phineas for demonstrating by means of his zeal that there are values that supersede unity and peace:

> God has promised His true peace not to weakness, the weak acquiescence which allows events to take their course, which is bold only where there is no resistance and will advocate the good cause only when it meets with general approval and needs no defenders; He has not promised the covenant of His rule to those who proclaim "peace, peace at any price." He has promised it to those whose highest and ultimate aim is true peace in Heaven and on earth. He has promised it to the zeal of Phineas, to the very man who is assailed by all the zealous adherents of a false peace as if he were a disturber of the peace; to him who in the name of God opposes every mocking departure from the law of God, the only power before which everyone has to bow; to him whose aim is to assert for the Law of God the sole rule over the acts and consciences of men.[105]

The compromise of other values is too high a price to pay for unity and there do exist overriding concerns in the face of which the ideal of unity must be swept aside.

SECESSION

In the last decades of the nineteenth century, German Orthodoxy became embroiled in an internal dispute which, in essence, involved a judgment of the extent to which communal unity could be preserved when it came into conflict with ideological principle. The most radical response to the emergence of Reform institutions was the policy of secession adopted and vigorously advocated by

---

[105]Samson Raphael Hirsch, *Judaism Eternal*, trans. I. Grunfeld (London: Soncino Press, 1959), 2:293.

Samson Raphael Hirsch.[106] The Jewish community in each city was
organized as a *kehillah* recognized by the government and supported primarily by a tax earmarked for religious purposes, which
was levied upon Jew and Christian alike. The governing board of
the *kehillah* was responsible for the administration of religious,
educational, social, and philanthropic institutions and organizations. The establishment of Reform institutions under the aegis of
the *kehillah* evoked a reaction from Hirsch demanding that the
Orthodox withdraw from the *kehillah* and establish their own
independent institutions. Hirsch contended that membership in
the communal organization constituted a form of endorsement or,
de minimis, conferred legitimacy upon the ideological positions
espoused by the institutions sponsored by the *kehillah*. Accordingly, Hirsch asserted that *halakhah* forbids such endorsement or
conferral of legitimacy and hence ruled that formal association with
any organization that denies the fundamental principles of Judaism
is forbidden. It must be noted that in formulating this position
Hirsch emphasized that his policy demanded, not disassociation
from individuals, but secession from a communal system that he
viewed as an institutionalized expression of heresy.[107]

However, as a practical matter, Hirsch was unable to act on his

---

[106]See the valuable discussion in Liberles, *Religious Conflict*, 165–226. It
is commonly assumed that separation as a policy of the Orthodox
community began in the 1870s with Hirsch. In fact, the idea of autonomous religious communities each practicing Judaism in accordance with
its own dictates dates from an earlier period and was viewed as a
desideratum by exponents of Reform. Thus in the 1830s Abraham Geiger
maintained that the only manner in which the Reform movement could
move forward at a suitable pace was by obtaining permission to form
autonomous religious organizations apart from the general community.
See Abraham Geiger, *Nachgelassene Schriften*, vol. 5 (Berlin, 1878), 54–55;
and Wiener, *Abraham Geiger*, 99–100.

[107]*Offener Brief an Sr. Ehrwürden Herrn Distrikts-Rabbiner S. B. Bamberger in Würzburg* (Frankfurt am Main: I. Kaufmann, 1877), 6ff. This
letter was included in *Gesammelte Schriften von Rabb. Samson Raphael
Hirsch* (Frankfurt am Main: I. Kaufmann, 1908), 4:316–43. An English

convictions immediately. Under German law, registration and membership in the local *kehillah* was automatic and a Jew could renounce membership only upon conversion to Christianity or upon a declaration that he was *konfessionslos* (without religion), a declaration that was widely regarded as tantamount to a renunciation of Judaism. Hirsch correctly considered this law to be an interference with the fundamental principle of freedom of religious conscience. As long as the law remained in effect the members of Hirsch's community had no choice but to retain their compulsory membership in the umbrella *kehillah* even after forming the autonomous *Israelitische Religionsgesellschaft*.

In 1873 the Prussian Parliament promulgated a law that enabled Christians of different denominations to disassociate themselves from the established church and to form their own religious communities. For Hirsch, passage of this law was the harbinger of a new era and signalled the possibility of establishing an independent and proud community that would be able to tap additional sources of revenue to be utilized in achieving enhanced spiritual and communal accomplishments.[108] To Hirsch, secession was a logical step

---

translation of this document as well as of Bamberger's response and Hirsch's counterreply may be found in Samson Raphael Hirsch, *The Collected Writings*, vol. 6, *Jewish Communal Life and Independent Orthodoxy* (New York and Jerusalem: Philipp Feldheim, 1990), 198–317.

[108]In the implementation of a policy such as secession, the sociological realities are often more dispositive than the theoretical or philosophical arguments. Liberles *(Religious Conflict)* quite correctly underscores the fact that secession was not "the cause of the strengthening of Orthodoxy in Germany. . . . Rather it was an expression of that strength." He concludes:

> All Orthodox leaders including Bamberger welcomed the law of separation, but only Hirsch approached it from a perspective of strength. For the others it was a guarantee of minority rights; for Hirsch it represented the right to be fully independent; . . . for Hirsch, emancipation was an opportunity. In that he was unique, as early as 1836 and as late as 1877. [pp. 225ff.]

since he was sincerely convinced that "within none of the Christian churches is there a deeper cleavage than between Reform Judaism . . . and Orthodox traditional Judaism."[109] Hirsch immediately began to lobby for a similar right to be granted to Jewish citizens. With the assistance of an influential statesman, Eduard Lasker, Hirsch finally succeeded in this endeavor. On July 28, 1876, the Prussian Parliament passed the Law of Secession granting Jews the right to withdraw from the organized community without renouncing Judaism and the concomitant right to form independent Jewish communities.

Following promulgation of the Law of Secession, Hirsch urged his congregants to secede from the established Jewish community of Frankfurt since it was now legally permissible for them to belong to the Orthodox community exclusively. Some congregants followed Hirsch's directive; however, a large number elected to remain within the general *kehillah* as well. To a large extent it was the relative newcomers to Frankfurt who followed Hirsch unconditionally while members of many of the older Frankfurt families who had a deep attachment to the historic *kehillah* and its institutions chose to maintain dual membership. Many of the latter were particularly loath to surrender their burial rights in the communal cemetery in which their forebears were interred.[110]

---

[109]*Denkschrift über die Judenfrage in dem Gesetz betreffend den Austritt aus der Kirche* (Berlin, 1873), 6. The essay was published anonymously but later included in Hirsch's *Gesammelte Schriften*, vol. 4 (Frankfurt, 1908), 250–65.

[110]See Liberles, *Religious Conflict*, 215–17. Of interest are analyses and reminiscences of the events in Frankfurt contained in *Historia Judaica* 10:2 (October 1948). In three articles—[Saemy Japhet], "The Secession of the Frankfurt Community under Samson Raphael Hirsch" (100–22); Isaac Heinemann, "Supplementary Remarks on the Secession from the Frankfurt Community under Samson Raphael Hirsch" (123–34); and Jacob Rosenheim, "Historical Significance of the Struggle for Secession from the Frankfurt Jewish Community" (135–46)—the developments in Frankfurt are discussed by natives of the city who were intimately involved in its

A very tense situation developed within the Frankfurt community, a situation that became exacerbated when the renowned Rabbi S. B. Bamberger of Würzburg issued a ruling supporting the decision of those who chose to remain within the general *kehillah*.[111] Much of the material contained in Bamberger's rebuttal

___

communal affairs. All three accounts provide intriguing background data but are highly subjective. An insight into Hirsch's thinking on secession and into the distinctions in approach between Hirsch and Hildesheimer may be obtained from the exchange of correspondence in Ezriel Hildesheimer, "Mi-tokh Hiluf ha-Mikhtavim beyn Maran R. Ezriel Hildesheimer Zatzal u-beyn Maran R. Shimshon Raphael Hirsch Zatzal u-Mekoravav," in *Yad Sha'ul: Sefer Zikaron al shem ha-Rav Dr. Shaul Weingort*, ed. J. J. Weinberg and P. Biberfeld (Tel Aviv, 1952), 233–51.

[111]Rabbi S. B. Bamberger, *Offene Antwort auf den an ihn gerichteten offenen Brief des Herrn S. R. Hirsch* (Würzburg: I. Frank'schen Buchhandlung, 1877). The sole rabbinic personality of stature to oppose Hirsch was Bamberger. Citation of Ettlinger's view by R. Zevi Yehudah Kook as recorded in *Hatzofeh*, December 29, 1972, is an obvious error of fact since at the time of the dispute between Hirsch and Bamberger over secession, Ettlinger was no longer alive. The rejoinder of David Henshke, "Mahloket le-Shem Shamayim," *Ha-Maayan* 13:4 (1973): 41–51, is very much to the point. Henshke also cites a similar error in Judah Leib Maimon, *Ha-Raiyah* (Jerusalem, Mossad ha-Rav Kook, 1965), 123.

In a communication to Bamberger urging the latter to reverse his ruling regarding the Frankfurt community, Maharam Schick (*Teshuvot Maraham Shik, Orah Hayyim*, no. 306) conceded that Hirsch had overstated the case in condemning as sinners those who did not join the secessionists since there were many devout individuals who hesitated to take that step for reasons that were entirely sociological in nature. Maharam Schick expressed his personal view, confirmed by his own experience, that, quite apart from the halakhic considerations involved in the question of secession, continued association with the nonobservant in a common *kehillah* structure would, in the course of time, prove deleterious. Furthermore, he stated that he was the recipient of a "tradition" handed down by Hatam Sofer that one should "distance oneself as much as possible from them and their cohorts and not be in one association with them."

of Hirsch's position, although intriguing and of weighty halakhic import, is a *non sequitur*. The only salient point is a fundamental and empirical disagreement with regard to whether continued participation in the *kehillah* did, or did not, constitute endorsement and legitimization of the views and policies espoused by institutions supported by the *kehillah*. Bamberger contended that the nature of the association with the Frankfurt *kehillah* was such that continued membership could not be construed as legitimization of heresy.

However, Bamberger was prepared to endorse retention of membership in the *kehillah* only in circumstances in which the Orthodox would be granted total autonomy in conducting the affairs of their own synagogues and religious organizations. As late as February 1877 he endorsed Hirsch's call for secession in Frankfurt[112] and reversed his position only when such autonomy was guaranteed by the *kehillah*. With regard to other communities in which the fundamental demands of the Orthodox were not granted, Bamberger ruled unequivocally that secession was not merely permissible but mandatory. In a responsum concerning the question of secession, Bamberger's son Simchah notes explicitly that only when the specified conditions were met did his father "agree that there is no obligation to separate from the Reform congregation in accordance with his reasoning. However, when these considerations are absent, his opinion has been recorded three and four times, namely, in the matter of Karlsruhe, Vienna, Wiesbaden and Frankfurt, that it is incumbent upon the law-abiding to separate themselves from the Reform congregation."[113]

Later, after concessions had been granted to the Orthodox community in Frankfurt assuring them of autonomy in matters of

---

[112]Bamberger, *Offene Antwort*, 14.

[113]*Teshuvot Zekher Simhah*, no. 230. Republished in Rabbi S. B. Bamberger, *Teshuvot Yad ha-Levi*, vol. 2 (Jerusalem, 1972). For a fuller analysis of Bamberger's position as well as of other considerations reflected in both sides of the dispute, see my "The Frankfurt Secession Controversy," *Jewish Action* 52:1 (Winter 1991–92): 22–27, 51–52.

religious practice, Bamberger ruled that *Austritt* (secession) was not mandatory in that community under the then prevailing circumstances. However, he did not view *Austritt* to be either forbidden or repugnant. He simply recognized the cogency of the familial, social, and emotional motives for remaining within the *kehillah*. While he fully recognized that remaining in the *kehillah* would minimize divisiveness within the community and provide opportunities for positive influence over others, he did not raise continued association to the level of an ideological imperative. Not so the leaders of the Frankfurt *kehillah*. For them secession was a breach of the unity of the community and unity was not only a cardinal principle but one with regard to which there could be no disagreement. Although tolerant of diverse theological positions with regard to all fundamentals of Jewish faith and practice, they regarded unity as the one dogma to which all must subscribe: "There will be no end to sectarianism if every tiny faction which does not agree with the forms recognized by the majority has the right, on that account, to withdraw from the whole."[114] Later, they wrote, "The religion of the majority alone, according to the principles of Judaism, is the true and legitimate religion."[115]

From that point on, the German Orthodox community was sharply divided. Following Hirsch's policy of *Trennungsorthodoxie* (separatist Orthodoxy) Jewish communities in several cities, notably those of Berlin, Wiesbaden, Darmstadt, and Mainz, established separatist Orthodox congregations. On the other hand, a large segment of Orthodoxy, whose position was considerably strengthened by Bamberger's sanction, chose to administer their own Orthodox institutions under the auspices of the overall community. Proponents of the latter policy, which came to be known as *Gemeindeorthodoxie* (communal Orthodoxy), established such com-

---

[114]From a memorandum of the Frankfurt *kehillah* board to the city Senate in 1854, cited by Liberles, *Religious Conflict*, 179.

[115]From a memorandum of the Frankfurt *kehillah* board to the city Senate in 1858, ibid.

munal arrangements in many towns, notably in Berlin, Cologne, Frankfurt, Hamburg, and Breslau.[116] Frequently, the very threat of secession appears to have had a significant effect in prompting the *kehillah* to accommodate the concerns of the Orthodox.[117] Cer-

---

[116]Despite the wealth of analytic comment in Noah Rosenbloom's *Tradition in an Age of Reform: The Religious Philosophy of Samson Raphael Hirsch* (Philadelphia: Jewish Publication Society, 1976), that work is marred by a partisanship that moves the author to interpret objective data in a manner that is not compelling. In particular, Rosenbloom's account of the controversy over secession is flawed. Rosenbloom is certainly entitled to regard secession as having been an unwise policy. But labeling Hirsch's action as "heedlessness" (p. 117) is hardly an appropriate designation if Hirsch believed he was "heeding" a higher imperative. The portrayal of those in other communities who followed Hirsch's secessionist policy as "malcontents" is also entirely unsupported and without basis in fact. Rosenbloom writes, "As expected, Hirsch's action was emulated by malcontents in other communities in Germany, such as Baden, Karlsruhe, Darmstadt, Wiesbaden, Giessen, Cologne, Bingen and Strassburg" (p. 119). The implication that those who—correctly or misguidedly—followed this policy were misanthropic, dyspeptic individuals, unhappy because of petty concerns or jealousies, can only reflect an unscholarly bias.

[117]Although, as noted above (n. 108), Liberles maintains that the Law of Secession was a manifestation of the strength of the Orthodox, its enactment certainly served to enhance that strength (cf. Liberles, 211). While the situation in Austria was not identical to that in Germany, the threat of *Austritt* served to curb radical Reform tendencies in that country as well. The Austrian government rejected a petition presented by the Orthodox members of the *Schiffschul* in 1872 for permission to secede and form a separate community. Nevertheless, the possibility that the Orthodox might eventually obtain such permission and act upon it influenced Vienna's Jewish communal leaders to desist from introducing ideological reforms in the communal synagogues. See Marsha L. Rozenblit, "The Struggle Over Religious Reform in Nineteenth-Century Vienna," *AJS Review* 14:2 (Fall 1989): 209–21. Significantly, Rozenblit demonstrates that the fear of loss of tax revenue was an important factor in the ultimate decision (p. 219).

tainly this was the case in Frankfurt itself where the various concessions granted the Orthodox within the *kehillah* were surely the result of the desire to limit the number who seceded. This rift within Orthodoxy did not heal with time and the two camps remained separate and distinct until the Holocaust decimated German Jewry.

Much has been written regarding the respective merits and failings of both approaches. The separatists have been taken to task for engendering a tragic waste of resources and for promoting divisiveness and disharmony. Hirsch's defenders, on the other hand, have maintained that were it not for the Law of Secession and the viable option of establishing autonomous Orthodox communities even *Gemeindeorthodoxie* would have been unable to wrest any concession from the general communities which were dominated by Reform elements. Very much to the point are the remarks of the Lithuanian rabbinic authority Rabbi Hayyim Ozer Grodzinski. R. Grodzinski hesitated to offer a definitive opinion with regard to what he viewed as a dispute whose resolution was contingent upon familiarity with the details of the local situation and subsequent determination of the wisest course of action under the circumstances, but nevertheless declared that in his opinion Hirsch's action was necessary for the preservation of Orthodoxy:

> There is no doubt that the sage and saint Rabbi S. R. Hirsch, of blessed memory . . . did a great thing in founding the admirable and outstanding *Religionsgesellschaft* which became an exemplary Jewish community. Had the God-fearing not separated themselves by means of a separate *kehillah*, due to their minority status they would have become submerged within the general community — [a development] which did not occur when they separated and developed on their own. Then even the general community was forced to improve itself and to conduct the general institutions in a sacred manner.[118]

---

[118]*Ahi'ezer: Kovetz Iggerot*, 1:243.

Whatever arguments may be presented in favor, or in criticism, of the wisdom and value of Hirsch's policy, several important points must be emphasized in the interests of historical accuracy. Hirsch's argument against enforced membership in, and taxation on behalf of, an overall religious superstructure was based upon considerations of freedom of conscience and infringement of basic civil liberties. Freedom of religion, argued Hirsch, entails not only freedom to desist from a form of worship which runs counter to an individual's convictions, but also freedom to refrain from actively supporting such forms of worship and the propagation of theological tenets offensive to a person's convictions. Thus, Hirsch claimed that the legal right of secession was based upon the fundamental principle of freedom of religious conscience which includes an individual's right to form his own independent community.

It is a distortion of fact to contend that Hirsch's practical policy of separation from the larger Jewish community was indicative of a lack of concern for individuals who did not accept the teachings of traditional Judaism.[119] Hirsch's *Nineteen Letters*, published in 1836, and a significant portion of his subsequent writings were addressed precisely to the questing and the nonobservant. Ultimately, the policy of separatism did in fact lead to an attitude of introversion and to an unfortunate erosion of interest in the well-being and welfare of the wider community. However, Hirsch himself cannot be faulted on that account. Quite to the contrary, Hirsch castigated those whose concern was limited solely to the religiously observant. Most revealing is Hirsch's discussion of the scriptural narrative of Abraham's quest for ten righteous men *within* the city of Sodom. He notes:

> The idea of a righteous man in the midst of Sodomite depravity which Abraham visualizes, for whose sake the city might be saved, is not one who keeps to his own four walls, in haughty pride of his superiority gives up the masses and just looks on at their ruinous moral lapses, who thinks he has done

---

[119]See the discussion in David Henshke, *Ha-Maayan* 13:4 (1973): 44–47.

quite enough if he saves himself and at most his own household. Yea, such a one Abraham would not class as righteous.
He would not consider that he had at all fulfilled the duty
which lies on every good man in bad surroundings. The ruin
of the masses whom he had long given up would leave such a
man cold. He might even possibly feel a certain smug satisfac-
tion in it. That is not Abraham's "righteous man" out of
consideration for whom the salvation of the city should be
effected. His righteous man is to be found "in the midst of the
city" and in lively connection with everything and everybody.
He never leaves off admonishing, teaching, warning, bettering
wherever and however he can. He takes everybody and
everything to heart; he never despairs, he is never tired of
trying, however distant the hopes of success may be. These are
the righteous ones whom he presumes must be "in the midst of
the city" who would feel grief and pain at the death of each
individual of these thousands. . . .[120]

Moreover, in formulating his position, Hirsch emphasized
that his policy demanded, not disassociation from individuals, but
secession from a communal system that he viewed as an institutionalized expression of heresy. In effect, Hirsch argued that the admonition "Do not associate with the wicked, even for purposes of
Torah" (*Avot de Rabi Natan* 9:4) is not applicable to the heretics of
the modern era and ruled that heretics and *apikorsim* such as those
with whom the Sages forbade all form of social contact no longer
exist in our time. The religious views of the nonobservant of
modern times have been shaped by parents, educational institutions, and a climate of opinion over which they have no control.
They are the products of their culture and are not to be held
responsible for what they are.[121] From a halakhic perspective they
are to be considered in a category identical to those *apikorsim* and
Karaites of whom Maimonides declared in *Hilkhot Mamrim*:

---

[120]Commentary on Genesis 18:24, English translation by I. Levi (London, 1959), 325–26.

[121]Cited by Hirsch, *Collected Works*, 6:207.

However, the children and grandchildren of these errants, whose parents have misled them, those who have been born among the Karaites who have reared them in their views, are like a child who has been taken captive among them, has been reared by them, and is not alacritous in seizing the paths of the commandments, whose status is comparable to that of an individual who is coerced; and even though he later learns that he is a Jew and becomes acquainted with Jews and their religion, he is nevertheless to be regarded as a person who is coerced for he was reared in their erroneous ways. Thus it is those of whom we have spoken who adhere to the practices of their Karaite parents who have erred. Therefore it is proper to cause them to return in repentance and to draw them nigh with words of peace until they return to the strength-giving Torah. [3:3]

Perhaps the best exposition of the arguments both for and against secession may be found in the previously cited letter of R. Hayyim Ozer Grodzinski. R. Grodzinski recognized the cogency of both positions as well as the sincere positive intentions of the protagonists. He wrote:

Regarding the question of association with sinners, in the opinion of the separatists they see in this a great danger to Judaism that [people] will learn from their actions and by their proximity they may influence the future generation in a negative manner. It is axiomatic that a matter that concerns the foundations of Judaism involves a grave proscription. However, in the opinion of the accommodationists, they see in this matter a great *mitzvah*, not to estrange a large portion of the Jewish people and bring them merit, and they see no loss in this for the faithful who are separated with regard to religious needs. And, thus, this does not involve a question regarding which one says, and do you tell an individual, sin in order that you bring merit to your friend? For, in the opinion of the accommodationists, this does not entail any sin or transgression, rather, to the contrary, it is a *mitzvah* to bring merit to the many. Accordingly, what the separationists see as a great transgression in uniting, in this, the accommodationists see a *mitzvah*. The doubt, according to this, is in the very act itself, whether it is a *mitzvah* or a transgression.[122]

What was apparent to R. Hayyim Ozer Grodzinski, writing in the early part of the twentieth century, has become even more evident as the events of recent history have vindicated the arguments of both proponents and opponents of secession.[123]

---

[122]*Ahi'ezer: Kovetz Iggerot* 1:243–44.

[123]Hirsch was not moved to formulate the policy of *Austritt* in the 1870s because of disinterest in the welfare of the nonobservant. His teachings and writings were addressed to that constituency and his concern for them was very real. However, if there is a shortcoming to be ascribed to the remarkable *kehillah* in New York City that has inherited the traditions of Frankfurt am Main, it is an insularity and isolationism, which is not the cause, but the product, of *Austritt*. Lack of contact over a period of years is bound to decrease a sense of concern and ongoing interest. With the passage of decades the *kehillah* has increasingly focused in an inward direction and has had little contact with individuals of different religious outlook and orientation. The result has been a sad loss for the wider Orthodox community. The standards, integrity, cohesiveness, and faith of the *kehillah* have produced outstanding educational and communal institutions greatly benefiting both residents of its environs and the entire city. But the general Orthodox community in the United States, not to speak of those beyond the pale of Orthodoxy, has not had the benefit of its guidance or leadership.

On the other hand, the ability of the *kehillah* to recreate itself on these shores after dislocation and war, despite relatively meager financial resources during its early years, and to develop into a community that is a model *kehillah*, stands as a tribute to the staunch advocates of *Torah im derekh eretz* among its adherents and to their total commitment to its religious ideals. It is a singular community in which the word of *Rav* remains unquestioned law, *kevod ha-rabbanut* is a meaningful phrase, and the label of the community, *K'hal Adas Jeschurun*, stands for a level of religious probity and reliability that is acknowledged by the entire spectrum of Orthodox Jewry.

Nevertheless, since as R. Hayyim Ozer Grodzinski noted, the decision to secede from the wider community is to be reached on the basis of a variety of considerations that depend on the needs and problems of the particular locale, the philosophy and rhetoric of secession of the 1870s may be sorely out of place in the 1990s. Of interest in this regard is a statement of a number of rabbis of the London Orthodox community issued in 1979 in opposition to joint communal programs to be undertaken under the auspices of Orthodox Jews in association with Jews in Liberal-Reform congregations. Noteworthy is not so much the decision itself, which may or may not be compelled by halakhic and/or socio-religious considerations, but the language in which it is couched. In a publication addressed to the broader general community, the Orthodox rabbis state: "Anyone who imagines that these dissenters can be brought back into the fold by consorting with them is deluding himself and misleading others. Indeed, such conduct will repel the Orthodox and those awaiting proper spiritual guidance."[124]

This is not a halakhic pronouncement but a descriptive statement of fact. Is this a statement that had validity in the 1980s? Will it be valid for the 1990s?

SELF-CRITICISM

Rare, but not entirely absent, in rabbinical writings of this period is the expression of a sense of responsibility bordering on guilt on the part of the rabbinic leaders themselves for the failings of the generation. In the earliest responsa focusing on Reform collected and published in *Eleh Divrei ha-Berit*, R. Eliezer of Triesch turned to his colleagues and admonished that the movement for reform in religious worship served as a sign that the Orthodox were indeed found wanting in precisely that aspect of religious life. If there were inadequacies in ritual and communal life it was rabbinic leaders

---

[124]*The Jewish Chronicle* (London), April 20, 1979, 21.

who bore the brunt of the responsibility for improvement. More-over, only individuals who were themselves of exemplary moral stature could hope to exert influence on the wayward.[125]

Of the various writings that focused on halakhic problems relating to the nonobservant, R. Tzevi Hirsch Chajes's *Minhat Kenaot* was unique in its scathing self-critique and indictment of the Orthodox rabbinate and its failure to respond to the needs of the time. In the opinion of Chajes, the early successes of the Reform movement were directly attributable to this deficiency.

It is on account of this self-critique that *Minhat Kenaot* occupied a position of unique importance in the polemical literature of the time and that it may have had a salutary impact. Most polemics fail to persuade since the argument is addressed to, read by, and accepted by only an already committed audience. In Reform-Orthodox polemics, the Orthodox preached to the Orthodox concerning the failings of the Reform rabbinate and the Ortho-dox agreed; the Reform preached to the Reform concerning Orthodox shortcomings and adherents of Reform agreed. In *Minhat Kenaot*, in an unusual *volte face*, an Orthodox writer castigated his Orthodox colleagues, in Hebrew, regarding their own failings.

Whatever hesitation and ambivalence Chajes may have experi-enced in pronouncing judgment upon exponents of Reform, he hesitated not a whit in his sharp critique and condemnation of his Orthodox colleagues. In *Minhat Kenaot*, he declared unequivocally: "I know the responsibility for the religious warping of the genera-tion rests solely upon our contemporary rabbis. Theirs was the obligation to stand on the look-out."[126] Again and again, he calls the rabbis to task in the words of the prophet Ezekiel, "But if the watchman sees the sword come and blows not the horn, and the

---

[125]*Eleh Divrei ha-Berit*, 94–96. Cf., also, comments in *Minhat Ani*, regarding the responsibilities of religious leaders, 5b, 87a–88a, 99a, 129b–130a.

[126]Chajes, *Minhat Kenaot*, 1019. See Chajes's almost identical language in the introduction to *Darkei Horaah*, 209.

people be not warned and the sword do come and take any person from among them . . . but his blood will I require at the watchman's hand" (33:6). In his analysis of the paralysis in Orthodox leadership Chajes differentiated between various categories of rabbinic leaders, all of whom he regarded as having fallen short of the mark. He divided those rabbis into four groups: to three of these groups he directed counterarguments and words of inspiration and encouragement; with regard to the fourth group he simply bemoaned the fact that he could find no common ground for discourse.

There are a significant number of rabbis among the Orthodox, wrote Chajes, who simply are unaware of the cataclysmic events taking place all around them. They have no knowledge of Reform circles in Germany; they have not followed the proceedings of the Reform Rabbinical Conferences as reported in the press and they are ignorant of the extent of the changes that have been instituted in various synagogues. In strongest tones, Chajes expressed disdain for such leadership:

> With such rabbis I can have no relationship whatsoever, since I know with certainty that they do not fulfill the obligations that devolve upon them by virtue of their standing in the community. Their standing demands of them not to be silent, bovine-like, concerned only with their immediate surroundings, unaware of what transpires among their people. Rather, an obligation devolves upon them to be informed.[127]

Complaints regarding know-nothingism among rabbis are a recurrent theme in Chajes's private correspondence. He repeatedly assailed defects in the religious education of the age. At an earlier date Chajes had authored a memorandum to the government containing practical suggestions regarding the training of rabbis and the responsibilities of their office in the community. In a

---

[127]Chajes, *Minhat Kenaot*, 1016.

private communication in which he described candidates for rabbinic office in Galicia, Chajes candidly wrote:

> Even that segment of the youth that prepare to devote
> themselves to a rabbinical career have not the vaguest notion
> of the scope of that office. . . . Of the vast corpus of the laws,
> of *Orah Hayyim* they study only the laws of Passover, and even
> that section not in its entirety . . . and then of *Yoreh De'ah*, the
> laws of ritual slaughter, *terefot,* milk and meat, and forbidden
> mixtures. This constitutes their entire course of study. If one
> of them has a smattering of proficiency in these areas, even if
> he does not know that David reigned after Saul, he will be
> recommended by the Rabbis as the most qualified rabbinical
> candidate for even the most prestigious cities.[128]

In another communication Chajes bemoaned in particular the lack
of appreciation of the importance of the study of history among
members of the Polish rabbinate: "In particular, among our coreligionists in the provinces of Poland, knowledge of the events of
history is regarded as a useless matter and they have no desire to
pursue it, deeming such study a waste of time and effort."[129]

However, the vast majority of Orthodox rabbis, Chajes
claimed, were indeed aware of the dangers of the innovators but,
nevertheless, had been unable to respond adequately. Chajes di-
vides those rabbis into three subgroups:

1. Those who were afraid to be vocal in opposition to Reform
lest their own response focus even more attention upon Reform

---

[128]The full text is cited in Herskovics, 367–68. See also N. M. Gelber,
Toldot Yehudei Brody (Jerusalem: Mossad ha-Rav Kook, 1955), 288.

[129]Herskovics, *Maharatz Hayes*, p. 215. Cf. Chajes, *Darkei Horaah,*
209–10, where Chajes observes that Maimonides did not utilize historical
research. For Chajes's own positive sentiments regarding this discipline,
see *She'elot u-Teshuvot Maharatz Hayes,* no. 12, 647–49; Herskovics,
Maharatz Hayes, 215, 280.

deviation and inadvertently enhance its success. Eastern European masses who had hitherto followed tradition unquestioningly might learn of innovations introduced by adherents of Reform and find them to be appealing. Accordingly, those rabbis regarded silence as the better part of valor.

2. A second group consisted of rabbis who were well aware of their own failings and lack of skill in the art of debate. They feared public confrontation lest their lack of expertise bring dishonor to their cause.

3. Finally, a third segment of the rabbinate consisted of talented and learned individuals who enjoyed positions of prestige in the community but considered themselves to be above the fray and believed it to be beneath their dignity to engage in debate with individuals who were not their equals in rabbinic scholarship.

Turning to the first two groups, Chajes stated simply that fear of publicity was vain. Regardless of what would or would not be done on the part of the Orthodox, the masses could not long remain in ignorance of the activities of Reform innovators. Chajes recognized adoption of an ostrichlike mentality to be ridiculous and candidly remarked, "Whether or not the innovators are knowledgeable or pious, they are assuredly most adept in the art of communication in public and they know how to present their programs in an attractive format."[130] Whoever would not hear about those matters from the periodicals and newspapers would not be likely to learn about them from learned scholarly debates. To the second group, Chajes offered advice and encouragement. He cautioned that fear of dishonor is but a defense mechanism and added that perhaps these individuals merely seek noble excuses to avoid challenge.

However, upon the third group, Chajes vented his spleen in language bespeaking pain and bitterness. He felt that they had abdicated their role as rabbis since they placed their personal honor

---

[130]Chajes, *Minhat Kenaot*, 1017.

and glory above the welfare of their communities. In the sharpest of tones he catalogued the shortcomings of the Orthodox rabbinate: their poor communication skills; their lack of pastoral technique; their failure to promote the welfare of their constituents; and their abysmal failure to understand the spirit that animates contemporary society and the very real social, ideological, and intellectual problems with which their coreligionists were confronted. In their self-absorption they had even failed to address the single most important need of the hour: establishment of appropriate educational institutions. Unfortunately, conceded Chajes, they were, and deserved to be, a target for the criticism of Reform adversaries: "Because of the behavior of the rabbis of our country, our adversaries have found a place to make claims against rabbis of the old school saying that those who follow talmudic Judaism are as sheep who have no shepherd or guide."[131] On the other hand, wrote Chajes, the leaders of the Reform movement had excelled in the very areas in which the Orthodox had failed so abjectly.

In a remarkable departure from the recriminatory style of Orthodox polemicists, Chajes candidly conceded the ability of Reform leaders to address the concerns of their followers and bemoaned the abysmal failure of most traditional rabbis to understand the very real ideological problems with which their constituents were confronted. In all honesty, one must admit, wrote Chajes, that whether or not the innovators are knowledgeable and while they may not be pious, "they certainly do have manners and culture and an ability to speak." No wonder, he added, that even formerly traditional congregations in large cities in Eastern Europe availed themselves of the services of these preachers.[132] Chajes's

---

[131]Ibid., 1018.

[132]Ibid., 1019. R. Meir Schapiro would later poke fun at modern rabbis and their penchant for sermonizing. In a play on the biblical verse Exodus 32:7 and the Yiddish "reden," preach—Hebrew "go down"—he commented, "*Lekh red,* When does one need to keep preaching? '*Ki shihes amkha,*' 'when your community is on a low level.' " *Zikhron Meir,* ed. A.

devastating critique of the Orthodox leadership and his intriguing analysis serve as a harbinger of what was to become the agenda for counter-Reform in the 1850s and 1860s.

One of the major rabbinic figures at the helm of the move- ment for counter-Reform and a creative leader in the revitalization of Orthodox educational institutions in Germany and Hungary was Azriel Hildesheimer. In many of these endeavors he was motivated by a visionary zeal shared by few of his contemporaries. He, too, turned a keenly critical eye upon the rabbinate and, in numerous letters and writings, sought to arouse his colleagues from their lethargy and to spur them to positive endeavors:

> The greatest enemies in our midst are fear, confusion and dread . . . our side is silent and continues to be silent. . . .[133] Indeed, I am assured that only with regard to what should not be done is there ever agreement among *Gedolei Yisrael*, but not with regard to what may be done; . . . always in our midst there is only "No" and "No." But . . . the main thing is to build.[134]

POSITIVE RESPONSES

Responses to Reform were by no means entirely negative in nature. In a limited sense the Reform movement occasioned salient intro- spection and self-criticism of the type called for by R. Tzevi Hirsch Chajes and improvements in such relatively minor matters as synagogue decorum. That reaction was prompted, in part, by recognition of the fact that these matters did indeed require correc-

---

Schapiro (New York, 1954), 63. Chajes had no such compunctions. He readily conceded that the strength of Reform leaders lay in their homilet- ical skills.

[133]*Iggerot Rabbi Ezriel Hildesheimer*, ed. Mordecai Eliav (Jerusalem: Rubin Mass, 1965), 30–31 (Hebrew).

[134]Ibid., 35.

tion but, primarily, out of a desire for containment, that is, to eliminate factors that might prompt further alienation and defection.

The prospect of the alienation of additional Jews, the aggregate number of whom could not be foretold, was certainly a matter of concern. But no less significant was the challenge of winning back the hearts and minds of those already attracted to the Reform movement. Many of the methods employed in that endeavor would also serve to stem the ongoing loss of those who, with the enticing availability of Reform as an option, were becoming disaffected with Orthodoxy. Although not all Orthodox leaders recognized that a positive program was imperative, some realized quite clearly that, ultimately, the only effective response to Reform and nonobservance was to be found in a positive approach, and that an effective agenda must include the founding of appropriate educational institutions, publication of journals and books for a popular audience, as well as the reopening of channels of communication and instruction.

One of the earliest rabbinic figures to express the need for such a positive approach was R. Jacob Ettlinger. His awareness of this need is articulated in a number of highly significant passages in *Minhat Ani*. In those comments Ettlinger called upon rabbinic leaders to concentrate their efforts upon a program of instruction and careful explanation geared to those whose faith had faltered. He stated emphatically that criticism and didacticism alone would continue to be ineffective; emphasis must be placed upon teaching and clarification of the practices and traditions of Judaism. Commenting on the double Hebrew expression for reproof (*hokhe'ah tokhiah*) employed in the biblical admonition "You shall surely reprove your friend" (Leviticus 19:17) and upon the dual connotations of the Hebrew term *hokhahah*, as meaning proof as well as reproof, Ettlinger notes:

> The repetition of [the word] *hokhe'ah* denotes that it is of the essence of reproof that when one says to one's friend, "Do not

do that" if he has committed a transgression or, "Do so and so" if he has ceased to observe a commandment, one should not do so without explaining the reason to him. . . . Rather, one should explain the matter to him so that he himself will understand the purpose of that which he admonishes him to do or to cease doing. . . . And that is what is meant by "You shall surely reprove" *(hokhe'ah tokhiah)*: with evidence and with logic you shall reprove him. . . .[135]

Ettlinger's positive approach undoubtedly molded the thinking of his disciples Samson Raphael Hirsch and Azriel Hildesheimer. Assuredly, the greatest accomplishments of these two leading ideologues of modern Orthodoxy in Germany were their innovative programs for dealing with the intellectual needs of their age.

Hirsch's first major literary works were the *Nineteen Letters,* published in 1836 under the pseudonym of Ben Uziel, and *Horeb,* subtitled *Essays on Israel's Duties in the Dispersion,* a compendium of *halakhot* and their underlying rationale and interpretive meaning, published in 1837.[136] In the case of the *Nineteen Letters,* in a sense,

---

[135]Ettlinger, *Minhat Ani*, 63a. See also, ibid., 5b, 87a–88b, 99a–100a, 129b–130a.

[136]Over a hundred years after their publication, the written works of Hirsch remain a treasured resource for the Orthodox student and scholar. If these works do not have the same magnetic effect upon some contemporary readers that they had in earlier decades, it is simply because of their particular potency in striking resonant chords that were uniquely nineteenth century in nature. The effectiveness of Hirsch's writings at the time of their publication is to be attributed, in part, precisely to the manner in which they captured the idiom, the mind-set, and the sensibilities of nineteenth-century Germany. Although to today's reader sections of these works may seem too forced, too heavy, or too didactic in tone, it is those very qualities that contributed to their popularity at a different stage in time.

The value of Hirsch's written works was fully appreciated by leading

the medium was the message; the format was as significant as the content. The letters were presented in the form of a dialogue via correspondence. In the first letter, a questioning and questing individual addresses a young rabbi and the rabbi replies in the following eighteen epistles. The salient feature is that there is a dialogue between two different individuals with two differing perspectives. The one doubts, hesitates, queries, questions. The other discusses, explains, argues, rhapsodizes, and interprets. At no time, however, does the respondent castigate or berate. The message of the format is clear and unequivocal: The author recognizes that there are different perspectives and, more significantly, that these differing perspectives are cogent and sincere. Hirsch is saying to the questioner: I realize that you have questions; I know that there are ample reasons to question; I wish to teach, to explain, and to provide answers. Your questions are well founded; I understand your doubts and hesitations. I even recognize that, in part, the shortcomings of our own community have caused your doubts to become even stronger. In the broad Orthodox community the neglect of spirituality has fostered a type of arid observance that is unattractive and hollow. No wonder that such rote observance has failed to inspire your confidence. But do not permit the failings of contemporary coreligionists to quench your own thirst for spiritu-

---

Torah scholars both of his own generation and of the generation that followed. Rabbi Israel Salanter sought to promote the translation of the *Nineteen Letters* into Russian. See Dov Katz, *Tenu'at ha-Mussar*, 3rd ed. (Tel Aviv: A. Zioni, 1958), 1:223. R. Hayyim Ozer Grodzinski, *Ahi'ezer: Kovetz Iggerot*, vol. 2, also commended translations of Hirsch's writings and wrote in superlative terms of "the *Gaon* and scholar, of blessed memory, who knew the ailments of the children of his generation and endeavored to cure them and was successful in drawing pure, living waters, waters of healing and refreshment for those who suffer maladies of the soul" (589–90). Cf. the encomium of Rav Kook, *Iggerot ha-Reiyah* 1:182: "The giant in knowledge, noble prince of God, the *Gaon*, R. Shimshon Hirsch, who with the saving might of his right hand preserved the remnant of Western Jewry."

ality and do not permit the failings of our coreligionists to becloud the beauty of the traditions of our people.

Although the dialogue is not continued and the doubter is not afforded an opportunity to challenge the answers provided in the form of the literary device of further letters, the message of the format is nevertheless not lost: The message is one of respect, of concern, of cordiality, and of availability. Moreover, although the questioner is afforded but one letter,[137] Hirsch, in his replies, frequently presents the opposing arguments and gives credence to many of the well-taken criticisms of exponents of Reform.[138] Indeed, perhaps the most powerful of Hirsch's methods is his utilization of the skilled debater's technique of stealing the opponent's thunder by conceding the opponent's best arguments in presenting them oneself.

Also noteworthy in terms of format is another stylistic characteristic which might easily be overlooked by a twentieth-century reader. Accustomed as we are to "equal opportunity" language, we may not notice the sensitivity to, and awareness of, the role of women and the conscious effort to address the concerns of "sons and daughters."[139] Such awareness and sensitivity is highly unusual in a nineteenth-century Orthodox writer.

----

[137]Indeed, this was Geiger's criticism of the *Nineteen Letters* and it is well-taken. See Geiger's review, "Rescensionen, *Iggerot Tzafon: Neunzehn Briefe über Judenthum*, Erster Artikel," *Wissenschaftliche Zeitschrift für jüdische Theologie* 2 (1836): 355; and Liberles, *Religious Conflict*, 122.

[138]For example, Samson Raphael Hirsch, *The Nineteen Letters of Ben Uziel*, trans. Bernard Drachman (New York: Bloch, 1942), 98–100, 147–148, 173, 185–87, 190–93, 195–96, 202–05. Cf. the letter from Hirsch to his friend Z. H. May in Hamburg included in *Horeb*, trans. I. Grunfeld (New York: Soncino, 1962), cxlii–cxliii.

[139]Hirsch, *Nineteen Letters*, 199, 201, 203, 220. The title page of the first edition of *Horeb* bore the dedication, "To Israel's thinking young men and women," and in the Foreword, the author writes, "I ventured to lay my essays before my brothers and sisters because the time seemed to demand something of the kind" (clxi).

Horeb presents a response to the challenge of Reform on an entirely different level. The basic thrust of Reform was radically antihalakhic, if not completely antinomian. Rather than debating fundamental questions of the theological or philosophical basis for the continuing binding force of halakhic rules or responding technically with involved arguments regarding the parameters of particular laws, Hirsch, in this work, adopted a quite different tactic. In *Horeb*, Hirsch undertook to delineate the laws, to teach their details, and to offer interpretations of their significance and symbolic or spiritual meaning. Rather than debate the case, Hirsch presented the law as a given. However, the detailed, precise, loving exposition of the law in its minutiae was, in itself, the answer to Reform. In effect, Hirsch was saying: This, the law, the 613 *mitzvot*, presented herewith in six divisions, is Judaism. This is the heart and soul of our religion. Reject the law and you are rejecting the heart and soul of Judaism.

Apart from his literary efforts, Hirsch played a major role in the modernization of Jewish education. In Frankfurt, Hirsch made establishment of a school that would offer a dual curriculum of religious and secular studies a matter of highest priority. Schools established by the Orthodox in Altona and Halberstadt had introduced the combined study of religious and secular subjects and use of current educational methodology.[140] Hirsch deemed such educational enterprises to be fundamental for the survival of Orthodoxy. Indeed, his earliest literary endeavors had been spurred by his concern to provide textbooks for teachers.[141] The school he

---

[140]Mordecai Eliav, *Ha-Hinnukh ha-Yehudi be-Germaniyah be-Yemei ha-Haskalah ve-ha-Emantzipatziyah* (Jerusalem: The Jewish Agency, 1960), 159–61, 232–35.

[141]In his letter to Z. H. May dated April 13, 1835, Hirsch writes, "I am in charge of a few hundred young souls; I have to provide teachers for them, of whom I have to ask that they introduce our youth into Judaism. But I cannot ask that of the teachers, because they themselves do not know what Judaism really means, and one cannot even really blame them

founded in Frankfurt in 1853, the *Unterrichtsanstalt der Israelitischen Religionsgesellschaft*, attracted a significant enrollment and became an important institution for the training of Orthodox laymen.[142]

The second major ideologue of the time, R. Azriel Hildesheimer, recognized that it was not sufficient to create institutions for elementary education. The need of the hour was for the training of rabbis who would be equipped to respond to the unique demands of the time. Writing to a group of lay leaders in May 1872, Hildesheimer, then in Berlin, extolled the positive achievements of a reinvigorated, restructured Orthodoxy and the establishment of independent congregations and journals. Yet, in a *cri de coeur*, he expressed his anxiety that, these developments notwithstanding,

> Where can we find . . . in our camp an institution that, in some measure, can respond to the destructive tendencies of our time and answer the needs of the hour? . . . Have we at all begun such an undertaking, even partially? . . . He who does not wish to deceive himself must see that in our stance there is a narrowness that may quiet matters momentarily but will not provide a substantive solution. . . . Whence shall we take rabbis? Whence shall we take teachers?[143]

Hildesheimer was not the first to perceive the need for a new type of institution for the training of rabbis. During the early years

---

for their ignorance. Moreover, there is no text-book available which I could give them for guidance" (*Horeb*, cxliv). Similarly, in the *Nineteen Letters*, Hirsch asserts, "I rejoice that the impulse to these essays was derived from the necessity of supplying the teachers of the schools under my supervision with a book in which they could read themselves into Jews before they began to rear young souls for Judaism" (p. 219).

[142]Eliav, *Ha-Hinnukh*, 227–32. See also Liberles, *Religious Conflict*, 152–55; and Rosenbloom, *Tradition*, 104.

[143]Published in Meir Hildesheimer, "Ketavim be-Dvar Yesod Bet ha-Midrash le-Rabbanim be-Berlin," *Ha-Maayan* 14 (1974): 14–15.

of the nineteenth century, the growth of *Haskalah* and impoverishment in some parts of Europe caused many of the *yeshivot* in Western Europe to close and the number of students in the ones remaining to dwindle.[144] Until that time, the *yeshivah*, with a curriculum of study consisting solely of Talmud and Codes, had served as the major source for the training of rabbis. The traditional *yeshivah* was an academic institution of higher learning concerned solely with rabbinic scholarship and made no effort to provide practical or professional training for rabbis. In response to cataclysmic change in the orientation of the Jewish community a demand arose for the establishment of a radically new type of educational institution that was to differ from the *yeshivah* in three basic respects: (1) There was to be a pronounced professional orientation with courses in homiletics and practical rabbinics. (2) The curriculum was to include secular studies as well. (3) The religious studies program was to be broadened to include Jewish philosophy and history and a somewhat positive attitude to modern Jewish scholarship and *Wissenschaft*.[145]

Throughout the course of the nineteenth century the question of professional training for the rabbinate was the focus of heated controversy within the Orthodox community. A number of innovative proposals were vigorously endorsed by some authorities only to be violently contested by others. The earliest suggestion for the establishment of a rabbinical seminary is found in a little known work entitled *Mosdot Tevel*, authored by Rabbi David Friesenhausen and published in Vienna in 1820. Friesenhausen claims to have submitted his novel proposal to government authorities as

---

[144]Ibid., 18–19; Eliav, *Ha-Hinnukh*, 237–38.

[145]Cf. the interesting comments and analysis of Mordecai Breuer, "Three Orthodox Approaches to *Wissenschaft*," *Jubilee Volume in Honor of Rabbi Joseph B. Soloveichik*, ed. S. Israeli, N. Lamm, and Y. Raphael (Jerusalem and New York: Mossad ha-Rav Kook and Yeshiva University, 1984), 2:856–65.

early as 1806, but he surmised quite correctly that "the majority of rabbis will oppose this matter."[146] The rabbinic leaders who originally endorsed the plan were prevailed upon publicly to withdraw their support.[147] More realistic proposals for the establishment of a rabbinical seminary were advanced by Rabbi Jacob Ettlinger as early as 1829[148] and again, in greater detail, in 1846.[149] For a variety of reasons those projects were abandoned[150] but many aspects of the proposed curriculum were later adopted by the Orthodox seminary established by Hildesheimer.

What for others was but a dream became a reality as the result of the creative leadership of Hildesheimer. *Die Rabbinerseminar für das Orthodoxische Judentum* established by Hildesheimer in Berlin in 1873 became a potent force in the Orthodox community. Decades later Joseph Wohlgemuth made the extravagant claim that the *Rabbinerseminar* had saved Orthodox Judaism in Western Europe and "only fools or zealots would not recognize this."[151] Apparently there are many whom Wohlgemuth would have considered to be fools and zealots since, despite its many successes, the *Rabbinerseminar* did not meet with universal approval in rabbinic circles.

Hildesheimer himself suggested that much of the opposition was based on previous negative experience with graduates of government-sponsored assimilationist seminaries and would dissipate when it became evident that his institution, staffed with an

---

[146]R. David Friesenhausen, *Mosdot Tevel* 91a.

[147]Ibid., 92a. See also R. Solomon Schuck, *She'elot u-Teshuvot Rashban al Even ha-Ezer* (Satmar, 1905), no. 157; and R. Moses Schick, *She'elot u-Teshuvot Maharam Shik, Orah Hayyim,* nos. 306, 307.

[148]Jaap Meijer, *Moeder in Israel: Een Geschiedenis van het Amsterdamse Asjkenazische Jodendom* (Haarlem: Bakenes, 1964), 80–81.

[149]*Der treue Zionswächter* 2 (1846): 241–45.

[150]*Die jüdische Presse* 3 (1872): 343–44.

[151]Cited in Moshe A. Shulvass, "Bet ha-Midrash le-Rabbanim be-Berlin," in *Mosdot Torah be-Europah be-Binyanam u-be-Hurbanam,* ed. Samuel K. Mirsky (New York, 1956), 697.

observant and dedicated faculty, was of a different genre.[152] But that was an oversimplification. Several of Hildesheimer's prominent colleagues in Germany remained notably cool toward the undertaking. Rabbi Samson Raphael Hirsch was unenthusiastic. Although the relationship between Hirsch and Hildesheimer may not have been free of tension, Hirsch's distrust of the seminary was based upon ideological considerations.[153] The venerable Rabbi Seligmann Baer Bamberger of Würzburg, as Hildesheimer himself conceded, was opposed as a matter of "pure ideological conviction with no personal animus whatsoever" simply because he did not favor the mingling of secular and sacred studies in a rabbinical academy.[154]

Many rabbinic authorities regarded the *Rabbinerseminar* as highly effective in preserving Orthodoxy in Germany but considered it to be unacceptable as an ideal.[155] In particular, R. Isaac Elhanan Spektor and Rabbi Israel Salanter praised Hildesheimer's achievements in Berlin.[156] Yet, repeatedly, reservations were ex-

---

[152]*Iggerot Rabbi Ezriel*, 34 (Hebrew).

[153]Shulvass, "Bet ha-Midrash," 694; Eliav, "Mekomo shel ha-Rav Ezriel Hildesheimer be-Maavak al Demuttah shel Yahadut Hungariyah," *Zion* 27 (1962): 85–86.

[154]*Iggerot Rabbi Ezriel*, 50 (Hebrew). See also Yitzchak Adler, "Minhagei ha-Rav Yitzchak Dov ha-Levi Bamberger Zatzal ve-Hanhagotav," *Ha-Maayan* 19 (1979): 35, 35 n. 2.

[155]Hungarian rabbis who had been vociferously opposed to Hildesheimer's earlier educational activities in Eisenstadt were muted in criticism of the Berlin seminary. See Eliav, "Mekomo," 66–67. Characteristic is an alleged comment of *Ketav Sofer* favoring Hildesheimer's Berlin endeavor because while "here he spoiled, there he will correct" (*Iggerot Soferim*, sec. 3, 41, n.).

[156]See Hildesheimer, "Ketavim," 34–37; R. Isaac Jacob Reines, *Shnei ha-Me'orot*, pt. 2 (Pietrkov, 1913), *Ma'amar Zikaron ba-Sefer*, sec. 1, 46. Cf. D. Hoffmann, "Festrede," in *Zum hundertjährigen Geburtstage des Rabbiners und Seminardirektors Dr. Israel Hildesheimer* (Berlin: Jeschurun, 1920), 5–12.

pressed regarding the suitability of such a program of study in Eastern Europe where Torah learning had not been diluted.[157] In a lengthy responsum in which, *inter alia*, he discussed the conditions under which secular studies might be included in the curriculum of communal schools, the head of the famed Yeshivah of Volozhin, R. Naftali Zevi Yehudah Berlin, cautioned that one should not expect such schools to produce rabbis and arbiters of the law for "it is the way of Torah to endure . . . and the goal of Torah study to be achieved, only in someone who devotes himself to it totally and exclusively."[158]

---

[157]On Rabbi Israel Salanter's reservations regarding professional schools for the rabbinate see Katz, *Tenuat ha-Mussar* 1:226–27; and Rabbi Jacob J. Weinberg, *Seridei Esh*, vol. 4 (Jerusalem: Mossad ha-Rav Kook, 1969), 234–35. Although R. Israel Salanter was opposed in principle to the establishment of rabbinical seminaries in Eastern Europe, he was a proponent of a vigorous educational program directed toward both the broad masses and the intelligentsia. He attempted to foster translations of the Talmud into a European vernacular as well as into Hebrew in order to popularize its study and mounted a campaign for the inclusion of talmudic studies in the curricula of European universities. See Katz, *Tenuat ha-Mussar*, 221–22; and Hillel Goldberg, *Between Berlin and Slabodka: Jewish Transition Figures from Eastern Europe* (Hoboken, NJ: Ktav, 1989), 30. Rabbi Israel Salanter believed that, apart from other benefits that might accrue, acceptance of Talmud in the academic curriculum of the university would lend it prestige in the eyes of assimilated Jews and might stimulate their own renewed interest in their heritage. He understood full well that they were enamored of secular and non-Jewish culture. Subjects held in esteem by non-Jews might arouse their own curiosity. If valued by non-Jews, then the Talmud might be seen as having enduring value by Jews as well. (It is related that when, on one occasion, a nonobservant *maskil* was called to the reading of the Torah in Brisk and recited the blessings, R. Joseph Baer Soloveichik, the *Beit ha-Levi*, commented pithily, "He certainly should recite the blessing 'who has given *us* the Torah' for had God given the Torah to the non-Jews, he would feel bound to observe its tenets." See Aaron Suraski, *Marbitzei Torah u-Mussar* [New York, 1977], 1:83.)

[158]*She'elot u-Teshuvot Meshiv Davar*, no. 44.

Decades later, some prominent Orthodox scholars continued to view rabbinical seminaries as, at best, an accommodation necessary to meet the needs of the Jewish communities of Western Europe. In the early 1930s, during the early years of the Hitler regime, a plan was formulated to relocate the Hildesheimer seminary—then in the sixth decade of its existence—to Palestine. Meir Hildesheimer, the administrator, traveled to the Holy Land on an investigatory mission. However, upon his return to Berlin, the Board of Directors and teaching faculty vetoed the proposal.[159] In all likelihood a principal reason for abandonment of this plan was the avowed opposition to transfer of the seminary expressed by leading Orthodox rabbinical authorities in Jerusalem and in Eastern Europe. An explicit record of this opposition is to be found in a series of letters discussing the projected move written by R. Hayyim Ozer Grodzinski of Vilna to the heads of the Berlin seminary as well as to his rabbinic colleagues in Palestine, including Rabbi Joseph Tzevi Duschinsky in Jerusalem and Rabbi Abraham Isaiah Karelitz, the *Hazon Ish*, in Bnei Brak.[160]

Rabbi Grodzinski enumerated his reasons for opposing establishment of a rabbinical seminary in Palestine, succinctly stating that: (1) While the Hildesheimer seminary fulfilled "the need of the hour, the time and the place," and was essential in an age and a locale that required Orthodox communities to appoint rabbis who had also received a university education, such a need was limited to the acculturated German community of the late nineteenth and early twentieth centuries. (2) Palestine in the twentieth century had no need, wrote Rabbi Grodzinski, for such a "factory for the production of rabbis." Palestine had great *yeshivot* of its own and did

---

[159]Shulvass, "Bet ha-Midrash," 712–13.

[160]*Ahi'ezer: Kovetz Iggerot* 2:443–47. Some of these letters are also to be found in Abraham I. Karelitz, *Kovetz Iggerot* (Bnei Brak, 1956), 2:170–74. See also *Pe'er ha-Dor: Hayyei ha-Hazon Ish* (Bnei Brak: Netzach Press, 1966), 1:315–16; and *Seridei Esh*, vol. 1 (Jerusalem: Mossad ha-Rav Kook, 1961), 307–08.

not require spiritual leaders to whom secular studies were primary and Torah studies secondary.[161] (3) Furthermore, in Rabbi Grod-zinski's opinion, neither could graduates of such a seminary prop-erly serve the Sephardic community in Palestine. Its graduates would not appeal to the traditional element among them. As for

---

[161]*Ahi'ezer: Kovetz Iggerot* 2:444. In 1950 Rabbi Herzog expressed a similarly negative opinion regarding the establishment of rabbinical sem-inaries in Israel. While he favored the establishment of a university under Orthodox auspices, he emphasized that he viewed the establishment of an Orthodox rabbinical seminary to be detrimental and wrote bluntly: "The seminaries have not as yet provided us with a single great scholar *(gadol)*. When great scholars entered them, some emerged as pygmies, while some emerged as great scholars. But it was not the seminaries that made them into great scholars." See Rabbi Isaac ha-Levi Herzog, *Tehukah le-Yisrael al pi ha-Torah*, vol. 3, *Hazakah, Hukkim ve-Takkanot ha-Rabbanut ha-Rashit*, ed. Itamar Wahrhaftig (Jerusalem: Mossad ha-Rav Kook and Yad Harov Herzog, 1989), 240. Cf., however, the assessment of Rabbi Weinberg, *Seridei Esh*, vol. 2 (Jerusalem: Mossad ha-Rav Kook, 1962), no. 30, who writes movingly, "It is proper to record that among the rabbis of Germany there were righteous, pious and holy men, who in other countries would have been pursued by tens of thousands of people seeking to benefit from their Torah and fear of God," and attests that, for these individuals, secular academic pursuits and attainments were secondary in nature and that they made use of their academic titles only in dealings with civil authorities or the assimilated.

Whatever may have been their attitude toward establishment of rab-binical seminaries, Torah scholars of every orientation exhibited an attitude of deep respect and fulsome appreciation for the contributions of both Hirsch and Hildesheimer. This attitude was based on the firm conviction that the synthesis of Torah and secular studies advocated by both Hirsch and Hildesheimer was predicated upon absolute and uncom-promising faith and fear of Heaven and an unshakeable sincerity of commitment to Torah and *mitzvot*. As Rav Kook wrote (*Iggerot ha-Reiyah* 2:27) of both Hirsch and Hildesheimer, they manifested "the ability to unite knowledge of the world and of life with a stalwart fear of God and love of Torah and *mitzvot*, with faith and a perfect heart."

nontraditional Sephardic Jews, it was not likely that their needs would be met by "rabbis of the Berlin type." (4) Implementation of the project could only lead to a lowering of the standards of Torah in Palestine. Clearly, the opposition expressed echoed the twofold negative view with which the idea of a rabbinical seminary had been received since the days of R. David Friesenhausen: (1) Rabbinical seminaries are merely professional schools for which there is now no real need. (2) Protestations to the contrary notwithstanding, graduates of these seminaries achieve proficiency in secular subjects but are solely lacking in rabbinic scholarship.

In his description of the aspirations of Hildesheimer, Rabbi Jechiel Jacob Weinberg, who served for decades as a member of the *Rabbinerseminar* faculty, noted that Hildesheimer had envisioned the growth of an Orthodox rabbinate that would assert itself in every aspect of public life and one that would publicize and explicate the Torah perspective with regard to the widest range of ethical and social questions. Hildesheimer had felt strongly that it was not sufficient for Orthodox rabbis to issue pronouncements on matters of ritual law alone. Rather, they must be thoroughly conversant with, and responsive to, the manifold sociological and philosophical issues that engage the attention of society.

Rabbi Weinberg stressed that, despite the name of the institution, Hildesheimer's goal had not been so much to establish a professional school as "to create an institution that would develop a religious intelligentsia."[162] The deterioration in the status of Orthodoxy in his generation was the result of the lack of precisely such a religious elite. The intelligentsia of the time consisted solely of the nonobservant who looked down on the Orthodox as lacking in culture and education. Torah scholars, for the most part, concentrated all their energies within the four ells of *halakhah*, and, as a result, had lost contact with the broad masses. They did not number among themselves Torah scholars such as Saadiah Gaon, Maimonides, Nahmanides, and Ibn Ezra of previous ages, scholars

---

[162]Weinberg, *Seridei Esh* 1:2.

who had mastered the secular wisdom of the day and responded to its challenges. It was Hildesheimer's hope that among the graduates of his institution there would be individuals suited to such a mission, persons capable of communicating with modern intellectuals and trained to transmit Jewish values in the modern idiom.[163] Whether or not Hildesheimer succeeded in that goal is a different question.

With the passage of time the need for rapprochement with the nonobservant became ever more compelling. It became increasingly evident to rabbinic leaders that positive approaches must be found in opening channels of communication. In a letter dated 25 Iyar 1912 addressed to those who were planning the first *Knessiah Gedolah* of the Agudath Israel movement, Rabbi Abraham I. Kook wrote that one finds "two spiritual strands . . . two opposites that cannot be united, holy zealotry and patient tolerance *(ha-kinah ha-kedoshah ve-ha-savlanut ha-metunah)*." But these two opposing vector forces of zealotry and calm patience must be reconciled if efforts for the greater good of *kelal Yisrael* are to be crowned with success. Only by fostering deep spiritual love for each member of the Jewish people can the tolerance and patience so sorely needed be acquired.[164]

In even stronger words than those used by Bamberger and Hirsch in the 1870s, Rabbi Kook argued that deviationists of modern times must be approached in a conciliatory manner. He vigorously opposed the view that had been adopted by "the great majority of [Torah] scholars that in our times it is fitting to abandon those children who have been turned from Torah ways and the faith by the raging current of the time. I say emphatically, that this is not God's way . . . !"[165] Such individuals must be

---

[163]Ibid., 1:2.

[164]Rabbi Abraham I. Kook, letter, 25 *Iyar* 1912, in *Sefer Hayovel: On the Occasion of the Thirtieth Anniversary of the Agudas Israel World Organization* (London: Agudas Israel Organisation, 1942), 57.

[165]Rabbi Abraham I. Kook, letter, May 20, 1908, *Iggerot ha-Reiyah* 1:170–71. An English translation of this letter may be found in *Rav A. Y.*

regarded in every respect as acting under *force majeure*. "They are coerced in every sense of the word," wrote Rabbi Kook, "and heaven forbid us from judging the compelled as we do the self-willed."[166]

Eighty-two years later the prophetic quality of the words penned by Rabbi Kook in 1908 becomes ever more evident. To the extent that rabbinic leaders erred in their assessment of, and response to, Reform, it was in the failure to develop avenues of communication with those whose deviation was intellectually motivated. The watchmen on guard on the watchtower, the *Shomrei Tzion*, had absorbed a siege mentality. But the watchmen referred to in Ezekiel are enjoined to be *tzofim*, those who stand on the lookout, those who look ahead to the future. Ultimately, as Rabbi Kook predicted,

> the transgressors and the rebels who are not prisoners of fashion but of misdirected reason will return at a highly exalted degree. For this reason, there is great hope for the vast majority of our children, so we must [hold] them and not forsake them "and it shall come to pass that, instead of that which was said to them, you are not my people, it shall be said of them, you are the sons of a living God." [Hosea 2:1][167]

Kook: Selected Letters, trans. and annot. Tzvi Feldman (Maaleh Adumim, Israel: Maaliyot Publications, 1986), 51–54.

[166]Rabbi Abraham I. Kook, *Iggerot ha-Reiyah* 1:171.

[167]Ibid., 171–72.

In Law and Thought

3

Rebuking a Fellow Jew: Theory and Practice

Yehuda Amital

The commandment of *tokhahah* (rebuke) requires Jews to repri-mand each other for sins they may commit. In an expression of mutual concern and responsibility, the Torah (Leviticus 19:27) bids every Jew to assist one another's observance of *mitzvot* with con-structive criticism. Clearly, such an imperative assumes that the entire community subscribes to the same law and authority, an assumption considered reasonable in premodern times. But is this *mitzvah* normative even when it is obvious that the object of the reproof will not heed the reproach? This issue is clearly relevant in contemporary times, and a clear analysis of it is urgently needed in today's Jewish world.[1]

It would appear that this question directly depends on the

---

[1]See *Hagahot Maimuniot, Mishneh Torah, Hilkhot De'ot* 6:3 for a prelim-inary discussion of the issue. However, only the views of the *Yere'im* and the *Semak* are cited there. See n. 4 below.

119

more fundamental matter of whether the goal of the rebuke—
helping one's neighbor to avoid sin and return to complete religious
observance—is part of the very definition of the *mitzvah* itself, or is
only the reason for the *mitzvah*, and therefore of no intrinsic
halakhic consequence.[2] If it is considered part of the obligation
itself, then the commandment cannot simply be understood as an
obligation to rebuke but must be expanded to include all means of
influence that could be brought to bear to help another person
avoid sin. Indeed, the vast majority of rabbinic authorities follow
this approach and therefore include other means, such as persuasion, under the mode of behavior required by this commandment.

Strikingly, and somewhat paradoxically, while this mode of
reasoning results in expanding the parameters of the *mitzvah* in one
respect, it circumscribes it in another. For if the purpose of the
mitzvah—bringing a fellow Jew closer to God—is an intrinsic aspect
of it, then it would not be required in a case where the end result will
not be achieved, such as when it is known that the rebukee will not
listen or respond. In fact, if it is clear that the sinner will not heed
the words of the rebuker, most authorities maintain that there is no
obligation to admonish. On the contrary, the obligation is to
refrain from saying something that will not be heeded.[3] Others

---

[2] This matter falls under the rubric of the more general question of
whether or not we may engage in *darshinan taama di-kra*, interpreting the
reason for a commandment, and investing that reason with halakhic
significance. The ruling is that we are not to engage in such activity and,
therefore, whatever is deemed to be *only* a reason for a *mitzvah* remains
outside its halakhic boundaries. See, for example, *Kiddushin* 68b and the
other references cited there in *Masoret ha-Shas*. The Hida, *Birkei Yosef*,
Orah Hayyim, no. 608, makes this connection explicitly. See, too, *She'elot
u-Teshuvot Avnei Nezer*, *Yoreh De'ah*, no. 461:4.

[3] See Rambam, *Sefer ha-Mitzvot*, Aseh no. 205; *Hilkhot De'ot* 6:7; *Semag*,
Mitzvah no. 11; Rashi, *Yevamot* 65b, s.v. *lomar davar ha-nishma*; Rif and
Meiri on *Yevamot* 65b; Rosh, *Betzah* 4:2; Tosafot, *Baba Batra* 60b, s.v.
mutav; *Shabbat* 55a, s.v. *ve-af al gav*; Rabad, cited in Hida, *Mahazik
Berakhah*, *Orah Hayyim* 208; *Shitah Mekubetzet*, *Baba Metzia* 31a; *Sefer*

disagree and maintain that there always exists an obligation to admonish a sinner, if only once, whether it will be effective or not.[4] However, the strength of the admonition depends on whether the reprimand is directed at an individual (where more of an effort is required) or at a group. Moreover, it is likely that even these authorities maintain that if it appears probable that a reprimand will be not only ineffective but counterproductive, that it will lead the sinner either to sin further or even only to hate the rebuker, then there is no obligation to fulfill the *mitzvah* of *tokhahah*.[5] If, for example, the sinner belongs to a community known to be unresponsive to criticism, then reprimanding him or her is treated in the same manner as communal reproof and should be avoided. In such a case, if it is clear that the collective group to which the individual belongs would not accept the reprimand, then there is no such obligation with respect to the individual within it either.

Yere'im ha-Katzar, no. 37; *Hagahot ha-Gra, Orah Hayyim* 608:4; *Sefer ha-Hinukh*, no. 239; *Sefer Hasidim*, no. 413 (no. 938, in another edition; although there the emphasis is on the negative impact such a rebuke may have [i.e., the rebukee might be motivated to sin even more], not its futility. See *Magen Avraham, Orah Hayyim* 608:3).

There is another related source for restricting the application of *tokhahah* based on the continuation of the verse "and you will not bear a sin over him" (Leviticus 19:17). Based on Targum Onkeles's interpretation, this means that a Jew will be held responsible for a sin committed by his friend only if he could have rebuked him and did not do so. This interpretation is echoed by Ibn Ezra and the Ramban in their biblical commentaries on this verse as well as by Rabbenu Yonah, *Shaarei Teshuvah* 3:59, 72, 196. Such accountability is reasonable only if such a rebuke would have been successful had it been attempted (see *Shabbat* 54b–55a). However, if one knows in advance that his rebuke will go unheeded, he is not obligated to go through with it.

[4]See *Yere'im*, no. 223; *Semak*, no. 114; Ritva and Nimukei Yosef, *Yevamot* 65b; Rama, *Orah Hayyim* 608:2. See too *Biur Halakhah*, ad loc.

[5]See *Sefer Hasidim*, no. 413; *Taz* on Rama, *Yoreh De'ah* 334:3; *Nekudot ha-Kesef*, ad loc.

A distinction must also be made between cases where those committing the sin are aware that what they are doing is prohibited and those where they actually believe their activity to be permissible. In the latter case, their unwillingness to heed the reproacher is not due to any obstinacy or rebelliousness, but simply to the fact that they have been trained to believe that their behavior is acceptable, and the person admonishing them must be considered to be unnecessarily stringent. With respect to those who are convinced that what they are doing is correct, some authorities maintain that there is no obligation of *tokhahah*.[6] If, however, the sinner is merely acting out of ignorance, then the commandment to correct his or her misconception does obtain.[7] Similarly, a distinction may exist depending on the nature of the violation, whether a Torah law is at stake (in which case rebuke is more seriously required), or merely a rabbinic ordinance;[8] and whether the violation was committed willfully *(bi-meẓid)* or mistakenly *(bi-shogeg)*.[9]

---

[6]See Mordekhai, *Betẓah*, no. 689. This distinction is also found in a responsum attributed to Rabbenu Hananel, printed in *Teshuvot Rashi* (ed. I. Elfenbein) (New York: Shulsinger Bros., 1943), no. 20, pp. 14–16; S. Hasidah, *Sefer Shibbolei ha-Leket*, vol. 2 (Jerusalem: Makhon Yerushalayim, 1988), no. 47, pp. 195–196.

[7]Interestingly, the Raavan (no. 25, end) applies the principle of *mutav she-yehiyu shogegin* (it is better that they sin out of ignorance) to such a circumstance and does not require rebuke even in a case where the possibility exists that they may respond favorably. He requires rebuke only when the efficacy of the act is assured in advance.

[8]Rama, *Darkei Mosheh*, *Orah Hayyim* 608 (based on the *Sefer ha-Itur*) requires rebuke whenever an explicit law of the Torah is being violated since, as he clearly assumes, there is no one who is ignorant of the Torah's lucidly formulated written laws and, therefore, the violation must have been committed willfully (see below). The Rashba understands the distinction based on the inherent severity of the commandment, considering a biblical law to be more serious than a rabbinic one.

[9]See *She'elot u-Teshuvot Avnei Neẓer*, *Yoreh De'ah*, no. 461:4; *Sefer Yere'im ha-Katẓar*, no. 37. There is also a distinction made between

All this, however, concerns only the obligation of an average individual Jew to reproach his or her fellow coreligionist. What about the obligation of the leaders of the community, such as rabbis, whose responsibility extends throughout the entire Jewish community? What are the limits, if any, to *their* obligation to rebuke?

On this subject, the insightful words of the Rashba (R. Solomon ibn Adret; c. 1235–1310) deserve careful attention:

> Be aware that a soft spoken word shatters bones, and different ways will clear a path before the people to remove obstacles from them. [Therefore,] one must progress from the easy to the difficult, and not attempt the entire package all at once. These words are directed towards the intentions of the heart, and you are already familiar with that which is stated in *Nazir* (23b), "A sin for its own sake is greater than a good deed not performed for its own sake."
>
> [Our Rabbis] have already shown us good and clear counsel, as it states in *Avodah Zarah* (15a) with reference to the house of Rabbi Judah the Prince which was under an obligation to send a fatted bull to the Caesar on the Roman holiday. Rabbi Judah then paid 40,000 coins to the Caesar for the concession that they would not sacrifice it on that day but on the morrow, then he paid another 40,000 for the concession that they would not sacrifice it at all. [The Talmud] comments on it that Rabbi Judah intended to uproot the entire practice, and therefore uprooted it slowly, bit by bit.
>
> Furthermore, you should know that it is impossible to deal with all people equally. Recall that David, our lord and king, decided to overlook the misconduct of Joab and Shim'i, even though they deserved death, . . . for to everything there

---

whether or not the rebuker has the power to enforce his will on the recalcitrant sinner. See *Bi'ur Halakhah, Orah Hayyim* 608, s.v. *mohin bi-yadam*, citing Hida, *Birkei Yosef*, ad loc.

is an appropriate time, and ignoring something sinful is occasionally a positive commandment, and everything must be measured by the need of the hour . . .[10]

While the Rashba's advice certainly applies to every individual, it was clearly intended for communal leaders, who are required to adapt their actions to contemporary exigencies all the more. Even though, generally speaking, it is improper to ignore the behavior of a sinner, at times it is a *mitzvah*, if the situation so requires. What emerges from this is that even in a case where the normative requirements of *tokhahah* call for an obligation to reprimand, if the leaders of the community believe that the times require refraining from such activity, then it is their obligation to do so. Indeed, the Rashba says further in the responsum: "And if silence, employed to ultimately yield positive results, is occasionally ineffective, the use of force will only engender the opposite."

THE VALUE OF PERSUASION

In light of the previous discussion, it is clear that there are a number of different reasons why there is no obligation to rebuke Jews who do not believe in the sanctity or binding force of the Oral Torah: (1) it is clear that they will not heed the words; (2) they are part of a group with respect to which it is said that "just as it is a *mitzvah* to speak words that will be heeded, so too it is a *mitzvah* not to speak words that will go unheeded" (*Yevamot* 65b); (3) in the sinner's own opinion, his conduct is permissible. In all of these cases, the authorities cited above do not require rebuke. Indeed, R. Yehiel Mikhel Epstein (1829–1908) deemed it obvious that with respect to such Jews, the entire notion of rebuking them simply does not apply:

Understand that all [the laws of rebuke] apply only to a Jew who believes but has been overtaken by desire to commit [his

---

[10]*She'elot u-Teshuvot ha-Rashba* 5:238.

sin]. In such a case [the *mitzvah* of] *tokhahah* applies. But with respect to those who totally deny the words of the Rabbis, reproach simply does not apply, for they are apostates and heretics and one should not argue with them.[11]

Nevertheless, even though formal reproof is ineffective and hence inappropriate, there is still room for other means of persuasion and influence. According to those who maintain that the aim of *tokhahah*—returning errant Jews to the path of Torah and *mitzvot*—is actually part and parcel of the definition of the commandment, then it is possible to expand the scope of the *mitzvah* to include the use of other kinds of persuasive means, as was suggested earlier.

Some might argue, however, that in order to fulfill this commandment, the other Jew at whom the persuasion is being directed must at least be considered "your neighbor (*amitekha*),"[12] a title nonobservant Jews lack according to R. Israel Meir Hakohen (the Hafetz Hayyim; 1838–1933).[13] However, as is well known, many great scholars have already dealt with the status of today's nonobservant Jews and determined that such an extreme position is inappropriate. For example, R. Jacob Ettlinger (1798–1871) wrote:

As to the sinners of our time, since, due to our overwhelming sins, [lack of observance] has reached epidemic proportions, such that the majority deem desecration of the Sabbath to be permissible, I do not know whether to treat them as those who

---

[11]*Arukh ha-Shulhan, Orah Hayyim,* no. 608:7.

[12]After all, that is the text of the biblical verse "Reproach your neighbor" (Leviticus 19:17). This is the opinion of *Tanna de-Vei Eliyahu.*

[13]See R. Israel Meir Hakohen, *Bi'ur Halakhah, Orah Hayyim* 608, where he takes the position that public violators of the Sabbath are not considered "neighbors" with respect to the observance of Torah and *mitzvot* and hence are not in the category of those toward whom an act of *tokhahah* would be a fulfillment of a *mitzvah.*

view their behavior as permissible (i.e., *omer mutar*) and do not willfully desecrate the commandments.[14]

It was his considered opinion that nineteenth-century German nonobservance was not to be treated as harshly as it should have been in earlier periods. Similarly, R. David Tzevi Hoffman (1843–1921) stated: "There is room to be lenient [in regard to counting *mehalelei Shabbat* to a *minyan*] for today they are not called public desecrators of the Sabbath, since the majority of them act thus."[15] Be that as it may, the views of R. Abraham I. Kook (1865–1935) and R. Isaiah Karelitz (the Hazon Ish; 1878–1952) are our most reliable guides: we must try to attract the unobservant and return them to Torah observance "with bonds of love."[16] Moreover, R. Joseph Babad (1800–c. 1874) implicitly disagrees with the Hafetz Hayyim's opinion and writes that "it appears to me that if there is a reasonable possibility that he [the unobservant Jew] will accept the reproof, then one is obligated to reprimand him, so that he may return to the correct path and be considered, once again, a brother."[17]

Therefore, even if the formal *mitzvah* of *tokhahah* may not be applicable, communal leaders have a special responsibility and a unique obligation to engage in other forms of persuasion. Further corroboration of this position is found in a passage of the Jerusalem Talmud. Commenting on the verse, "Cursed be the person who does not fulfill the words of this Torah to observe them, and the entire nation will say 'Amen' " (Deuteronomy 27:26), it states:

> Rabbi Asi said in the name of Rav Tanhum bar Hiyya: If one learned, taught, observed and performed [*mitzvot*] but was in

---

[14]See *She'elot u-Teshuvot Binyan Tziyon* 2:23, end.

[15]*Sefer Melamed le-Ho'il, Orah Hayyim*, no. 29.

[16]This term is found in *Hazon Ish, Yoreh De'ah* 2:16. See also Rabbi Abraham Kook, *Iggerot ha-Reiyah*, vol. 1 (Jerusalem: Mossad ha-Rav Kook, 1961), no. 138, pp. 170–72.

[17]See *Minhat Hinukh, Mitzvah* no. 239.

a position to encourage others in their observance and did not do so, such a person is included in this curse. This is interpreted as referring to the king and the Nasi who, by virtue of their power, have the ability to force violators of the Torah to observe it. Even if he [i.e., the leader] was an impeccably righteous person in his own conduct, but had in his power to encourage Torah observance among the wicked and did not, then he is accursed.[18]

Clearly, these words are applicable also to those who have the ability to enhance Torah observance through persuasion. In fact, one's responsibility in this regard is measured precisely according to the degree of one's powers of persuasion, as the Talmud (*Shabbat* 54b) states: "Anyone who is able to protest the behavior of his family members and does not, is held responsible for his family members; [if he is able to protest the activities] of the members of his town and does not, then he is held responsible for the conduct of the people of his town; if for the whole world, then he is held responsible for the entire world." "Protest" here refers not only to rebuke in the conventional sense but also to the use of persuasion.[19]

ARGUMENTS FOR TEMPERING REBUKE

However, the effective use of persuasion to help the unobservant return to Judaism raises a number of halakhic problems that we must consider. The Rambam (1135–1204) writes in connection with the Great Sanhedrin that "if they see that the situation requires the suspension of a positive commandment or the violation of a negative one in order to bring many back to proper observance, or to save many Jews from stumbling in other areas, they may enact

---

[18]See *Talmud Yerushalmi* (*Sotah* 7:4). This passage is cited by the Ramban in his *Commentary on the Torah*, Deuteronomy 27:26.

[19]See Rashi, *Shabbat* 54b, s.v. *bikhol ha-olam kulo*.

whatever they feel the moment requires."[20] The problem that the Rambam identified in connection with "many" Jews (a *"rabbim"*) may also arise in our day when dealing with individuals. At times, in order to assist individual Jews to return to observance, and to spare individuals from stumbling, there is a need to ignore certain violations of rabbinic or even Torah laws; at times, there is a need to rule permissively, and even to abet the violator indirectly. Such halakhic questions arise daily, as we shall shortly see. Moreover, the halakhic considerations in any given case cannot be exercised in a vacuum, limited exclusively to the particular situation under discussion. Every deliberate overlooking of a sin, and every dispensation given in a specific case, may result in a cumulative negative affect with regard to the public at large. There is a need for tremendous caution and a large measure of divine assistance to help us refrain from destroying in one case when we want to improve in another. In the same vein, many questions arise in the domain of "putting a stumbling block before the blind" and "assisting sinners," where the one who is doing the influencing may himself be violating the law, as will be shown below. As a result, persuasion as an alternative to rebuke is a dangerous route, "on which the righteous travel safely but the frivolous stumble."[21]

In his responsum cited above, the Rashba afforded us wide latitude in overlooking a sinner's misconduct, based on a consideration of long-term goals. He explicitly noted that "looking the other way from the sinner is, at times, a positive commandment." Indeed, it is standard procedure to ignore a whole host of violations when dealing with penitents at the outset of their return to observance (*hozerim bi-teshuvah*), out of a concern that if the burden imposed upon them is too heavy at the beginning, they might become frustrated and revert to their former (mis)behavior. I heard from a reliable source that one of the leading halakhic authorities in Israel instructed those who work in *kiruv* not to discuss the laws of family

---

[20]*Hilkhot Mamrim* 2:4.

[21]This is a play on the words of Hosea 14:10.

purity with those married individuals taking their first steps toward renewed observance. Furthermore, he suggested that even if the subject is broached by the penitent him/herself, the instructor should plead ignorance.

Rabbi Dov Katz relates that when R. Israel Salanter (1810–1883) arrived in a port city in Germany, he discovered that those Jewish merchants who had business at the port would load and unload their goods on the Sabbath as on any other day. When R. Salanter arrived in the synagogue where those merchants prayed, he asked if he could give a sermon about the Sabbath. However, after discovering that there were Lithuanian visitors present, he refrained from doing so. On the next Sabbath, after he had determined that there were no such guests, he delivered an inspiring sermon on the importance of the Sabbath which was perfectly suited to his audience. He concluded the sermon by saying that "while loading and unloading at the port is necessary, writing is not," and the merchants accepted his suggestion and refrained from writing on the Sabbath. After several Sabbaths, R. Salanter offered another sermon in that same synagogue and told his audience that "removing one's goods [at the dock] is essential, but surely loading is not," and the merchants accepted this as well. A while later, he again delivered the sermon, and spoke of the prohibition of unloading also, and thus those Jews were slowly brought to observe the Sabbath properly.[22] The novelty of this tale is that it allows for much more than simply looking the other way. Indeed, R. Salanter explicitly permitted behavior which was prohibited by law in order to attract his audience to observe Shabbat completely.[23]

Quite frequently, Orthodox synagogues do not refrain from allowing unobservant Jewish families to celebrate their *bar mitzvah*

---

[22]See D. Katz, *Tenuat ha-Musar*, 5th ed. (Jerusalem, 1974), 1:184.

[23]I am aware that this book on the *Musar* movement is not a halakhic work, despite the well-known erudition of its author. Nonetheless, I think that it is appropriate to mention this story because it is relevant to our subject.

celebrations in them. They do so even though it is obvious that many members of the family will drive to the synagogue on the Sabbath. As long as they park their vehicles out of the sight of the synagogue, the rabbi and congregants ignore the Sabbath desecration that such celebrations necessarily entail. They are clearly not concerned with violating the prohibitions of "putting a stumbling block before the blind" or "assisting sinners" in their transgressions. Moreover, it is also an everyday occurrence in Israeli rabbinical courts, on which sit very distinguished Torah scholars, to spare no effort in trying to reconcile an unobservant couple which has come to them for a divorce despite the fact that they obviously do not observe the laws of family purity.

Apparently, in both of these cases the rabbinic authorities are relying on a statement in the *Mishnah*: "Bet Shammai says that one should not sell a cow for plowing to those who work their fields during the Sabbatical year (when the law requires the land to lie fallow), and Bet Hillel permits it, for the buyer may slaughter it (and not use it for plowing)" (*Shevi'it* 5:8). R. Ovadya Bartenura (c. 1450–before 1516; ad. loc.) explains Bet Hillel's reasoning by noting that "if any conceivable possibility can be suggested (that will not entail violation of the law) we accept it." So too in these cases of the potential violation of either Shabbat or *taharat ha-mishpahah*, we consider any possibility, however remote, that will not necessarily result in any violation of the law.

However, R. Abraham Gombiner (the *Magen Avraham*; c. 1637–1683) stipulates that one may not lend tools to a person suspected of doing work on the Sabbath unless there exist permitted uses for these tools that are not farfetched but standard. If, however, their use for permissible purposes is only unlikely, then such lending is forbidden, unless refusal to lend will lead to strife (*"mipnei darkei shalom"*).[24] According to this, it would appear that a more stringent position would also have to be taken in the cases

---

[24]*Magen Avraham, Orah Hayyim* 347:4. See, too, *Mahatzit ha-Shekel*, ad loc.

above, as well, where the possibility of not violating Torah law is highly unlikely. Nevertheless, one may distinguish between the two circumstances, claiming that in the cases under discussion here the demands of peace in the home or the intention of drawing the unobservant to Torah is identical to the consideration of *"mipnei darkei shalom,"* thus allowing for the overlooking of probable Torah violations, as long as it is possible—however unlikely—that they will not take place.

Incidentally, an occurrence similar to the one described by the *Magen Avraham* occurred to me about twenty-five years ago. An observant, God-fearing Jew asked me whether he could buy a truck in partnership with a nonobservant Jew, where the latter had conditioned his participation on his being allowed to use the vehicle to take his family to the beach on the Sabbath. I consulted two great rabbinic scholars and both upbraided me, for opposite reasons. The first, who is no longer alive, claimed: "I don't understand your question. What argument can possibly be made to permit this?" The other, the great Rabbi Shlomo Zalman Auerbach, claimed: "I don't understand you? What argument can possibly be made to forbid this?" I asked him if his permissive stance was based on the consideration described above, that is, that we consider any feasible possibility in such a case, and he answered: "Yes," despite the fact that the other Jew had openly stated his intention to drive the truck on the Sabbath.

PUTTING A STUMBLING BLOCK BEFORE THE BLIND

One of the more common problems that arises today is whether or not one is permitted to invite an unobservant Jew to a Sabbath meal when it is clear that he will be returning to his home by car and will thus violate the Shabbat. With regard to the Friday night meal, most rely on the famous ruling that if we offer such a Jew a place to sleep, thereby affording him the opportunity not to desecrate the Sabbath, then we need no longer concern ourselves about his violation, even though it is clear that he will decline such an invitation. There are situations, however, where such a reasoning cannot be employed. It is well known that in a number of communities around the world, many Jews have been influenced by the B'nei Akiva movement to return to observant Judaism. The major activity of this movement is *Shabbat* afternoon meetings, and it often happens that teenagers who live quite a distance from the meeting location apply for membership in B'nei Akiva. The question, of course, is whether to accept them and ignore their probable desecration of the Shabbat or not, and thereby run the risk of "losing" them entirely. On the one hand, there is more room to be lenient here, for what is at stake is merely a rabbinic prohibition against riding on a bus. On the other hand, we are dealing with a regular, ongoing violation, not a one-time event. In addition, there is also the issue of the public nature of this conduct, since the other members of the group will surely be aware of it. Moreover, such behavior may also at times result in violating the Torah prohibition against carrying in the public domain, which the young adult may do.

Rabbi Shlomo Zalman Auerbach suggests an approach with regard to the prohibition against "putting a stumbling block before the blind" that has far-reaching and novel halakhic consequences. He suggests that while we do not allow someone to commit even a minor violation in order to save others from a greater sin, nevertheless it is permitted to "put a stumbling block before the blind" (e.g., offer food to someone who will not make a *berakhah* and thereby cause him to violate a particular detail of the law) in order to help him avoid stumbling over an even greater "obstacle" (i.e., doing something that may result in distancing him entirely from Torah and *mitzvot*, the concern being that if he is not offered the food, he will totally reject Judaism). The reasoning behind this is that "it turns out that there is no sin here at all, for in this case there is no obstacle being set. On the contrary, it is the removal of a very great obstacle, by actively exchanging it with a less serious one."[25] Similarly, he writes that if someone sees his friend drink the wine of *orlah*,[26] and is totally unable to prevent him from violating this biblical prohibition unless he hands him, instead, either wine from untithed grapes *(tevel)* or wine made by non-Jews *(stam yayin)*, which are only rabbinically prohibited, he does not violate the prohibition of placing an obstacle before the blind since he is sparing his friend from an even greater stumbling block.

The basic question is how far can we extend the scope of Rabbi Auerbach's insight, a subject which demands a thorough analysis. For example, does this mean that we can allow a woman to immerse herself in a *mikveh* without washing her hair, a procedure normally prohibited, because she refuses to do so and would not immerse herself at all otherwise? Would we permit a woman to count only the "seven clean days" after her period, but not the five days of her menstrual flow itself, before resuming sexual relations with her husband if otherwise she would not "count any days" at all? The range of considerations here extends beyond the limited scope of "placing a stumbling block before the blind," and discussions of this subject have already appeared in the responsa literature of earlier generations.

Simply put, are we permitted to instruct sinners to violate minor infractions of the *halakhah* in order to prevent them from committing greater sins or even just to bring them closer to observance and belief in general?

The Rambam was the first to address this issue. A Mishnah in *Yevamot* states explicitly: "One suspected of having relations with a maidservant who was later freed, or with a non-Jew who later

---

[25]See Rabbi Shlomo Zalman Auerbach, *Sefer Minhat Shlomo* (Jerusalem: Makhon Sha'arei Ziv, 1986), no. 35:1. This principle had already been formulated by R. Akiva Eger in his commentary to *Shulhan Arukh, Yoreh De'ah* 181:6.

[26]*Orlah* is the Torah prohibition against deriving any benefit from the fruit of a tree during the first three years after it was planted. This applies to vines and their grapes as well.

converted, should not marry her, but if he did, we do not force him to divorce her" (24b). In his *Mishneh Torah*, the Rambam ruled in accordance with this Mishnah.[27] In one of his responsa, he addressed the question as to whether a Jewish court was obliged to coerce a man to send a non-Jewish maid with whom he had sexual relations out of his house. He wrote:

> It is clear that according to Torah law, he must remove her, even while she is still non-Jewish, for the Torah made concessions only to man's strongest desires, and this is not the proper way [of satisfying them]. . . . Therefore, the Jewish court, after hearing such a report, must use every means at its disposal to force the person either to send the girl away, or free her (by which means she becomes Jewish) and marry her. And even though we rule that a person may not marry a freed maidservant with whom he has been suspected of fornication, here we rule the opposite in order to facilitate his repentance, saying it is better that he eat gravy and not the fat itself, and we rely on the statement of the Rabbis: When there is a need to act for the sake of God, then [one may] violate His Torah. So here he is permitted to marry her, and may God in heaven atone for our sins.[28]

Subsequent scholars relied on this responsum to permit the conversion of a non-Jewish woman who had married a Jew civilly, when her intention is to marry him in accordance with Jewish law after she had converted. R. Hayyim Ozer Grodzinski (1863–1940), for example, permitted the conversion of a non-Jewish woman under these circumstances, writing that "the Rambam's words are a fundamental principle."[29] R. Hayyim of Sanz (1793–1876) apparently had not seen this responsum of the Rambam and neverthe-

---

[27]*Hilkhot Gerushin* 10:14.

[28]See Ramham's book of responsa, *Sefer Pe'er ha-Dor*, no. 132.

[29]See R. Hayyim Ozer Grodzinski's *Teshuvot Ahi'ezer* 3:26.

less, in a similar case, wrote that "we permit him a minor violation so that he will not come to commit more serious ones. . . . Many have leaned towards leniency in such matters. . . . But we should not, God forbid, permit this easily, and it requires the consent of the rabbis in your surrounding area."[30]

However, in regard to the Rabbis' edict (*Yevamot* 42a) prohibiting one from marrying a pregnant or nursing woman until her child is 24 months old (the age an infant usually finishes nursing), there is a disagreement as to whether or not this prohibition can be waived in the event that the woman would engage in promiscuous behavior while single. In this case, R. Yosef Karo (1488–1575) maintained that it is not permissible to suspend this minor prohibition in order to prevent the violation of an even greater one (promiscuity). He considered the view which permits a promiscuous nursing mother to marry to be "an errant decision" and called upon "all wise scholars whose hearts have been touched by God to strongly oppose it."[31] R. Yehudah Mintz (c. 1408–1506), however, did permit such a woman to marry before her child reached 24 months. Although he acknowledged the novelty of his lenient decision, he felt that the circumstances necessitated such a ruling.[32] Based on R. Mintz's ruling, followed by R. Moshe Isserles (the Rama; c. 1525–1572), R. David ha-Levi (the Taz; 1586–1667) ruled that one should not excommunicate someone who would most assuredly cease observance as a result of the excommunication.[33]

---

[30]See R. Hayyim of Sanz's *She'elot u-Teshuvot Divrei Hayyim, Even ha-Ezer*, no. 2:36.

[31]See R. Yosef Caro, *She'elot u-Teshuvot Bet Yosef, Even ha-Ezer*, in the responsa following the Laws of *Ketuvot*, no. 1.

[32]See R. Yehudah Mintz, *She'elot u-Teshuvot Mahari Mintz*, no. 5. This dispute is cited in the *Shulhan Arukh* (*Even ha-Ezer* 13:11). Rabbi Yosef Caro is consistent with the opinion expressed in his responsum and forbids such behavior while R. Moshe Isserles follows the opinion of R. Mintz.

[33]*Taz, Yoreh De'ah* 334:7.

However, two caveats must be considered if we choose to follow this more lenient position: (1) R. Yehezkel Landau (1713–1793) pointed out that the Rama permitted only such a violation if it would be temporary, but if a lenient ruling would lead to the individual permanently violating the law then it could not be followed.[34] (2) The *Otzar ha-Posekim* records that most rabbinic decisors also reject the Rama's lenient position in cases where the couple will live together in violation of the laws of family purity.[35] One must therefore be very careful in drawing any inferences from the Rama's ruling.

R. Naftali Tzevi Yehudah Berlin (the Netziv; 1817–1893) was asked about a case in which a woman who was suspected of not having observed the laws of family purity was "now moved by a desire to cleanse herself in pure waters," but only on the condition that she be allowed to immerse during the day, and not at night, which is the lawful time for immersion. If permission was not granted her, she claimed that she would continue to sin and not immerse at all. Despite the fact that immersing during the day is a relatively minor prohibition, the Netziv was unsure whether such behavior could be permitted, even under such circumstances, in light of the fact that the very prohibition was instituted lest other women see her immersing during the day and think that on the seventh day (rather than after seven complete days, i.e., the eighth night) a woman is permitted to immerse. The response implies that if the considerations had been limited only to the conflict between a minor violation and a more serious one he would have permitted it. However, the Netziv concludes his response by stating that "the principle that one may suspend one prohibition for the sake of another must be exercised most sparingly."[36]

R. Yehiel Yaakov Weinberg (1885–1966) was approached by a

---

[34]See R. Yehezkel Landau, *Noda bi-Yehudah, Mahadura Tinyana, Even ha-Ezer*, no. 34.

[35]*Even ha-Ezer*, ad loc.

[36]See R. Naftali Tzevi Yehudah Berlin, *Meshiv Davar*, no. 2:43, 44.

French ritual slaughterer, appointed to be in charge of the community's butchers, who saw that those belonging to the more liberal segments of the community were not concerned at all with the laws of *trefot*.[37] If he were to check the animals and inform the butchers which ones were not kosher, they would eat the meat themselves anyway and also sell it to others, thereby violating a Torah prohibition. He asked whether, under these circumstances, it would be better not to check at all and rely on the fact that the majority of animals are not blemished in a way that would render them unfit for eating, for Torah law allows an animal to be eaten even without checking. In his response, R. Weinberg deals at length with the definition and scope of "putting obstacles before the blind" and "abetting sinners," leans towards a lenient position, but then concludes that "all I have written is for academic purposes [only], and not for a practical ruling. The final decision should come from the leading scholars of the generation, in Israel and the Diaspora."[38]

Similarly, Rabbi Ovadiah Yosef (b. 1920) was approached by a slaughterer who had been asked by a nonobservant Jew to slaughter a chicken for him. In the course of handling the bird, the slaughterer detected that its wing was broken near the joint next to the ribcage, a defect that renders it automatically unkosher. However, he felt that were he to refuse to slaughter the bird, the owner would slaughter it himself with a regular kitchen knife (which is invalid for ritual slaughter), and would eat the chicken despite the warnings of the slaughterer. Should he therefore slaughter the blemished chicken himself or not? Rabbi Yosef cited the responsum of R. Tzevi Pesah Frank (1873–1960) who was asked by a slaughterer for a kibbutz that did not observe *kashrut* whether or not he had to check the animals. He concurred with R. Frank's decision not to

---

[37]If a blemish is found on an animal, usually on the lung, but also on other organs and tissues, such that the animal would most likely have died within twelve months had it not been slaughtered, then the animal is not considered to be kosher (e.g., it is *trefah*), and cannot be eaten by Jews.

[38]*Seridei Esh*, no. 2:57.

require it, and added parenthetically, "and I ruled similarly here in Tel Aviv to allow ritual slaughter without an inspection of the lungs, in order to spare some from the potential prohibition ('obstacle') of slaughtering the animal with their own invalid knives." Rabbi Yosef cited many responsa of recent scholars who absolutely forbid the suspension of a rabbinic ordinance in order to spare someone from a more serious offence. Yet, he concludes:

> The principle of permitting a minor violation for the sake of [avoiding] a more serious one must be exercised most sparingly. Just like in the case of healing the body, a doctor sometimes decides to amputate the hand to prevent the spread of the disease to the rest of the body, and sometimes decides to leave things as they are, all decided upon with the counsel of other doctors, so too should this procedure be followed with the healing of the soul. One must consult many erudite and esteemed Torah scholars, so that the decision should not cause any damage, God forbid.[39]

It is noteworthy that a large proportion of the recent responsa dealing with such matters relates to problems arising with individuals who may become entirely unobservant if we do not permit them a certain leniency, or refer to nonobservant individuals whom we want to help avoid more serious violations. The major question for us is whether, in our time, given the grave situation in which Judaism finds itself, the general, more strict considerations here outlined should be reconsidered and, as a broad guiding principle, we should be required to adopt a more lenient posture, in order to draw the hearts of Jews nearer to God.

---

[39]*Yabia Omer, Yoreh De'ah*, no. 6:3.

A more elaborate Hebrew version of this essay will appear in the *Sefer ha-Yovel le-Mordekhai Breuer*.

4

Loving and Hating Jews as Halakhic Categories

Norman Lamm

The feeling of love that is expected from every individual Jew for his people *(ahavat Yisrael)* is an existential fact that sometimes assumes mystical proportions. Associated with this love for Israel is its obverse, the injunction against hating one's fellows in his heart. And the exception is the commandment to hate the *rasha,* the evil-doer.

These are themes which stir passions and, indeed, have played a not insignificant role in the political polemics of our day, both enriching and obscuring the rhetoric of intra-Jewish dialogue.

Concomitant with these problems, and deeply intertwined with them, is that of Jewish identity, often phrased as who does and who does not belong to *kelal Yisrael,* the Jewish people.*

---

*This is not the same as the current "Who is a Jew?" question, which refers to one's individual identity as a Jew. Our problem is that of, as it were, citizenship in the Jewish people. This will be clarified in the course of the chapter.

But these are also biblical or rabbinic commandments, and it is instructive as well as enlightening to view them more dispassionately as halakhic categories. Such a treatment, as the reader will surely notice, is not without its problems, but it is well worth theenterprise. At the very least, such an objective legal focus will make possible a modicum of calm analysis, certainly more than is otherwise likely in dealing with such fateful questions.

"Thou shalt love thy neighbor[1] as thyself" (Leviticus 19:18) is the biblical source of *ahavat Yisrael*, the commandment to love one's fellow Jews, as codified by Maimonides[2] and the author of *Sefer ha-Hinnukh*.[3] What is the scope of this *mitzvah*? There is, according to *halakhah*, a *mitzvah* to "hate" evil-doers and, *prima facie*, love and hate are mutually exclusive. Are, then, evil-doers outside the pale?

We will divide our consideration of the issue into two parts, dealing first with the theoretical halakhic aspects and then moving to the contemporary implications of these *halakhot*.

HALAKHIC ASPECTS

The Position of *Hagahot Maimuniyyot*

In *Hilkhot De'ot*, Maimonides writes:

> It is incumbent on everyone to love each individual Israelite as himself, as it is said, "Thou shalt love thy neighbor as thyself." Hence, a person ought to speak in praise of his neighbor and be careful of his neighbor's property as he is careful of his own

---

[1]The translation of *le-re'akha* is problematic. We shall here adopt the conventional "thy neighbor" for the sake of convenience. The proper definition of this term is a major concern of this essay. The question of whether non-Jews are included in this commandment, important as it is, is not treated here and must be left for another occasion.

[2]Maimonides, *Mishneh Torah, Hilkhot De'ot* 6:3; *Sefer Ha-Mitzvot, aseh* no. 206.

[3]*Sefer ha-Hinnukh*, no. 243.

property and solicitous about his own honor. Whoever glorifies himself by humiliating another person will have no portion in the world-to-come. [6:3]

Hagahot Maimuniyyot offers the following gloss:

[One must love his neighbor] only if he is a "neighbor" with regard to Torah and [performance of the] commandments. However, as far as a wicked person who does not accept rebuke is concerned, the *mitzvah* is to hate him, as it is written, "The fear of the Lord is to hate evil" (Proverbs 8:13). And so too, "Shall I not hate, O Lord, those who hate Thee?" (Psalms 139:21).

And, writing in a similar vein, the medieval biblical exegete and talmudist, R. Samuel ben Meir (Rashbam), comments on Leviticus 19:18 as follows: " 'Thou shalt love thy neighbor as thyself.' He is thy neighbor if he is good, but not if he is evil, as it is written, 'The fear of the Lord is to hate evil' (Proverbs 8:13)." Abraham ibn Ezra, however, seems to allow for broader parameters for the term *neighbor*. He writes that the end of the verse, "I am the Lord," explains why one should love his neighbor: "I am your God who created all of you [good and bad]" (commentary to Leviticus 19:18). Thus, love is not dependent upon the quality of the neighbor but rather flows from the principle of the unity of God; the same God who created both light and darkness is the One who created all humankind, both the righteous and the evil-doers.

The point of departure for the restrictive view of *Hagahot Maimuniyyot* is Maimonides' *Hilkhot Evel*.

The following positive commands were ordained by the Rabbis: visiting the sick; comforting the mourners; joining a funeral procession; dowering a bride; escorting departing guests; etc. These constitute deeds of loving-kindness performed in person and for which no fixed measure is prescribed. Although all these commands are only on rabbinical authority, they are implied in the precept, "Thou shalt love thy neighbor as thyself," that is: what you would have others do unto you, do unto him who is your brother in the Torah and [in the performance of] the commandments. [14:1]

It seems, however, that these statements do not correlate with Maimonides' own views as expressed in *Hilkhot Rotze'ah*, chap. 13. He writes in *halakhah* no. 13 (based on the principle that unloading an animal takes precedence over loading another animal in response to the *mitzvah* to minimize pain to animals):

If one encounters two animals, one crouching under its burden and the other unburdened because the owner cannot find anyone to help him load, he is obligated to unload the first to relieve the animal's suffering, and then to load the other. This rule applies only if the owners of the animals are both friends or both enemies [of the person who comes upon them]. But if one is an enemy and the other is a friend, he is obligated to load for the enemy first, in order to subdue his evil impulse. [13:13]

In the next *halakhah*, Maimonides defines "enemy":

The "enemy" mentioned in the Law [cf. Exodus 23:5] does not mean a foreign enemy but an Israelite one. How can an Israelite have an Israelite enemy when Scripture says, "Thou shalt not hate thy brother in thy heart" (Leviticus 19:17)? The Sages decreed that if one all by himself sees another committing a crime and warns him against it and he does not desist, one is obligated to hate him until he repents and leaves his evil ways. Yet even if he has not yet repented and one finds him in difficulties with his burden, one is obligated to help him load and unload, and not leave him possibly to die. For the enemy might tarry because of his property and meet with danger, and the Torah is very solicitous for the lives of Israelites, whether of the wicked or of the righteous, since all Israelites acknowledge God and believe in the essentials of our religion. For it is said, "Say unto them: As I live, saith the Lord God, I have no pleasure in the death of the wicked but that the wicked turn from his way and live" (Ezekiel 33:11). [13:14]

If, then, one is required to be solicitous of the transgressing Israelite, why does Maimonides in *Hilkhot Evel* apparently exclude him as an object of love, restricted to "your brothers in the Torah and the [performance of the] commandments"?

Character Building and *Halakhah*

At first blush, one might suggest that the moral imperative to "subdue his evil impulses" (at the end of *Hilkhot Rotze'ah* 13:13) and to perfect one's character is the reason one must first unload the burden of one's enemy's animal before loading that of one's friend. This moral imperative would even override the halakhic prohibition of causing animals undue pain *(tzaar baalei hayyim)*. Indeed, this seems to be R. Abraham Maimonides' sense of this law.

> The verse means to say that although he is hated because of his sins, nevertheless we have to strengthen him financially because possibly he will repent or he will leave his possessions to children who are upright in their deeds. From this we learn that the purpose of this and similar *mitzvot* is not only solicitude for the property owner, but also in order to acquire for himself virtuous traits.[4]

According to this principle of R. Abraham, one may override a specific biblical law to achieve the goal of ethical and moral perfection. The students of R. Isaac Luria, centuries later, also

---

[4]See Rabbi M. M. Kasher, *Torah Shelemah, Mishpatim* (vol. 17), addenda, 202, quoting the excerpts of R. Abraham Maimonides' Commentary, as printed in the *Jubilee Volume in Honor of Rabbi David Zevi Hoffman*.

exhibited this predilection to value the goal of moral perfection over the performance of *mitzvot*. R. Hayyim Vital held that virtue resides in the lowly soul *(ha-nefesh ha-yesodit)*, whereas the drive to perform the commandments rests within the rational soul. Yet the rational soul does not have the power to perform commandments without the assistance of the bedrock soul. While individual virtues are not reckoned within the 613 biblical commandments, virtuous behavior is the necessary propaedeutic to performance of all the *mitzvot*. For him, "it is more important to avoid non-virtuous behavior than it is to perform the *mitzvot*."[5]

It is difficult, however, to accept R. Hayyim Vital's position as normative halakhic practice. R. Hayyim of Volozhin's words on this score are well known. In his work *Ruah Hayyim*, commenting on the Mishnah in Tractate *Avot* (1:2),[6] he makes the remarkable comment that the three attributes of Torah, worship, and loving-kindness—the "three foundations upon which the world rests," according to the Mishnah—existed as independent variables only prior to the giving of the Torah. Subsequent to the revelation at Sinai, worship and kindliness became meaningless when separate from Torah. Hence, if one acts in a seemingly virtuous manner but contrary to *halakhah*, he has strayed from the proper path of life and has lost his way. The *Taz*[7] offers a graphic example of this principle. Before the revelation of the Torah at Mount Sinai, one who lent money at interest performed a virtuous act; when the Torah prohibited usury, however, it redefined its moral nature as well. Lending money at interest became a vice and, as a result, any subsequent offender became eternally damned.

Hence, the improvement of ethical qualities and the attainment of a moral character, important as they are, may not override

---

[5]R. Hayyim Vital, *Shaarei Kedushah* (Bnei Brak, 1967), 15.

[6]R. Hayyim of Volozhin, *Ruah Hayyim* to *Avot* 1:2. See my *Torah Lishmah* (New York: Yeshiva University Press/Ktav, 1989), 87, on this work.

[7]*Yoreh De'ah* 160.

the formal *halakhah*. How, then, can we formulate Maimonides' position—that the suppression of one's evil impulses overrides the injunction against causing pain to animals—in strictly halakhic terms?

Love and Hatred

One must, I believe, subsume the moral act of subduing one's evil impulses under the formal rubric of a *mitzvah*. If this act is categorized as a technical *mitzvah*, one can understand why it overrides the prohibition of causing undue pain to animals. That *mitzvah* is none other than the commandment to love one's fellowman. But if so, we must also reckon with the obligation to hate evil-doers. How can this positive *mitzvah* of love override two other *mitzvot* (in this case, the prohibition against inflicting needless pain upon animals and the obligation to hate evil-doers)? Even if the commandments to love one's neighbor and to hate evil-doers neutralize each other, there remains the prohibition of causing undue pain to animals. How, then, may one load the burden of his enemy, the evil-doer, before unloading for his friend, and thereby allow the animal of his friend to suffer pain?

We can suggest the following formulation. The positive commandment to love one's neighbor (which, in this case, is to load his enemy's donkey first) overrides only the prohibition of causing unnecessary pain to animals. It does not override the *mitzvah* to hate evil-doers (which *mitzvah*, however, does not diminish the imperative to help the evil-doer's animal). Analyzing the matter further, we can posit the following reconstruction of both the rejected hypothesis and the conclusion of the germane talmudic passage which forms the basis for Maimonides' ruling.[8] Originally,

---

[8]*Baba Metzia* 32b. "Come and hear: If a friend requires unloading, and an enemy loading, one's [first] obligation is towards his enemy, in order to subdue his evil inclinations. Now if you should think that [relieving the suffering of an animal] is biblically [enjoined], [surely] the other is prefer-

the Talmud thought that when one is faced with the live option of unloading one's friend's animal or loading one's enemy's animal, one should pursue the first option for two reasons. First, the prohibition against causing unnecessary pain to animals (in this case, delaying the act of unloading the friend's animal) dictates that one should immediately perform the act of unloading. Second, the *mitzvah* to hate evil-doers should require that one should first attend to the animal of one's friend (i.e., an observant Jew). But when the Talmud concludes that the goal of subduing one's evil inclination (i.e., the formal *mitzvah* of loving one's neighbor which applies to everyone) mandates that one help his enemy first, this *mitzvah* overrides the prohibition of causing undue pain to animals. Although the *mitzvah* to hate evil-doers remains in full force, it is irrelevant to the imperative at hand—to subdue the evil inclination. We thus remain with two commandments: to love and hate the very same person.

But how is it possible for the Torah to command to love someone and, at the same time, to hate the same person? One may offer two explanations for this apparent conundrum. First, the law to "love" one's neighbor is purely functional, restricted to the practical sphere, and makes no demands upon one's emotions. Contrariwise, hatred of evil-doers is a *mitzvah* which focuses upon one's psychological attitude only. Nahmanides, in his commentary

---

able! . . . Even so, [the motive] in order to subdue his evil inclination is more compelling."

"Come and hear: The enemy spoken of is an Israelite enemy, but not a heathen enemy. But if you say that [relieving] the suffering of an animal is biblically [enjoined], what is the difference whether [the animal belongs to] an Israelite or a heathen enemy? . . . Do you think that this refers to 'enemy' mentioned in Scripture? It refers to 'enemy' spoken of in the Mishnah."

See *Hebrew-English Edition of the Babylonian Talmud*, trans. Salis Daiches and H. Freedman, ed. I. Epstein (London: Soncino Press, 1962), *Baba Metzia* 32b.

to Leviticus 19:18, writes: "This is an expression by way of over-statement, for a human heart is not able to accept a command to love one's neighbor as oneself. . . . Rather the commandment of the Torah means that one is to love one's fellow being *in all matters* as one loves *all good* for oneself." The Torah could not demand, according to Nahmanides, that one emotionally bestow the same degree of love that he feels for himself upon others. Rather, the verse means that one must *act lovingly* to one's fellow; he must conduct himself *as if* he loved him. In this vein Nahmanides explains why the preposition *et* is not used.[9] According to this distinction between the *mitzvah* of love and the *mitzvah* of hate, it is understandable for Maimonides to rule that one simultaneously hate someone with respect to attitude but perform acts of love toward him as a practical matter.

This analysis, however, cannot suffice for our reconstruction of Maimonides' position, for he clearly rejects a dichotomy between the nature of the *mitzvot* of love and hatred. According to Maimonides, the *mitzvah* to love one's neighbor includes one's emotional orientation toward him. In *Sefer ha-Mitzvot* (ed. Kapah), Maimonides writes:

> By this injunction we are commanded that we are to love one another even as we love ourselves, and that a man's love and compassion for his brother in faith shall be like his love and compassion for himself, in respect of his money, his person, and whatever he possesses and desires. Whatever I wish for myself, I am to wish the like for him; and whatever I do not wish for myself or for my friends, I am not to wish the like for him. This injunction is contained in His words (exalted be He), "thou shalt love thy neighbor as thyself." [no. 206]

---

[9]See also Meiri to *Yoma* 75b: "One should not let hatred of his fellow deter him from helping him as much as he can." See Maharam Shick's work on the commandments, *Mitzvah* no. 244.

He reiterates this view in *Hilkhot De'ot* 6:3 and in *Hilkhot Evel* 14:1, both cited above.

In sum, Nahmanides perceives the essence of the *mitzvah* of love and the means of its implementation to lie in the practical sphere. Maimonides, however, holds that while the means of implementation are functional or practical in nature, the *essence* of the commandment, which defines its fulfillment, is emotional, a feeling of love. This feeling, and not the act per se, constitutes the essence of the fulfillment of this *mitzvah*. Our original question then, remains: How can Maimonides conceive of a simultaneous *mitzvah* of love and hatred, both on the emotional level?

Maimonides believes, in my view, that it is psychologically and therefore legally possible to maintain a position of ambivalence.[10] *Halakhah* can demand that one both love and hate the same person. Hence, one must love even the evil-doer, even while one is also halakhically required to hate him.[11]

Maharam Schick points out that the Torah formulated the *mitzvah* of love with the term *neighbor*, not the usual *brother*. He believes that this demonstrates that one most love even those who are not God-fearers. In support, he cites the talmudic statement (*Sanhedrin* 52a) that the *mitzvah* of neighborly love obligates us to choose an "easy death" for those condemned by the Sanhedrin to die. There certainly can be no greater evil-doer than one who

---

[10]This analysis is opposed to that of R. Barukh Halevi Epstein who, in his *Torah Temimah* (Leviticus 19:18), classifies love as the opposite of hatred. According to our analysis, Maimonides thus antedated the "discovery" of ambivalence by psychoanalysis by over 700 years.

[11]See *Tanya* (*Likkutei Amarim*), chap. 32, who, in a famous passage, asserts that even those whom we must hate we must simultaneously love. Our hatred is directed to the element of evil in them; our love is focused upon the good that they contain. This view, of course, has roots in the famous talmudic record of the dialogue between R. Meir and his wife Beruriah, in which he accepted her distinction between praying for the destruction of sinners and praying for the eradication of sin: David's plea in his Psalms was for the latter, not the former. See *Berakhot* 10a.

merited the death penalty, yet we are commanded to love him. One of the early medieval halakhic authorities, R. Meir Abulafia, in his commentary *Yad Ramah to Sanhedrin* 52b, deduces the same principle from the Hebrew spelling of the term that connotes neighbor. *Neighbor* includes, he writes, even the evil among the Jews. Indeed, the word for *neighbor* and the word for *bad* are spelled identically in Hebrew *(ra)*.

Your Brother in Torah and *Mitzvot*

However, it yet remains for us to reconcile our analysis of the aforementioned passage—in opposition to the interpretation of *Hagahot Maimuniyyot*—with Maimonides' remarks in *Hilkhot Evel* which limit the *mitzvah* to love one's fellow Jew to the Jew who is "your brother in Torah and *mitzvot*." Are not the latter the very source of *Hagahot Maimuniyyot?*

This key phrase must be understood not in terms of actual observance, which is the literal sense in which it was read by *Hagahot Maimuniyyot*, but as a metaphor for those who are *obligated* to study Torah and observe *mitzvot*—Jews. Interestingly, the Yemenite manuscript of Maimonides' *Hilkhot De'ot* substitutes "children of the covenant" for "Israelite."[12] We suggest that "your brother in Torah and *mitzvot*" is another such honorific synonym; it only excludes non-Jews, and is not meant to limit the *mitzvah* to those who are totally observant Jews.

The literalist reading of the phrase "your brother in Torah and *mitzvot*" presents insuperable difficulties. Where does one draw the line? If one who is inadequately observant of *mitzvot* is excluded, what of one who does not satisfy the criterion of the first half of the phrase, one who is not a scholar and cannot study Torah, and is therefore not "your brother in *Torah?*" Moreover, everyone has sinned at one time or another in his life ("For there is not a

---

[12]See Maimonides, *Mishneh Torah*, ed. Cohen and Liberman (Jerusalem: Mossad ha-Rav Kook, 1964), ad loc.

righteous man upon earth who doeth good and sinneth not"
[Ecclesiastes 7:20]). In face of the *reductio ad absurdum* that would
impose massive limitations upon the scope of the *mitzvah* and
effectively make it inoperative, it is preferable to interpret the
phrase "your brother in Torah and *mitzvot*" in the manner we have
here suggested.

Different Classifications of Evil-doers

We cannot complete our analysis of Maimonides' position without
referring to his concluding remarks in *Hilkhot Rotze'ah*: "The Torah
is very solicitous of the lives of Israelites, whether of the wicked or
of the righteous, since they acknowledge God and believe in the
essentials of our religion." The point of these remarks, of course, is
to make a drastic distinction between different types of evil-doers.
Perhaps our previous contentions hold only for the evil-doer who
still believes in the fundamentals of the Jewish faith, one, that is,
who transgresses but has not strayed theologically.

Of course, the distinctive literary character of Maimonides'
concluding words to all his fourteen books of the *Mishneh Torah* is
well known. In light of this tendency to stylistic flourish, it is
conceivable that the word "they" does not refer to specific Jews,
whether observant or nonobservant of *halakhah*, but pertains,
rather, to Jews as a whole. All Jews, even sinners, are regarded by
the Jewish tradition "as full of *mitzvot* as a pomegranate"; and *all*
Jews collectively constitute the people of Israel which in its ideal
state is pure and holy. Hence, all Jews are included in the group of
those who "acknowledge God and believe in the essentials of our
religion" and are therefore deserving of compassion. The *mitzvah* to
love one's fellow Jew applies to all.

Support for our contention may be found in the law, formulated by Maimonides in *Hilkhot Avodah Zarah* 5:4, that the commandment to love one's fellow Jew does not apply to one who
attempts to persuade his neighbor to worship idols.

The execution of the enticer devolves upon the one he attempted to entice, as it is said, "Thy hand shall be first upon him to put him to death" (Deuteronomy 13:10). The latter is forbidden to love the enticer, as it is said, "Thou shalt not consent unto him" (Deuteronomy 13:9). Since, in reference to an enemy, it is said, "Thou shalt surely help with him" (Exodus 23:5) it might be supposed that this person [the enticer] should also be helped. It is therefore said, "Nor hearken unto him" (Exodus 13:9).

The source for this law is the *Sifre:* " 'Thou shall not consent unto him' (Exodus 13:9): Because of what is said elsewhere, thou shalt 'love thy neighbor as thyself' (Leviticus 19:18), you might think you must love this one too; hence the verse says, 'Thou shalt not consent unto him, nor hearken unto him' " (*Piska* 89). (Parenthetically, Maimonides' use of this passage in the *Sifre* – defining "thou shalt not consent" as "thou shall not love" – in his formulation of the law of loading and unloading in *Hilkhot Rotze'ah,* may also lend credence to our contention that the commandment to "subdue his evil impulse" is that of neighborly love.) If the *Sifre* is viewed as presenting the only exception to the universal rule to love one's neighbor, then it follows that all other evil-doers, even those who deny the fundamentals of Jewish belief, do fall under the scope of this law. Even with regard to such people, one must adopt a simultaneous posture of love and hate.[13] Barring the lone exception of the "persuader" to idolatry, the *mitzvah* to love one's fellow Jew is absolute.

However, Maimonides, in his *Commentary to the Mishnah,* after enumerating his formulation of the thirteen principles of Judaism, does indeed distinguish between classes of evil-doers.

If a person holds all these principles to be sound, and he truly believes in them, he is then part of that "Israel" whom we are

---

[13]See n. 11, above.

to love, pity, and treat, as God commanded, with love and fellowship. Even if a Jew should commit every possible sin, out of lust or mastery by his lower nature, he will be punished for his sins but will still have a share in the world-to-come. He is one of the "sinners in Israel." But if a person holds one of these principles to be defective, he has removed himself from the Jewish community. He is an atheist, a heretic, and unbeliever who "cuts among the plantings." We are commanded to hate him and destroy him. Of him it is said: "Shall I not hate, O Lord, those who hate Thee?" (Psalms 139:21).[14]

Thus, Maimonides might accept that the commandment to love one's neighbor applies to one who sins out of moral weakness if he still subscribes to the thirteen fundamentals of Jewish belief, but he excludes the Jewish heretic from the fellowship of Israel.

The aforementioned *Sifre* stands in stark opposition to Maimonides' position just cited. One may deduce from it that one must even love his neighbor who is a heretic; the only exception is the "enticer." Apparently, however, the heretic is in many respects worse than one who persuades others to idolatry. True, when Maimonides writes (in Chapter 2 of *Hilkhot Avodah Zarah*) that with regard to many *halakhot*, the heretic and the *apikores* are no different from one who incessantly worships idols, and he does not mention as well that the *mitzvah* to love one's fellow man does not apply to the heretic, this supports our previous contention that only the persuader to idolatry is not subject to the *mitzvah* to love

---

[14]Maimonides, *Commentary to the Mishnah*, tractate *Sanhedrin*, chap. 10, ed. J. Kapah, 145. Parenthetically, we have here one of the first mentions of the term *kelal Yisrael* in halakhic literature. In contemporary parlance, this is a composite noun indicating, *the collectivity of Israel*, or, *the Jewish community*. This is not, however, strictly the sense in which Maimonides uses the term. For him it might better be translated, "the category of 'Israel,' " meaning, the very definition or identity of one's Jewishness. See below, p. 153, and n. 15.

one's fellow man. However, we cannot escape the conclusion that Maimonides' own words on the heretic in his *Commentary to the Mishnah* militate against our interpretation of his position in the *Mishneh Torah.*

In truth, Maimonides holds that the heretic does not only lose his share in the world-to-come; he is removed from the class of those fellow Jews whom one is commanded to love and, indeed, he is not considered part of the Jewish people (*kelal Yisrael*, literally, "the category of 'Israel.'" This is the original meaning of the term so often used today).[15] With regard to the principle of the resurrection of the dead, Maimonides writes: "The resurrection of the dead is one of the cardinal principles established by Moses our Teacher. A person who does not believe in this principle has no real religion and no connection with the Jewish people" (*Commentary to the Mishnah, Sanhedrin*, chap. 10).

In *Mishneh Torah, Hilkhot Rotze'ah*, he writes:

> It was at one time deemed meritorious to kill apostates—by this are meant Israelites who worship idols or who provocatively do other sinful things, for even one who provocatively eats carrion or wears clothes made of mingled stuffs is deemed an apostate—and heretics, who deny the authenticity of the Torah or of prophecy. If one had the power to slay them publicly by the sword, he would do so. If not, one would plot against them in such a way as to bring about their death. Thus, if a person saw that such a one had fallen into a well containing a ladder, he would remove the ladder, giving the excuse that he wanted it to get his son down from the roof, and would bring it back afterward, and do similar acts. [4:10]

These words are consistent with his opinion in his *Commentary to the Mishnah*, cited above. R. Menahem ha-Meiri, in his commen-

---

[15]See Arthur Hyman, "Maimonides' 'Thirteen Principles,'" *Jewish Medieval and Renaissance Studies*, ed. A. Altmann (Cambridge, MA: Harvard University Press, 1967), 119–44.

tary on this Mishnah in tractate *Sanhedrin*, also writes in the same vein: "Since he believes what is proper for one to believe, and is thus included among the people (Hebrew: *am*), his many sins do not exclude him from the class of virtuous people. . . ." Meiri seems to agree with this limited classification of the term *people of Israel*.

Although Maimonides' position is clear, there do seem to be inherent difficulties with it, especially with his equation of those who will receive no share in the world-to-come with those who are not part of "Israel."

For one thing, why did the Mishnah itself not adopt the Maimonidean formulation and write, "All of Israel has a share in the world-to-come . . . and these are not included in Israel . . ."? Perhaps the Mishnah did not want to reach this extreme conclusion and only stated the fact that these people, while remaining part of Israel, do not possess a share in the world-to-come; while those who do maintain Judaism's cardinal beliefs will merit a share in the world-to-come.

Another difficulty: In *Avot de Rabbi Natan*, we find the following remark: "Seven have no share in the world-to-come, to wit: Scribes, elementary teachers, (even) the best of physicians, judges in their native cities, diviners, ministers of the court, and butchers" (30:5). Later in the same chapter, still others of such type are added to this category. Now, this presented a problem for the Tosafists. In their commentary to *Sotah* 5a (s.v. *kol*), they ask why the Mishnah in *Sanhedrin* did not mention the many others who do not share in the world-to-come according to various views in the Talmud, such as: the haughty;[16] those who die outside the Land of Israel;[17] the ignorant, if they do not at least help support Torah scholars;[18] those who lend money at interest, and the like (in addition to the seven enumerated in *Avot de Rabi Natan*). Certainly it is unthinkable that these people would not be counted as belonging to *kelal*

---

[16]*Sotah*, ad loc.

[17]*Ketubot* 111a.

[18]*Ketubot*, ad loc.

Yisrael, yet their exclusion is the inevitable result of Maimonides' exclusion from the fellowship of Israel of those who are assumed to have forfeited their share in the world-to-come.

Moreover, when Maimonides lists the twenty-four categories of sinners who will not receive a share in the world-to-come, he mentions those who violate the prohibition of *leshon ha-ra*, gossip or tale-bearing. The Talmud states that no one can escape the "dust" of *leshon ha-ra* even for one day.[19] According to Maimonides' own rules, few indeed would merit a share in the world-to-come, while the overwhelming majority would be considered hateful, undeserving of our love, and meriting severe oppression. This would seem to contradict the plain sense of the Mishnah which states that everyone (implying only a few exceptions) will merit a share in the next world.

Maimonides, it appears, was aware of this difficulty. In *Hilkhot Teshuvah* 3:24–25, he states: "There are transgressions less grave than those mentioned, concerning which, however, the Sages said that whoever habitually commits them will have no portion in the world-to-come. One should therefore avoid and beware of such transgressions. They are: one who gives another a nickname, etc." If Maimonides felt that these people are not part of Israel, even as they do not merit a share in the world-to-come, why does he not spell out the consequences of those who violate these comparatively "light" sins? If he believed that these people do not merit a share in the world-to-come but are still considered a part of *kelal Yisrael*, as opposed to those enumerated in the Mishnah in *Sanhedrin*, he certainly should have made that distinction explicit. Does he take this latter view for granted in the *Mishneh Torah?*

Even more difficult for the Maimonidean assumption is the opinion of R. Akiva (*Sanhedrin* 108a, 110b) that the "generation of the desert," Moses' contemporaries who worshiped the golden calf, have no share in the world-to-come. Now, if that implies the loss of status as Jews, how did the Jewish people continue? Furthermore,

---

[19]*Baba Batra* 165a.

when Maimonides in *Hilkhot Teshuvah*, chap. 3, classifies those who will not receive a share in the world-to-come, he does not include the remark that these people are not counted as part of Israel.[20] Moreover, Maimonides himself fails to apply in practice the principle that theological heresy removes from one his status as a Jew. Thus, for instance, his codification as *halakhah* the law that an apostate Jew who has married a Jewess is considered married (*Hilkhot Ishut* 4:15); in the immediately preceding *halakhah* he declares as null and void any marriage contracted between a Jew and a non-Jew. Finally, the Maimonidean equation of "no share in the world-to-come" with exclusion from *kelal Yisrael* is upset by the famous teaching of the Tosefta (*Sanhedrin*, chap. 11) that the pious Gentiles *(hasidei umot ha-olam)* have a share in the world-to-come. Maimonides codifies this in *Hilkhot Melakhim* 8:11. Hence, if non-Jews have a share in the world-to-come, it follows that the right to such eternal bliss is not a sure sign of one's status as a Jew.

In the final analysis, we must accept the stark truth that Rabbi Moses ben Maimon differentiated between different degrees of "wickedness" in his *Commentary to the Mishnah*. One who does not accept the fundamentals of Jewish belief excludes himself from the class of individuals the *halakhah* tells us to love and, in addition, is excluded from *kelal Yisrael*, the fellowship of the people of Israel. It is possible, however, that with regard to the equation of those who forfeit their share in eternal life with those who lose their status as Jews, he changed his mind when he later wrote his immortal code, *Mishneh Torah*; at the very least, there is enough material in his halakhic code to support the contention that he was no longer as

---

[20]In Maimonides' *Treatise on the Resurrection of the Dead*, the author did not repeat the remarks he had made in his *Commentary to the Mishnah*. This is the work Maimonides wrote to counter those who erroneously maintained that he did not believe resurrection to be a cardinal principle of the Torah and that he took figuratively the instances where the rabbis mentioned resurrection. It seems that in this treatise he softened the stand he originally took in classifying heretics.

certain then that heresy leads to exclusion from the Jewish people[21] as he was when he wrote the *Commentary to the Mishnah.*

It is, at first, quite astonishing that Maimonides takes such a hard line on orthodox adherence to the Thirteen Principles. Any deviation results not only in the loss of eternal life, but of member-ship in *kelal Yisrael.* However, upon reflection, this is not at all surprising. Systems that hold that the acme of Judaism is attained in formulating correct ideas and true notions about God, as opposed to proper conduct, will consider any divergence from such correct opinions to be severe violations of the integrity of the faith. Rationalism is closely linked to dogmatism. Since Maimonides is the supreme rationalist, who holds that metaphysics is beyond *halakhah,* and that the loftiest goal is the forming of correct concepts about the Deity, it is in the area of ideas and theory that the test of faith takes place. It is in that realm, rather than in behavior, that one stands or falls as a Jew.

CONTEMPORARY IMPLICATIONS

The halakhic implications of the issue we have been discussing are of great import to the Jewish community today. Are we, in fact,

---

[21]I am indebted to Dr. Jacob J. Schacter for alerting me to the article by Dr. Menachem Kellner on this subject (in *Tura* [1989], 249–60 [Hebrew]). Kellner attempts to solve the problem of the inconsistency in Maimonides in a rather novel manner by linking it to a supposed Messianic dimension of Maimonides' thought. But while that could possibly explain Maimo-nides' insistence on theological purity in his *Commentary,* it does not adequately explain the apparent contradictions in the *Code.* While I have no better way of systematically explaining away all the latter, I prefer to think that Maimonides had, at that stage of his life, begun to question the certainty of his earlier convictions (the *Commentary* was begun by Maimo-nides at the age of 23 and concluded when he was 30 years old) and therefore ruled in all *practical* issues in the *Mishneh Torah* that heresy does not exclude one from the fellowship of Israel.

commanded to exclude all those who reject the fundamentals of Jewish belief from the *mitzvah* of love and from membership in *kelal Yisrael*?[22] If indeed this is what we are bidden to do, the ramifications are nothing short of cataclysmic. But if one is not sure that the *halakhah* is indeed such, but decides to act toward Jews who have abandoned the creed of Judaism as if they were enemies, he is not being *mahmir* (adopting the stringent view); he is illicitly being *meikil* (adopting a lenient view) on the *mitzvah* of the love of one's neighbor, a *mitzvah* which involves potential defamation of God's Name, "Thou shall love thy neighbor as thyself—I am the Lord," and a commandment which Hillel, in a famous passage (*Shabbat* 31a), considered the fundamental principle of Judaism even in its negative formulation.

Our analysis will show that there are four cogent reasons for concluding that the *mitzvah* to love one's fellow Jew applies to virtually all Jews today, even those who do not believe in the basic tenets of Judaism. Recent halakhic authorities *(Aharonim)* have already proposed two reasons, which we shall here cite, and we shall assert two additional reasons for this decision as well.

The Prevailing Zeitgeist as a Form of "Coercion"

How do we classify one who does not accept the fundamentals of Jewish belief (whether Maimonides' Thirteen Principles or the various other dogmatologies proposed by other medieval Jewish

---

[22]This was indeed explicitly published as the policy of Agudath Israel in an article by Rabbi Moshe Blau in *Kol Yisrael* in 1923: "Only one who believes in the God of Israel and in the Torah of Israel is entitled to be called by the name 'Jew' *(Yisrael)*. One who violates the Sabbath openly or proudly and brazenly announces that he is not religious, is not [part of] *kelal Yisrael*, neither according to Halakhah nor according to Jewish logic." That same theme was reflected more recently in the pages of *Ha-Mahaneh ha-Haredi* (August 1987), the organ of the Belzer Hasidim, where the editor declared that the total population of *kelal Yisrael* in our days amounts to no more than about a million people. . . .

authorities) if his dissension issues neither out of his personal philosophical conviction nor out of spite, but simply because of mindless conformity to the prevailing norms and values of the ubiquitous secular culture? In other circumstances, had he been nurtured by a loving family committed to Torah, and educated by competent and religiously inspired teachers, he might well have grown up firm in his commitment to God, Torah, and the Jewish tradition. Can we not claim for such people the halakhic status of "children who were taken away into captivity amongst the heathen" that the Talmud categorizes as *ones* (coerced transgressors) and, hence, exonerated from willful heresy, and included amongst those we are commanded to love?

Rabbi Abraham Isaac ha-Kohen Kook maintained that the category of the sinner by coercion applies as well to the realm of faith and beliefs.

> Just as the Tosafists remark in *Sanhedrin* 26b (s.v. *he-hashud*) that someone who is suspected of an act of sexual immorality because he was seized by passion is not disqualified as a witness because "his passion coerced him" and, by the same token, the Tosafists in *Gittin* 41b (s.v. *kofin*) write that seduction by a maid-servant is considered a form of coercion, we may say that the *Zeitgeist* acts as an evil intellectual temptress who seduces the young men of the age with her charm and her sorcery. They are truly "coerced," and God forbid that we judge them as willful heretics.[23]

Once we grant that in matters of faith, as in the realm of sexual misconduct, extenuating circumstances do exist along with the consequent halakhic categories of lack of intention, coercion, and ignorance of the law, we must then proceed to investigate carefully every case of a person to whom we would deny the biblical mandate of love, making sure that he willfully rejected Judaism

---

[23]Rabbi Abraham Isaac ha-Kohen Kook, *Iggerot ha-Reiyah* 1:71.

because of his free personal decision rather than his seduction by the overwhelming might of the cognitive majority in his environment.[24] The *mitzvah* to love one's fellow is, as R. Akiba is quoted in *Sifra* to Leviticus (19:18), a *kelal gadol*, or fundamental principle of the Torah.

Hence, we dare not, in our paganized generation, glibly assume that any particular person is not a "child who has been taken captive among the heathen" and is thus excluded from the circle of those we are commanded to love and from the fraternity of Israel. Moreover, not only is it wrong to condemn whole sections of the Jewish people to this status but, given the intellectual climate in which we live — its pervasive secularism, hedonism, agnosticism, and materialism — each individual Jew who has strayed from Torah must be presumed to be "coerced" and thus not regarded as a willful heretic or *apikores*. "And it shall be forgiven all the congregation of the children of Israel . . . seeing that all the people were in ignorance" (Numbers 15:36).

Rabbi Abraham Isaiah Karelitz, known as the Hazon Ish, arrived at the same conclusion. His words deserve close attention:

> I believe that the law that we drop (into a well, i.e., kill) an
> *apikores* (heretic) only existed in an epoch when divine Prov-
> idence was perceived by all as self-evident, as in those times
> when overt miracles were abundant and the Heavenly Voice
> *(bat kol)* was heard, and when the righteous men of the

---

[24]By the same token, there is no special merit in faith and obedience in the presence of revelation or, derivatively, in circumstances when the *Zeitgeist* moves an individual to belief and observance. In both cases, the environment exercises a form of duress on the individual. The maximum opportunity for freedom of choice, and therefore for credit or blame, occurs when circumstances are neutral, equidistant from both extremes. See my *The Royal Reach*, chap. 2 ("Neither Here Nor There"), where I develop this idea based upon the talmudic linkage of Purim to Sinai. Hence, this exculpation by Rav Kook would apply selectively, depending upon one's individual circumstances.

generation were under the specific Providence that was visible to all. The heretics of that day were particularly spiteful in their rejection (of Torah) and pursuit of hedonistic values and amorality. Then, the eradication of wicked people was a way to protect the world, for everyone knew that the waywardness of the generation brought destruction upon the world: pestilence, war, and famine. However, in a time when God's Providence is hidden and when the masses have lost faith, the act of eradicating unbelievers does not correct a breach in the world; on the contrary, it creates a larger breach, for it will appear to others as nothing more than wanton destruction and violence, God forbid. Since [the purpose of the law of dropping into the well] is meant to repair, this law does not apply when it fails to repair. We must instead woo back [those who have strayed] with love and enable them to stand upright with the strength of Torah insofar as we can.[25]

The Hazon Ish thus asserts that in our generation, a time when "God's face is hidden" and when "heresy rules the world," laws which sanction the oppression of heretics are counterproductive and no longer apply. Instead, love and friendship must prevail. The grounds of analysis differ—Rav Kook is more anthropological, focusing on this secular age as one in which the intellectual temptress seduces, while the Hazon Ish is more theological, considering our epoch as an age of the hiding of divine Providence—but the conclusion is the same. And what is true for individuals holds true for the community as a whole.

Indeed, Maimonides himself, in spite of the harsh attitude so evident in his remarks in his *Commentary to the Mishnah* in *Sanhedrin*, does mention in his *Mishneh Torah* that one who rejects the fundamentals of Jewish belief out of force of habit or out of defective education is halakhically not considered a heretic. In *Hilkhot Mamrim* 3:3, he writes concerning the exclusion of an individual

---

[25]*Hazon Ish* 13:16 (or to *Yoreh De'ah, Hilkhot Shehitah,* no. 2:16).

from *kelal Yisrael* and the punishment of being cast into a well and not being rescued from it,

> that this applies only to one who repudiates the Oral Law as a result of his reasoned opinion and conclusion, who walks lightmindedly in the stubbornness of his heart, denying first the Oral Law, as did Zadok and Boethus and all who went astray. But their children and grandchildren, who were misguided by their parents and were raised among the Karaites and trained in their views, are like a child taken captive by them and raised in their religion, whose status is that of an *anus* (one who abjures the Jewish religion under duress) who, although he later learns that he is a Jew, meets Jews, and observes them practice their religion, is nevertheless to be regarded as an *anus*, since he was reared in the erroneous ways of his fathers. Thus it is with those who adhere to the practices of their Karaite parents. Therefore, efforts should be made to bring them back in repentance, to draw them near by friendly relations so that they may return to the strength-giving source, i.e., the Torah.

Maimonides could not have been any more explicit in exculpating those who were raised by their parents and teachers (and, presumably, society) on a diet of rejection of or indifference to Judaism. The category of *ones* (duress, coercion) thus applies to the realm of religious faith. Indeed, this view is already prefigured by Maimonides in his *Commentary to the Mishnah, Hullin:*

> Know that the tradition, as we have received it from our forefathers, is that since we are living in an age of exile, we no longer practice capital punishment in all other capital crimes. However, in cases of religious sedition—to wit: heretics, Sadducees, and followers of Boethus—those who initiated the rebellion against the Torah are punished by death. They are to be executed in order that they not mislead Israel and

destroy the Jews' faith, etc. But their followers who were born and educated into these ideas are considered as coerced *(ones)*, and the applicable law is that of children who were taken into captivity by the heathen. All their sins are deemed inadvertent, as we explained. However, those who initiated the heresy are considered intentional and not inadvertent. [1:1]

The Lack of Proper "Rebuke"

Secondly, we must consider the decision of the *Hazon Ish* relating the *mitzvah* to hate evil-doers to the commandment to rebuke the sinner: "Thou shalt not hate thy brother in thy heart; *thou shalt surely rebuke thy neighbor,* and not bear sin because of him" (Leviticus 19:17). The *halakhah* considers the negative consequences that flow from a transgression to be contingent upon prior proper rebuke of the sinner. He quotes earlier halakhic authorities, such as Maharam of Lublin and R. Jacob Molin (or Molln), who rule that the *mitzvah* of hating the evil-doer applies only after one has properly rebuked the sinner and the latter still refuses to obey. On the basis of the talmudic discussion in *Arakhin* 16b, that nowadays there is no one sufficiently capable of delivering proper rebuke *(tokhahah),* one arrives at the conclusion that today we must act toward those who have strayed as people who have not yet been rebuked properly, and hence, even though they explicitly reject Torah, as still deserving of love. The lack of proper rebuke places them in the category of *ones.* Thus:

> The *Hagahot Maimuniyyot* wrote that one may not hate the heretic until he has disregarded rebuke. At the end of his book *Ahavat Hessed* (by Rabbi Israel Meir Ha-Kohen, author of the classic work *Hafetz Hayyim*), the author cites R. Jacob Molin (Molln) to the effect that we must love the sinner. He also quotes the responsa of Maharam of Lublin to show that we must consider the sinners as those who have not yet been rebuked, for we no longer know how to rebuke properly, and

hence one must treat them as transgressors under duress. As a result, we cannot exempt these sinners from [standard Jewish] obligations such as levirate marriage and other *halakhot.*[26]

According to this analysis, not only must one love the sinner (even the heretic), but one must desist as well from hating him as an evil-doer. Consequently, to hate such a person is to violate the injunction against hating one's neighbor in one's heart (the first part of the same verse in Leviticus 19:17).

It must be noted that the Hazon Ish's ruling is based on the premise that we are incapable of fulfilling the requirement of rebuke in our generation. Such is, in fact, the opinion of most decisors and most *Rishonim.* They follow the Mishnaic teachers R. Tarfon, R. Elazar b. Azariah, and R. Akiba, all of whom, for different reasons, arrive at the same conclusion. However, Maimonides (*Hilkhot De'ot,* chap. 6) decides the law in favor of R. Yohanan b. Nuri, who "called heaven and earth as witnesses" that one may indeed fulfill the *mitzvah* of rebuke in the present generation.[27]

Doubt and Denial

I have suggested elsewhere that those who *doubt* the fundamentals of Judaism should not be classified together with those who categorically *reject* the truths of Judaism. (The gist of the argument is repeated here, in somewhat different form, because of its obvious relevance to our theme.)

Support for this contention may be found in the Talmud (*Shabbat* 31a):

---

[26]See *Hazon Ish, Yoreh De'ah,* no. 2:28. See, as well, *Hazon Ish* on Maimonides' *Mishneh Torah, Hilkhot De'ot* 6:3, and references cited ad loc. See too *Sefer ha-Hinnukh,* no. 238.

[27]See my chapter on this subject in my *Halakhot ve-Halikhot* (Jerusalem: Mossad ha-Rav Kook, 1990), 168–75.

Our Rabbis taught: A certain heathen once came before Shammai and asked him, "How many Torahs have you?" "Two," he replied: "the Written Torah and the Oral Torah." "I believe you with respect to the Written, but not with respect to the Oral Torah; make me a proselyte on condition that you teach me the Written Torah [only]." [Shammai] scolded and repulsed him in anger. When he went before Hillel, he accepted him as a proselyte. On the first day he taught him [the alphabet:] *Alef, bet, gimmel, dalat.* The following day he reversed [them] to him. "But yesterday you did not teach them to me thus," he protested. [Hillel replied:] "Must you then not rely upon me? Then rely upon me with respect to the Oral [Torah] too."

Rashi comments:

"He converted him"—and relied upon his wisdom, that in the end he will persuade him to accept [the Oral Torah]. This is not to be compared to the case of one who accepts Judaism except for one law. The man (in our case) did not willfully deny the Oral Law; he just did not believe in its divine origin. Hillel was confident that after he would teach him, he would rely upon him.

Rashi clearly draws a line of demarcation between the heretic and the individual who simply does not believe.[28]

One critic has argued against the thesis here presented, maintaining that Rashi's focus is on the words "divine origin" (literally, "from the mouth of God"). On this view, the proselyte was willing to commit himself to practice all the *mitzvot* of the Oral Law, but

---

[28]See my *Faith and Doubt* (New York: Ktav, 1971), 186ff. nn. 24–27, where I bring proof for my assertion. See too *Migdal Oz* to Maimonides, *Hilkhot Teshuvah,* chap. 3, and R. Abraham Isaac Kook, *Iggerot ha-Reiyah* 1:20.

was unwilling to grant its divine origin. This idea of the Oral Law's divine origin is thus the content of the "belief" as yet unattained by the proselyte. The phrase "did not willfully deny the Oral Law" then refers to his acceptance of the Oral Law in practice. If so, Rashi's distinction is between belief and practice, rather than between faith and doubt.

This proposed explanation, however, is untenable. Besides violating the plain sense of Rashi, it offers no explanation as to why Rashi shifted from the phrase "willfully deny" to the phrase "did not believe." Rashi intended with these two different phrases two different and opposite concepts, two sides of the same coin. Moreover, the talmudic passage does not mention at all the phrase "deny" or any similar term. The only phrases used are "I believe you" and "I do not believe you." Furthermore, what would be the source of this bold distinction between the practice of laws of the Oral Torah when accompanied and when unaccompanied by belief in its divine origin, the consequence of which was that Hillel was prepared to convert him even though he did not believe in the Oral Law's divine origin? If one is a heretic, even with regard to the theoretical basis of the Oral Law, his mechanical performance of *mitzvot* carries no weight.

Our interpretation of Rashi does not suffer from these difficulties. According to our analysis, both "did not willfully deny" and "did not believe" refer to the axiom of the Law's "divine origin," and "to accept" means to consent to this article of faith; there is no reference intended here to the question of whether or not one commits to a course of action without belief in its ultimate authenticity. Rashi proposes a distinction between deliberate apostasy and lack of positive conviction, doubt but not willful heresy.

Most people, especially in our days but in days of yore as well, abandon religion not because they are sure that it is false. They leave it because they are unconvinced, in doubt, and perhaps uncertain whether any kind of certainty can ever be attained. Such pervasive doubt is founded upon the Cartesian principle of *de omnibus dubitendum*—doubt everything. In other words, they are not "deniers" but "nonbelievers."

On the basis of this distinction, we maintain that the great majority of nonbelievers of today are not equivalent to the *apikores* of talmudic times.

Love and Brotherhood

Finally, a note on Maimonides' formulation in his *Commentary on the Mishnah* to *Sanhedrin* is in order. Maimonides, it will be recalled, there stated that "if a person holds all of these principles to be sound—he is then part of 'Israel,' " but "if a person holds one of these principles to be defective, he has removed himself from the Jewish community." Maimonides thus demands positive theological commitment as the price for inclusion in *kelal Yisrael*. If we take his words literally, we reach the astonishing conclusion that he who observes *mitzvot* but has not reflected upon their theological basis would also be excluded from the Children of Israel. Spelling out the consequences of this position, we would be forced to conclude that not only heretics but unreflective and intellectually indifferent Jews, and children, would not be included in the "people of Israel"; as a result, they would not only not receive a share in the world-to-come, but other Jews would not be permitted to love them and would, indeed, be commanded to hate them.

These words of Maimonides, however, are not repeated in his *Mishneh Torah*, and, except for the citation from R. Menahem ha-Meiri referred to above, to my knowledge this view is not repeated by any other medieval Jewish authority.

From his remarks, especially in *Hilkhot Mamrim* cited above, we see that with regard to the Karaites of his day, Maimonides did not repeat his position as expressed earlier in his comments to tractate *Sanhedrin*, requiring positive affirmation of the Thirteen Principles of faith as prerequisite to inclusion in *kelal Yisrael*, and considering the absence of conscious rejection of such principles as inadequate. This follows from his ruling that children of the original Karaites and other sectarians are accepted as part of the fellowship of Israel; presumably, no such positive affirmation of rabbinic Judaism can be expected of the later Karaites. "Coercion" as a halakhic category exists as an exemption; it does not substitute for a needed prerequisite.

According to the other *Rishonim*, must one declare his adherence to the principles of Jewish belief as a *conditio sina qua non* to be counted as a Jew? Alternatively, is one reckoned a Jew from birth, remaining so until he commits a positive act of heresy similar to that performed by the "wicked son" in the Passover Haggadah?

To analyze this controversy which separates Maimonides from most other *Rishonim* (and which, as was indicated above, may well be Maimonides' position in his later *Mishneh Torah* as well), we must focus upon the parameters of inclusion in and exclusion from the community of "Israel."

One who does not believe in all the fundamentals of Judaism is certainly still obligated to observe all the commandments incumbent upon a believing Jew. I have elsewhere[29] developed the thesis that in *halakhah*, especially according to Maimonides, the term *Israelite (Yisrael)* admits of two different definitions: as an individual per se, a "son" of his heavenly Father with Whom he has a relationship expressed halakhically in the form of specific obligations and prohibitions; and as a brother to other Israelites, which in turn is manifested in a different set of halakhic norms. Only with regard to the second moment, the fraternal aspect of Jewishness, do heretics lose their status as *Israelites*. Thus, for example, wine that heretics touch is to be considered as wine that a non-Jew handled and hence forbidden; and Jewish courts do not have the obligation to prevent them from committing sins.[30] Their obligations toward

---

[29]See my "May A Transgressing Kohen Perform the Priestly Blessing?" *Ha-Darom* 10 (*Elul* 5719 [1959]): 95–103 (Hebrew).

[30]See *Siftei Kohen, Yoreh De'ah* 141, and *Responsa Avnei Nezer, Yoreh De'ah*, no. 127.

God as individual Jews, however, remain in full force. In this limited sense, their status as Israelites remains uncompromised, and their obligation to observe the Torah remains undiminished irrespective of their theological perplexities.[31]

A responsum by R. Israel of Bruna, which distinguishes between the halakhic implications of the terms "Jew" and "Israelite," is most relevant.

> There was a case of a young man by the name of Loewe of Passau who vowed never to play (i.e., gamble) with any Jew. . . . Now, in Neustadt there was (a converted Jew) and Loewe asked R. Israel Isserlin if he is permitted to play with him. He permitted him to do so, for a Jew who is converted out of the faith is not called a Jew, even though "an Israelite even if he sinned remains an Israelite" (*Sanhedrin* 44a). Nevertheless, he is not called a "Jew," and therefore the vow does not apply to him. I can support this (ruling) with proof from a talmudic passage in *Sanhedrin* upon which Rashi comments that, "whoever denies idolatry is called a Jew" (*Megillah* 13a).

---

[31]This conforms with Maimonides' views in his famous *Iggeret ha-Shemad*. See references in my article, "A Transgressing Kohen." See, too, *Keren Orah* to *Yevamot* 17, concerning the talmudic statement that the Rabbis classified the Ten Lost Tribes (who had totally assimilated into their idolatrous milieu) as idol-worshipers. He writes: "Perhaps with respect to marriage laws were they classified as non-Jews; in other respects, however, they could not be classified as such, for halakhically they remained Jews." Our analysis supports his conclusion that the ten tribes became non-Jews only with regard to the brotherhood of the Jewish people, which includes marriage law. *Keren Orah* (ad loc.) quotes Maharsha, Maharshal, and the Mordekhai on this topic, and suggests that only at the time of the assimilation of the ten tribes, the age of Prophecy and the availability of the divine Spirit, could the reclassification of the ten tribes as idol-worshipers have been effected. See also the surprising comment by R. Moshe Sofer, *Hagahot Hatam Sofer* to *Shulhan Arukh, Orah Hayyim* 29:4.

Thus, a converted Jew who denies the God of Israel and worships an idol is not called a "Jew."[32]

R. Isserlin does not attempt to distinguish halakhically between the terms *Israelite* and *Jew*; he merely observes that with regard to vows (which halakhically follow the common usage of the average person), renegade Jews were not meant to be included in the term *Jude*, Jew, as used in Germany at that time. Hence, his permission for Loewe to gamble with the apostate of Neustadt.

However, R. Israel of Bruna does make an essential distinction that is valid regardless of time and place, as evidenced from his citation of the talmudic passage in *Megillah* to buttress his position. In his view, "Israelite" designates one's lineage as a Jew, which is essential and eternal and which concomitantly obligates performance of *mitzvot*, notwithstanding one's apostasy. *Jew* (or *Jude*) refers to his relationship with the rest of the Jewish community. The former is what we have referred to as a Jew *qua* an individual, and the latter as a Jew who is a brother to other Jews, part of the fraternity of Israel. One who apostasizes loses his connections and his rights vis-à-vis the rest of the Jewish people. "An Israelite even if he sinned remains an Israelite," but he is no longer a Jew because he has forfeited the privileges attendant upon such status. Hence, one who vowed not to gamble with Jews did not refer to such an apostate.

The *mitzvah* to love one's neighbor is, of course, the quintessential *mitzvah* of brotherhood. At first blush it appears puzzling that the heretic who sinned against God but not against man should be deprived of his halakhic ties of brotherhood to the rest of the Jewish people. We suggest that this punishment does not follow from the heretic's rejection of God; such matters are the concern of the omniscient Creator who alone knows the innermost thoughts

---

[32]R. Israel of Bruna, *She'elot u-Teshuvot Mahari mi-Bruna*, no. 35. The text is slightly corrupted, but the sense of the responsum is unaffected by these textual difficulties.

of all His creatures. It is, instead, a direct response to a sin against the Jewish people in its entirety. The Sinaitic covenant, which the Jewish people accepted with respect to God, also involved the element of Israel's brotherhood. The formal expression of the covenant, it is true, is reflected in the *mitzvot maasiyyot* that individual Jews perform; but its foundation is the faith in Him by Jews as a collectivity, a nation. One who rejects this faith sins not only against the Holy One, but equally destroys the entire foundation of Judaism by weakening the fabric of the Jewish covenantal community as a whole. Without this faith in God we, as a people, are not worthy of being the covenantal partners of God. The heretic thus severs the unique metaphysical chain that binds the Jewish people together as the people of God, the "holy nation and kingdom of priests." It is fitting that, as a punishment, he should be denied all expressions of Jewish brotherhood, a fraternity which he has treated with contempt.

Now Maimonides in his *Commentary to the Mishnah* holds that only one who has explicitly accepted the fundamentals of Jewish belief can join the brotherhood of Israel and be a part of the Jewish fraternity based upon the commonality of belief. Such a Jew merits all the privileges of Jewish brotherhood, including the *mitzvah* of neighborly love. But one who rejects such fraternity, even if only by the absence of explicit acceptance of the fundamental principles of Jewish faith in God, has read himself out of this brotherhood. One who is thereby not part of this voluntary fraternity, however, is still *qua* individual classified as a Jew. Other *Rishonim* (and probably Maimonides himself in *Mishneh Torah*) maintain that one's classification as a Jew automatically confers upon him the rights of membership in the Jewish fraternity. Those who are sons of God are *ipso facto* brothers to each other. Only those who intentionally remove themselves from the community, by actions such as outright and positive rejection of Judaism, are denied the rights of the Jewish fraternity. One is not required to love a person who explicitly removed himself from the Jewish faith-community.

According to the foregoing analysis, only in a historical epoch

when the great majority of the Jewish people are religiously observant and God-fearing, such that heresy constitutes a demonstrative
denial of Jewish identity, does the corresponding removal of the
apostate from the Jewish fraternity make sense. However, when the
majority of the Jewish people themselves are ignorant of Torah and
indifferent to its commandments, the heretic's denial of Judaism's
theological principles is not destructive of the communal Jewish
identity per se. On the contrary, many Jewish nonbelievers today
affirm their "Jewish identity," are proud of their lineage, and contribute their effort and substance for the welfare of the Jewish people.
They certainly cannot be said to intend harm to Jewish fraternity by
means of their heresy. They may be classified along with those who
have not consciously and positively denied Judaism's tenets; they
must be presumed simply not to have paid much attention to matters
of faith. Their Jewishness is natural, not intellectual or spiritual;
their conscious status as part of the community is intuitively assumed and is not felt to be in need of demonstration or corroboration.

It is not out of place to cite a more recent source, one which
explicitly confirms the Jewishness of any Jew who calls himself a
Jew, regardless of the content of such self-identification. What
follows is a passage by R. Zadok ha-Kohen of Lublin, a profound
and influential hasidic rebbe of the nineteenth century:

> The essence of Judaism is the name of "Israel" (Jew). This is
> what Isaiah says: "One shall say, I am the Lord's, and another
> shall call himself by the name of Jacob and designate himself
> by the name of Israel" (Isaiah 44:5). This means that a Jew who
> has no greater distinction than this, that he calls himself a
> Jew—that is enough.
>
> We find in the Talmud that a non-Jew who was con-
> verted amongst Gentiles (and thus failed to observe the
> commandments), later has to bring a sin-offering for eating
> non-kosher food, drinking blood, violating Shabbat, and
> bowing to idols (*Shabbat* 68b). Obviously, he was unaware

that these things are forbidden—even Shabbat and idolatry; thus he knew nothing at all about Torah. In what way, then, is he considered a Jew such that he must bring a special sacrifice for these infractions? Obviously, it is *because he calls himself a Jew.*

Thus we may understand as well why the law requiring martyrdom applies to one who converts to Islam, even though that religion prohibits idol worship, immorality, and the shedding of blood. . . . So: abandoning the name (or: identity) of "Jew" alone, is considered as serious as the violation of all the other commandments of the Torah, including the three most heinous of all sins, namely, idolatry, immorality, and murder. . . . So too, [our ancestors] once worshipped idols but they never denied they were Jews [and so they remained Jews indeed].[33]

One can hardly make a more cogent case for breaking the necessary bond between theological error and membership in *kelal Yisrael.*

For this reason we can assume that in our contemporary era, even one who consciously rejects the principles of Judaism (but still maintains his "Jewish identity") is not halakhically defined as an *apikores* of the kind that flourished in the talmudic period.

CONCLUSION

To summarize, there exist four reasons why the stringency of the laws concerning treatment of a heretic should not apply to nonbelievers in our age:

1. Heretics today are "coerced" by the *Zeitgeist* we live in, which ineluctably affects their *Weltanschaaung.*

---

[33]R. Tzadok ha-Kohen, *Tzidkat ha-Tzaddik ha-Malei* (Jerusalem: "A" Publishers, 1968), 40, no. 54 (editor anonymous; presumably Eliyahu Kitov).

2. One may be classified as a heretic only if he has rejected halakhically valid "rebuke"; most *Rishonim* decide in favor of the majority of *Tannaim* that one cannot deliver proper rebuke in our times. As a result, there is no official status of "evil-doer."

3. Heresy in our day is most often not a positive rejection of Jewish principles of faith but a lack of conviction or belief; this doubt, according to Rashi's gloss, is not equivalent to heresy.

. 4. Heresy is applicable to a time when the majority of the people of Israel are themselves religiously observant. It does not constitute a traitorous act vis-à-vis the Jewish people under present conditions. Consequently, the reason why the heretic should lose his status as part of the Jewish fraternity does not apply. One forfeits the love of his fellow Jew if and only if he himself has first deserted the Jewish people.

On the basis of all of the above, we may conclude that according to most *Rishonim*, the *mitzvah* of hating "evil-doers" does not apply to the overwhelming majority of nonobservant and nonreligious Jews in our times. (Indeed, the prohibition against hating a fellow Jew in one's heart might apply to those who practice hatred of the sinners.) Such Jews are indeed full members of *kelal Yisrael*. Even if we grant Maimonides' early position on the need for explicit commitment to the Thirteen Principles in order to be accepted in the Jewish fraternity and thereby merit neighborly love, and hence affirm the relevance of the *mitzvah* of hatred (of evil-doers) in our generation, the *mitzvah* to love one's fellow Jew applies universally (except in the case of one who tempts his fellow Jew to worship idols) simultaneously with the *mitzvah* to hate evil-doers.[34] And even if we grant Maimonides' acceptance of the applicability of the *mitzvah* of rebuke in our day and age (and thereby rendering

---

[34]See the beautiful and uplifting comments of R. Naftali Tzevi Yehudah Berlin (the Netziv), *Teshuvot Meshiv Davar*, vol. 1, no. 44. His words deserve wide dissemination. The Netziv here exemplifies the truthfulness of the saying of the Sages that "Torah scholars bring peace to the world."

irrelevant the second principle which we have enumerated), most Jews today should be classified as fully within the Jewish people and therefore exempt from the onus of being hated, according to the other three parts of our analysis.

A NOTE ON TRANSLATIONS

Translations of many of the Maimonidean and other rabbinic texts cited in this article were derived from the following sources, with occasional changes for purposes of clarity or emphasis:

1. Chavel, Charles B., trans. *The Commandments: Sefer Ha-Mitzvoth of Maimonides*. Vol. 1, *The Positive Commandments*. London: Soncino, 1940, p. 220.

2. _____ . *Ramban's (Nachmanides) Commentary on the Torah: Leviticus*. New York: Shilo, 1974, pp. 292–93.

3. Epstein, I., ed., and H. Freedman, trans. *Hebrew-English Edition of the Babylonian Talmud: Shabbath*. New York: Soncino, 1972, 26b.

4. Goldin, Judah, trans. *The Fathers According to Rabbi Nathan*. New Haven: Yale University Press, 1955, p. 151.

5. Hammer, Reuven, trans. and intro. *Sifre: A Tannaitic Commentary on the Book of Deuteronomy*. New Haven: Yale University Press, 1986, p. 139.

6. Hershman, Abraham M., trans. *The Code of Maimonides: Book 14. The Book of Judges*. New Haven: Yale University Press, 1949, p. 200.

7. Hyamson, Moses, ed. and intro. *Mishneh Torah: The Book of Knowledge by Maimonides*. Jerusalem: Boys' Town, 1965, 55a, 71b, 85a.

8. Klein, Hyman, trans. *The Code of Maimonides: Book 11. The Book of Torts*. New Haven: Yale University Press, 1954, pp. 234–36.

9. Twersky, Isadore, ed. and intro. *A Maimonides Reader*. New York: Behrman House, 1972, pp. 414–22.

Some of my translations of passages from Maimonides' *Commentary to the Mishnah* received the benefit of critical review by Prof. Joshua Blau of the Hebrew University and Prof. Richard Steiner of Yeshiva University. I am grateful to them for their wise suggestions.[35]

---

[35]An earlier version of this chapter appeared in *Tradition* 24:2 (1989): 98–122.

5

All Jews Are Responsible for One Another

Nachum L. Rabinovitch

The obligation of one Jew to be responsible for the spiritual well-being of another is as old as the Bible itself. "And they shall stumble over one another" (Leviticus 26:37) was understood by the rabbis to mean, "not [literally] over one another, but over one another's sins. This teaches us that all Jews are responsible for one another *(melamed she-kol Yisrael arevim zeh ba-zeh)*."[1] The Talmud further clarified (and restricted) this principle so that "it applies only if they have the ability to prevent the sin, and do not do so" (*Shevuot* 39a). This is spelled out in a celebrated talmudic passage: "Whoever is able to prevent the members of his household from sinning and does not do so is held accountable for their sins; [if one is able to prevent] the members of his city [from sinning, and does not,] he is held accountable for their sins; [and if he is able to prevent the sins]

---

[1]*Sifra* on Leviticus 26:37.

of the entire world [and does not,] he is held accountable for their sins" (*Shabbat* 54b).

From the continuation of the Talmud's treatment there, it is clear that the expression "the entire world" should not be taken literally. Rav Papa had stated that the Exilarch was held accountable "for [the sins of] the entire world," and Rashi, in his commentary on that passage, understood the term to mean "the entire *Jewish* world, such as the case of a king or *nasi* who can prevent [violations of the law], for the populace fear them and follow their commands."

The Rambam also accepted this view, for he cited this passage in the context of the *mitzvah* of rebuking one's neighbor (*mitzvat tokhahah*), a *mitzvah* which applies only to Jews. He also slightly altered the talmudic text to read: "and whoever who has the ability to prevent the sin and does not do so is held accountable for the sins of *everyone whom he was able to prevent*."[2] The Rambam leaves out the category of "the entire world," for that would be misleading. It is thus clear that the basis for holding accountable someone who neglects to prevent another's sin is the concept of *arevut*, as the aforementioned verse from Leviticus and talmudic commentary indicated.

This concept of *arevut* also has other, more positive, implications. The Talmud states: "Ahavah the son of R. Zera taught, Any blessing which one has already recited on behalf of himself, he can recite again on behalf of others" (*Rosh Hashanah* 29a). Rashi explains that the reason is "because all Jews are responsible (*arevin*) for one another's fulfillment of *mitzvot*." The Ritva goes even further, stating that "all Jews are responsible (*arevin*) for one another. They are all like [parts of] one body and like a guarantor (*arev*) who repays the debt of his friend."[3]

This notion of *arevut* lies at the heart of a cluster of commandments which the Rambam presented together in *Hilkhot De'ot*, and

---

[2]*Hilkhot De'ot* 6:8.
[3]Ritva, *Rosh Hashanah*, ad loc.

which he incorporated into his list of the commandments included in the introduction to his *Mishneh Torah* as follows:

> Positive precept no. 206: To love everyone of the covenantal community *(mi-benei berit)*, as it says, "and you shall love your neighbor as yourself" (Leviticus 19:18);
>
> Negative precept no. 302: Not to hate in the heart, as it says, "Do not hate your brother in your heart" (Leviticus 19:17);
>
> Positive precept no. 205: To reprove the sinner, as it says, "Indeed shall you reprove your neighbor" (ibid.).[4]

One may add to this list a commandment of much wider scope which, unlike the notion of *arevut*, is not limited to the Jewish people:

> Negative precept no. 299: Not to cause the naive *(tam)* to err while on his way, as it says, "Do not put a stumbling block before the blind *(lifnei iver lo titen mikhshol)*" (Leviticus 19:14).[5]

There is a great deal of discussion among rabbinic authorities as to whether the biblical prohibition of *lifnei iver* applies only if the abettor's assistance is actually indispensable for the violation to have occurred, or if it is applicable even if his involvement merely

---

[4]From the full Maimonidean formulation in the *Sefer ha-Mitzvot*, it would appear that this *tokhahah* could only be done with words and not through physical force. See Netziv, *Haamek She'elah, Parshat Vayeshev, She'ilta* 27, nos. 6–7, who identifies this also as the opinion of the *She'iltot* and the *Geonim*. See, too, *idem, Meromei Sadeh, Baba Kamma* 28a. Cf. *Rama, Hoshen Mishpat* 421:6, 13. There is also a discussion as to whether this obligation applies only to a *bet din* of *mumhin* or to every individual Jew as well. See *Ketzot ha-Hoshen* 3:1; *Netivot ha-Mishpat, Bi'urim*, no. 1; *Meshovev Netivot*, ad loc.

[5]For the relevance of *lifnei iver* to Gentiles, see *Pesahim* 22b; Rambam, *Guide for the Perplexed* 3:17.

facilitates the potential violator in committing a sin which he could otherwise also have committed unaided. There are those who maintain that if the person can commit his sin without the Jew's assistance, then this prohibition does not apply.[6] Others maintain, however, that anyone who even minimally assists a sinner in the performance of his *averah (afilu bi-dibbur mu'at)* is guilty of *lifnei iver*, even if the sin could have been committed anyway without this outside help.[7] Another issue that is raised in this context relates to when the assistance takes place: while the sin is being committed (certainly prohibited), before it is done (possibly permitted since

---

[6]This is *Tosafot's* understanding of the talmudic discussion in *Avodah Zarah* 6a, which requires a situation of "two banks of a river," where the sinner is on one side, the instrument of violation is on the other, and someone is needed to get the object across the river. Since the sin cannot be committed without this assistance, then the one who offers it violates the prohibition of *lifnei iver*. See *Tosafot*, loc. cit., s.v. *minyan; Shabbat* 3a, s.v. *bava; Hagigah* 13a, s.v. *ein; Kiddushin* 56a, s.v. *aval*. See, too, *Rama, Yoreh De'ah* 151:4.

[7]This is Rabbenu Hananel's interpretation of the passage in *Avodah Zarah*, ad loc. It is clear that this is also the Rambam's opinion. He discusses the prohibition of *lifnei iver* in a number of places in his writings. See *Perush ha-Mishnah, Shevi'it* 5:6; *Terumot* 6:3; *Demai* 3:2, 5; 6:12; *Avodah Zarah* 1:7; *Sefer ha-Mitzvot, Lo Taaseh* nos. 236, 299; *Mishneh Torah, Hilkhot Avodah Zarah* 9:8, *Hilkhot Roze'ah* 12:12–14, *Hilkhot Isurei Biah* 22:5–6; *Hilkhot Kilayim* 10:31; *Hilkhot Nezirut* 5:20 (and *Radbaz*, ad loc.); *Hilkhot Gezelah ve-Avedah* 5:1; *Hilkhot Hovel u-Mazik* 5:13; *Hilkhot Malveh ve-Loveh* 2:7, 4:2; *Hilkhot Avel* 3:5 (and *Radbaz*, ad loc.). Rashi also agrees with this position. See Rashi, *Kiddushin* 56a, *Avodah Zarah* 22a. See, too, *She'iltot, Parshat Noah*, no. 6; *Sefer Halakhot Gedolot* (Warsaw, 1874), 135b, no. 68; *Hiddushei ha-Ran, Avodah Zarah* 6a, s.v. *ibaya; Shulhan Arukh, Yoreh De'ah* 151:1 and *Bi'ur ha-Gra* 151:8.

For more on this opinion, see my "Sho'el ki-Inyan," *Ha-Darom* 30 (5730): 61–64, and my *Yad Peshutah* (Jerusalem: Maaliyot Press, 1990) to *Hilkhot Avodah Zarah* 9:8.

there is still a possibility that it will not come to pass), or after it is done (certainly permitted).[8]

As noted earlier, the obligation to reprove a sinner *(tokhahah)* is related to the notion of *arevut*. We are responsible to see to it that another person does not sin, and, if there is a reasonable chance that he or she will sin, we are obligated to try to prevent it. But what if it is clear that the rebuke will not be effective and the sinner will proceed with his or her behavior anyway? It would appear from the Rambam that, in such a case, *tokhahah* would not be required.[9] The act of rebuke itself would be a violation of *lifnei iver* and therefore counterproductive for, thereby, the violator will be informed of the sinful nature of his act, and "better they be unintentional [sinners] than be intentional ones."[10] In such a circumstance, reprimanding the person will yield the opposite results, effectively rendering him or her a deliberate sinner.

There is, however, one opinion that makes a distinction between a law that is derived from the text *(midi de-ati mi-derashah)* and one that is expressly stated in the Torah. If the law is merely derived, then the individual about to violate it is best left in ignorance. But if an explicit Torah prohibition is at stake, then there is *always* an obligation to reprimand, even to punish, until the person desists

---

[8]See Mishnah *Gittin* 5:9 and *Avodah Zarah* 4:9 and Rambam, *Perush ha-Mishnah*, ad loc.; *Mishneh Torah, Hilkhot Shemittah ve-Yovel* 8:1–7; *Hilkhot Bikkurim* 8:13; *Hullin* 107b; *Hilkhot Berakhot* 6:19; *Shulhan Arukh, Orah Hayyim* 169:2 and commentaries of *Taz* and *Levush Mordekhai*, ad loc.

[9]See *Sefer ha-Mitzvot, Aseh* no. 205: "It is incumbent upon every person to rebuke him and to stop him *(le-hokhiho u-lemone'o)*." It would appear from this that the obligation only applies if the rebuke will lead to stopping. See also *Mishneh Torah, Hilkhot De'ot* 5:7; 6:7, based on *Yevamot* 65b. See, too, *Hagahot Maimuniyyot, Hilkhot De'ot* 6:3.

[10]See Rambam, *Mishneh Torah, Hilkhot Shevitat Asor* 1:7. See, too, *Tosafot, Baba Batra* 60b, s.v. *mutav; Shabbat* 55a, s.v. *ve-af al gav*.

from his violation of the law.[11] The basis of this distinction between a derived law and an explicit law requires explanation. Indeed, why should the source of a law determine the scope of the *mitzvah* of *tokhahah* relevant to it?

It would appear that this distinction stems from a dispute over the definition of the *mitzvah*, which in turn lies in differing perceptions of the essence of *arevut*. In the normal case of *arevut*, there are two possible ways of understanding the responsibility of a third person who serves as the guarantor of a loan from one party to another. One way is to see the *arevut* as being essentially for the benefit of the borrower, because the guarantor *(arev)* makes it easier for the borrower to obtain the money. It is even likely that the *arev* himself would have lent his friend the money, but at the time did not have the cash available. In order to help his friend, the *arev* is prepared to convince the lender to supply the needed money to the borrower. The alternative is to see the *arevut* as primarily serving the interests of the lender. The latter is concerned that he might not get back his money, and he has no desire to get involved in a complex legal process to retrieve it once the loan comes due. Therefore, he seeks further guarantees for his money, and that is provided to him by the *arev*. At times, the guarantor is even paid to accept this responsibility, for he is not interested in helping the borrower, but rather is prepared to offer a guarantee to the lender, for the latter's benefit, for a small profit. Thus, from this perspective, the goal of having a guarantor is to insure the return of the lender's money, and it is the guarantor who will determine how, ultimately, to extract the money owed him by the borrower.

Similarly, the concept of *arevut* of one Jew for another can be understood in two ways. One may view this as a responsibility incurred essentially for the benefit of the other Jew. Since every Jew must love every other Jew and actively work for his or her benefit, one is obligated to act in a way which will benefit him or her spiritually and certainly should try to prevent the serious negative

---

[11]See Rosh, *Betzah* 4:2, citing the *Baal ha-Ittur*.

consequences of sinning. According to this understanding, the commandment to reprove one's neighbor is an expression of one's *arevut*, which is, by definition, done only for the other's benefit. It is therefore obvious that, if in a specific situation the rebuke will be counterproductive, then it is better that the other Jew be left in ignorance and not be turned into a deliberate sinner. After all, it is forbidden to create any obstacle even for a non-Jew for whom there is no notion of *arevut*, all the more so in the case of a Jew where that concept is very much relevant.

But there is also another possible approach. One may view the *arevut* relationship as one in effect between man and God, as it were. In other words, all Jews are responsible for one another in order to ensure the complete observance of the Torah and its commandments, thereby sanctifying God's name in the world. One way of fulfilling this obligation is through the commandment of *tokhahah*, which requires one Jew to prevent another from sinning. Just as a guarantor who is unsuccessful in getting the borrower to pay the loan must pay it himself, so too the reprover who has no possibility of persuading the sinner of correcting his ways is nonetheless still responsible to reprove him, for he must at least demonstrate his concern for the violation and, as it were, pay something of the loan.

Given this second approach, it is now possible to understand the distinction made above between a law which is explicitly mentioned in the Torah and one which is only derived from it. In the former case, since the law is commonly known, even if the sinner may be unaware of it, the transgression assumes a public character, God's name becomes desecrated, and it therefore behooves the rebuker/guarantor to correct this to at least some extent, even if he knows that his action will not be efficacious. However, a law which is derived by the rabbis is not generally known, and its violation is not as widely recognized. As a result, as long as most people are unaware that such conduct is sinful, then no desecration of His name will have occurred, and therefore there is no *arevut* for the sake of God. On the other hand, if we were to publicize the fact that a violation has taken place, and if those responsible were nevertheless to persist in their rebellion, then, indeed, God's name would be desecrated. Therefore, from the perspective of *arevut* with respect to God, in those cases where the law is derived by a *derashah* and therefore not well known, better that the sinners be left in ignorance rather than be rendered deliberate transgressors by the act of *tokhahah*.

WHO IS INCLUDED IN *AREVUT*?

According to Rambam:

> Those who are included in the category of Israel—we are obligated to love them and care for them and do everything God has commanded us concerning love and brotherhood. Even if a Jew committed any sin due to his lust and the overpowering nature of his evil inclination, he is punished according to the severity of his transgression, but still has a portion [in the world-to-come], and he is deemed a "sinner of Israel *(mi-poshe'ai Yisrael)*."[12]

On the other hand, he ruled elsewhere that those labeled heretics, deniers, or apostates "are not of the community of Israel *(enam bi-khelal Yisrael)*."[13] Since we are not concerned here with these exceptions, we will focus on those Jews who, despite being called "sinners of Israel," are nevertheless considered Jews in every regard.

The starting point for any discussion of this nature is the ruling of the Rambam in *Hilkhot Mamrim*:

> . . . [Zadok's and Boethus's] children and grandchildren, who, misguided by their parents, were raised among the Karaites and trained in their views, are like a child taken captive and

---

[12]*Perush ha-Mishnayot, Sanhedrin, Perek Helek*, beginning.
[13]*Mishneh Torah, Hilkhot Mamrim* 3:2.

raised by them [*ki-tinok she-nishbah benehem*]. Such a person is not anxious to observe *mitzvot* for he is like an *anus* (one who abjures the Jewish religion under duress). Although he later learns that he is a Jew, and observes Jews practice their religion, he is nevertheless to be regarded as an *anus*, since he was reared in their erroneous ways. Thus it is with those whom we are discussing, who adhere to the practices of their Karaite parents who have erred. Therefore, efforts should be made to bring them back in repentance, to draw them near through words of peace that they may return to the strength-giving source, the Torah. [3:3]

There are also two extant responsa of the Rambam dealing with the Karaites. In the first, he maintains that as long as they respect the Rabbinite tradition and do not demean either its bearers or its laws and customs, Karaites should be treated as full Jews. Other Jews should honor them, go to greet them (even in their homes), circumcise their sons (even on the Sabbath), bury their dead, comfort their mourners, distribute charity to them, and even drink their wine. Since they have not denied God, they should not be treated as heretics or non-Jews, for their children may one day return to the true tradition. The Rambam notes that such a reasoning was already expressed by Rav Hai Gaon and Rav Yehudah Gaon who allowed for the circumcision of Karaite sons on the Sabbath.[14]

There are those who denied the authenticity of this responsum, claiming it to be inconsistent with what is known to be the Rambam's view regarding Karaites.[15] However, a second responsum of the Rambam belies this assertion. In that text, he

---

[14]See *Teshuvot ha-Rambam*, ed. J. Blau, vol. 2 (Jerusalem: Mekize Nirdamim, 1960), 729, no. 449; *Iggerot ha-Rambam*, ed. Y. Shilat, vol. 2 (Jerusalem: Yeshivat Birkat Mosheh, 1988), 669–72. This responsum is also cited by the Radbaz and Rabbi Eliyahu Mizrahi. See ibid., 668.

[15]For a detailed discussion of this, see ibid., 668–69.

addresses the question as to whether Karaites may be included in the required quorum of ten for prayer or of three for *Birkat ha-Zimmun*. In response, the Rambam determines that their inclusion vis-à-vis a particular commandment depends solely on whether or not they accept its validity and are prepared to follow its dictates correctly. In these cases, therefore, since they do not believe in the concept of a quorum of ten for prayer or of three for *zimmun*, they cannot be included in any of these practices.[16] However, the ruling that they can participate in any activity that they do accept and acknowledge is consistent with the stipulation made in the previously cited responsum. That is why the Rambam there added the condition that the prayer service that takes place at the home where the child is to be circumcised is to be conducted "according to our custom, with nothing of it being altered" and that the *mohel* be appointed by the local (Rabbinite) Jewish court. Clearly he did not mean to allow them to be counted to the *minyan*, for if the prayer service were to proceed according to their customs, no *minyan* would be required. In those areas where they do accept the Rabbinite tradition they are to be treated as full-fledged Jews, he ruled.

Rabbi Eliyahu Mizrahi points to a statement of the Rambam in his *Perush ha-Mishnayot* where he treats Karaism harshly and that he considers to be, to some degree, contradictory to the impression forthcoming from his responsa.[17] However, in a manuscript of that passage in the *Perush ha-Mishnayot*, written in the Rambam's own hand, we find a treatment of the Karaites entirely consistent with his discussion in *Hilkhot Mamrim*:

> Those born into this tradition and trained in accordance with it are to be seen as *anusim*. They must be treated as children taken captive *(tinok she-nishbah)* among non-Jews, whose every

---

[16] See *Teshuvot ha-Rambam* 2:502–04, no. 265; *Iggerot ha-Rambam*, 611.

[17] See *She'elot u-Teshuvot Rabbi Eliyahu Mizrahi*, no. 57, citing *Perush ha-Mishnayot*, *Hullin* 1:2. Yet, when it comes to practical *halakhah*, he relies on the position as reflected in the responsa.

transgression is inadvertent (*shegagah*), as we have explained (*Shabbat* 68a). But the first person [to deviate] is considered a deliberate transgressor and not an inadvertent one.[18]

What clearly emerges from all the above citations of the Rambam is that someone who was raised and trained in a religiously nonobservant or theologically incorrect atmosphere is still included within the concept of *arevut*, and all Jews are responsible for him or her as well. Consistent with his view, the Rambam maintains that even if that person later hears or learns of proper Jewish behavior and does not immediately begin to act accordingly, he or she is still deemed a *tinok she-nishbah*, "whose every transgression is inadvertent." As a result, one who wants to reprove such individuals must be aware that, due to their background and upbringing, they will not accept direct rebuke regarding specific violations. On the contrary, if one does reprimand them in this fashion, not only will it achieve nothing positive but it will most likely cause them to deliberately continue their sinful behavior. That is exactly why the Rambam wrote in *Hilkhot Mamrim* (cited above): "Therefore, efforts should be made to bring them back in repentance, to draw them near by words of peace (*bi-divrei shalom*) that they may return to the strength-giving source, the Torah." The Rambam thus carefully instructs us how to handle those who commit sins due to ignorance, habit, and poor education. It is obvious that telling them that "such and such an action is against *halakhah*" will not motivate them to repent. On the contrary, such specified reproof only causes them to sin deliberately, resulting in the rebuker having violated the commandment against "putting a stumbling block before the blind." Rather, such transgressors must be "drawn by words of peace . . . to the strength-giving source." We must draw them near to Torah and observance in general, and only as they slowly progress in their acceptance of its binding nature does it become appropriate to specify the details which they should

---

[18]See Rabbi Y. Kapah's translation of the *Perush ha-Mishnayot*.

begin to observe. But without first attracting them to the Torah in general, they will never come to full repentance.

In his commentary to the *Tur*, Rav Yosef Karo cites the Rashba's statement that, if someone is suspected of violating a law of which most people are unaware, he will not be held accountable (*"kasher hu la-kol"*).[19] It is true that in the Rashba's time, this notion could never have been applied to the public desecration of the Sabbath, which all knew to be prohibited. But R. Karo continues:

> Furthermore, Rabbenu Yonah quoted French scholars who ruled regarding an apostate *(mumar le-avodah zarah)* who travels from place to place, acknowledging in one the idolatrous deity in the presence of non-Jews and in the other place entering Jewish homes and claiming to be a Jew, that since he informs us that he is a Jew, he is taken to be one and does not render wine unfit for use . . . and when he tells us that he is a Jew, he is speaking honestly. . . .

His contrary actions do not disqualify him. Rather, we assume that in the presence of non-Jews he acts as if under duress, or as if unaware of the serious nature of his transgressions. As a result, even apostasy can, under certain circumstances, be viewed as unintentional.

"CHILDREN TAKEN CAPTIVE"

In our generation, the majority of Jews were raised and educated in the absence of Torah and *mitzvot* and consequently are not aware of most of the Torah's prohibitions. Nevertheless, many of them wholeheartedly want to be affiliated with the Jewish people, some proving this with great dedication and sacrifice in the rebuilding of the State of Israel and in its defense against its enemies. Over the

---

[19]See *Bet Yosef, Yoreh De'ah* 119, s.v. *katav ha-Rashba*. The responsum is found in *She'elot u-Teshuvot ha-Rashba*, vol. 1, nos. 430, 657.

last two hundred years, many Torah scholars have dealt with the status of such Jews, focusing primarily on the fact that they do desecrate the Sabbath publicly. After all, the law has already stated:

> The [observance of the] Sabbath and [the prohibition against] idolatry are each deemed equivalent to the entire corpus of commandments. The Sabbath is the eternal sign of the covenant between the Holy One, Blessed be He, and us. Therefore, anyone who violates any of the other commandments is considered one of the transgressors of Israel (*bi-khelal rish'ei Yisrael*), but the public desecrator of the Sabbath is identical with an idol worshipper, and both are considered as non-Jews (*goyim*) in all respects.[20]

Nevertheless, modern decisors have not been as extreme toward them as this ruling would warrant. Already in 1861, Rabbi Jacob Ettlinger dealt with this dilemma and ruled:

> As to Jewish sinners (*poshei Yisrael*) of our time, I do not know how to treat them now that, due to our overwhelming sins, the disease has spread so widely that the majority of them deem the desecration of the Sabbath to be permissible. Perhaps they have the status of one who thinks what he is doing is permitted (*omer mutar*) and who is considered to be only close to the status of a deliberate sinner (*karov li-mezid*). Some of them pray on the Sabbath and recite the Kiddush, and then violate the Sabbath by performing activities forbidden both by biblical and rabbinic law. Now, a Sabbath desecrator is considered a heretic because by denying the Sabbath he denies Creation and the Creator, but this individual [obviously] acknowledges [these beliefs] by virtue of his praying and reciting the Kiddush.

---

[20]Rambam, *Mishneh Torah, Hilkhot Shabbat* 30:15.

Moreover, their children who follow after them, who never heard of the laws of the Sabbath, are identical to the Sadducees, who were not deemed heretics even though they violated the Sabbath, for they are merely acting as they were trained by their parents. They are considered like a child taken captive (*ki-tinok she-nishbah*) among non-Jews. . . .

Many of the sinners of our generation are similar to them, and are [even] better than they. The reason Rabbi Shimshon was stringent with respect to the Karaites, to the point of treating their wine like the wine of non-Jews (*yayin nesekh*), was not that they kept a different calendar of holidays, which is tantamount to [desecrating] the Sabbath. Rather, the reason was that they denied many of the fundamental principles of Judaism, such as the way they circumcise, and their rejection of the laws of marriage or divorce which consequently turn their children into bastards. [However,] with regard to these [laws], the majority of today's sinners have not breached [them].[21]

Many great scholars followed this lead, and the late Chief Rabbi Isaac Halevi Herzog summed up this approach as follows: "Recent Torah authorities distinguished between those countries where the majority of Jews desecrate the Sabbath, so that the violator cannot be seen as denying Creation, [and others where this is not the case]."[22]

An important precedent for this notion can be found in the words of the Rambam at the conclusion of his *Iggeret ha-Shemad*,

---

[21]See his *She'elot u-Teshuvot Binyan Tzion ha-Hadashot*, no. 23. R. Ettlinger cites R. Isaiah di-Trani, who writes (*Mabit*, no. 37): "It is also possible that Sadducees who were not accustomed [to living] among Jews, do not know the essentials of the faith, and do not speak with disrespect about the scholars of the generation, are not deemed to be deliberate sinners."

[22]*She'elot u-Teshuvot Hekhal Yitzhak, Orah Hayyim*, no. 2.

where he writes about a country in which the number of observant Jews has decreased due to harsh persecutions against them:

> It is also inappropriate to distance Sabbath desecrators or treat them repugnantly. Rather, one should draw them near and encourage them in the observance of *mitzvot*. Our rabbis have already instructed us that when a deliberate violator comes to the synagogue to pray he is to be accepted and not treated with disdain. They linked their advice to the words of Solomon: "Do not despise a thief even if he steals" (Proverbs 6:30), [which they interpreted to mean] do not despise Jewish sinners when they come to pray secretly and "steal" some *mitzvot*.[23]

If we are required to adopt this attitude toward deliberate sinners, all the more so must we do so with regard to Sabbath violators who transgress inadvertently as a result of never having been trained properly, for they are similar to *anusim*.

The Hazon Ish concurred with this assessment of contemporary nonobservant Jews, writing that "we are obligated to bring them back with bonds of love (*bi-avotot ahavah*) and to place them in the rays of the Torah's light, to the extent we possibly can."[24]

In conclusion, there is no doubt that the vast majority of today's Jews who do not observe *mitzvot* have the status of "children taken captive." Even if they subsequently see observant Jews, the latter appear to them to be an abnormal, strange group, God forbid, and not those who are the true bearers of the original Sinaitic tradition. Therefore, even if we inform them of certain specific *mitzvot* and reproach them with regard to their observance, the admonishment is futile. We have already noted that such rebuke only serves to distance them further and arouses bitterness

---

[23]*Iggerot ha-Rambam*, 59.
[24]See *Hazon Ish, Yoreh De'ah* 2:16; see also 2:28.

and anger, thus fostering a terrible hatred against religion. Nevertheless, as we have already explained, we are still not absolved from the obligations toward them associated with the notion of *arevut* and we therefore must deal seriously with the question of how to bring them closer to Torah and Jewish observance in positive, constructive ways.

THE EXAMPLE OF THE KARAITES

The Rambam provided us with a general guiding principle in one of the responsa cited above. He ruled that "any [Torah] observance whose obligation and authority they affirm, we are permitted to have them participate jointly with us. And anything whose obligation and authority they do not affirm, we are forbidden to allow them to participate with us." Most secular Jews in Israel or Conservative and Reform Jews in the Diaspora arrange to have their sons circumcised by an observant *mohel*, just as the Karaites of Babylonia and the Islamic countries did, as the Rambam reports in the name of Rav Hai Gaon. Therefore, in keeping with this principle, we are allowed to circumcise their sons, and to do so even on the Sabbath.

However, there are significant differences in other areas between "secular Jews" today and the medieval Karaites as there are between "secular Jews" in Israel and those who identify with non-Orthodox denominations in the Diaspora. For instance, the overwhelming majority of secular Jews in Israel turn to the official rabbinate regarding matters of marriage and divorce, thereby eliminating any cause for concern in these areas. In contrast, outside of Israel, there are those who perform marriages that are not halakhically valid and there are couples who divorce civilly, but without a Jewish *get*. The matter of marriages performed by Conservative and Reform rabbis has been the subject of much attention by Torah authorities of the previous generation and Rabbi Moshe Feinstein's decision not to deem their marriages valid[25] has been widely accepted in Orthodox circles. This is in contrast to the case of Karaite marriages, which the Rambam ruled were legitimate and required a divorce, while considering the Karaite writ of divorce to be invalid.[26]

One of the more frequently encountered problems is that of a prayer service that includes people who are not Sabbath observers. The Rambam maintained that we should not rebuff them if they come to pray in the synagogue. Moreover, the Talmud (*Keritut* 6b) considers the list of ingredients of the incense offered on the altar in the Temple as symbolic of the constituency necessary for a complete ritual act: some with a pleasant aroma (i.e., righteous people), but one *(helbenah)* with an unpleasant odor (i.e., a sinner). It states: "R. Hana b. Bizna said in the name of R. Shimon Hasida: Any fast day which does not include the transgressors of Israel *(mi-poshei Yisrael)* is not a proper fast day, for *helbenah* odor is foul, and yet Scripture counted it as one of the spices of the incense." However, the Maharsha comments that the malodorous spice could only be included if without it there were still ten other fragrant ones in the recipe, indicating that ten observant Jews were required to constitute a quorum, only after which could nonobservant Jews be included. He wrote: "It can be learned that there were eleven types of [spices in the] incense, ten whose aroma was pleasant, and one—*helbenah*—whose odor was foul. Therefore, the sinner may be included, provided there is a quorum of righteous Jews *(edah kedoshah)* without him, but he is not to be included in the ten." He goes on to say that this is suggested by the behavior of Abraham, who, when bargaining with God over the fate of Sodom, stopped after asking God not to destroy the city if there were ten righteous persons there, but did not pursue the matter beyond that.[27]

Many have addressed this issue of including Sabbath desecrators

[25]See *Iggerot Mosheh, Even ha-Ezer,* nos. 76–77.

[26]See *Teshuvot ha-Rambam* 3:140, no. 351; *Iggerot ha-Rambam,* 613.

[27]Maharsha, *Hiddushei Aggadot,* ad loc., s.v. *she-harei.*

in a quorum. Rabbi Herzog permitted their inclusion.[28] Rabbi Moshe Feinstein also did, with the qualification that, although *Kaddish* and *Kedushah* may be recited, the service will not technically be considered a *"tefillah bi-tzibbur."*[29] However, in my opinion, all this is irrelevant to our subject. After all, we have already noted that the Rambam ruled that Karaites may not be included in the quorum, either for prayer or for *Birkat ha-Zimmun*, only because they do not consider these practices as a valid part of the tradition, since their origins lie in the Oral Law which they reject. The fact that the Karaites violate the Sabbath and Festivals alone is insufficient to disqualify them because, in this regard, they are to be treated as "children taken captive."[30] Were it not for the fact that they did not subscribe to the notion of a quorum, they would have been acceptable for inclusion even though they were *mehalelei Shabbat*.

Applying this principle to our contemporary situation, we would conclude that, while contemporary nonobservant Jews desecrate the Sabbath, they *do* come to the synagogue to pray and they *do* accept the requirement of praying with a quorum to be binding. As a result, they *should* be allowed to be included in it. However, a corollary of this is that if there are some groups today who, like the Karaites of old, do not believe in the binding nature of a quorum for prayer, and who require neither ten, nor adults, nor men, then these individuals, like the Karaites, are not to be included in the quorum. Furthermore, based on this principle, if someone does not

---

[28]*She'elot u-Teshuvot Hekhal Yitzhak, Orah Hayyim*, no. 2.

[29]See *Iggerot Mosheh, Orah Hayyim*, vol. 1, no. 23; vol. 2, no. 19; vol. 3, no. 14. Rabbi Feinstein also cites the interesting and novel ruling of R. Israel Rozin (the author of the *Tzofnat Paane'ah*) that sinners may be included in any quorum except for the Musaf service, which is recited today in lieu of the sacrifice brought in ancient times. That is because a sacrificial offering must be accompanied by penitence to be acceptable.

[30]The Rambam himself made this clear. See *Perush ha-Mishnayot, Hullin*, above, n. 17.

believe in prayer but is willing to help make a *minyan* as an act of kindness, neither may he be included as one of the requisite number of ten men required for public prayer to take place.[31]

EDUCATION: THE ROAD BACK TO TORAH

It is, however, not possible for us to fulfill our obligation of *arevut* merely by welcoming nonobservant Jews when they happen to enter the synagogue. Our essential task is to go out and attract them to Torah and religious observance. Here, too, our rabbis provided us with very useful guidelines and we need only to follow their advice.

In many respects, our age parallels that of the return to Zion in the era of Ezra and Nehemiah. An explicit verse describes the experience of those days: "Also at that time I saw that Jews had married wives of Ashdodite, Ammonite, and Moabite women. And their children spoke half in the speech of Ashdod and they could not speak in the Jews' language, but according to the language of each people" (Nehemiah 13:23-24). How did the men of the Great Assembly cope with all those children born from these intermarriages who clearly did not have any concept about Judaism?

The Rambam explains:

> When the people of Israel went into exile in the days of the wicked Nebuchadnezzar, they mingled with the Persians, Greeks, and other nations. In those foreign countries, children were born to them, whose language was confused. Everyone's speech was a mixture of many tongues. No one was able, when he spoke, to express his thoughts adequately in any one language, otherwise than incoherently, as it is said,

---

[31]See *Tashbetz*, vol. 3, no. 309. See, too, R. Moshe Feinstein, *Iggerot Mosheh*, *Orah Hayyim*, vol. 3, no. 12; vol. 2, no. 51, for rulings allowing sinners to receive *aliyot* and other synagogue honors.

"And their children spoke half in the speech of Ashdod and they could not speak in the Jews' language, but according to the language of each people" (Nehemiah 13:24).

Consequently, when any one of them prayed in Hebrew, he was unable adequately to express his needs or recount the praises of God, without mixing Hebrew with other languages. When Ezra and his council realized this condition, they ordained the Eighteen Benedictions in their present order.

The first three blessings consist of praises of God and the last three of thanksgiving to Him. The intermediate benedictions are petitions for the things which may stand as prototypes of all the desires of the individual and the needs of the community. The object aimed at was that these prayers should be in an orderly form in everyone's mouth, that all should learn them, and thus the prayer of those who were not expert in speech would be as perfect as that of those who had command of a chaste style. For the same reason, they arranged in a fixed form all the blessings and prayers for all Jews so that the substance of every blessing should be familiar and current in the mouth of one who is not expert in speech.

They similarly instituted that the number of prayers . . . [32]

The scholars of that generation implemented a wide-ranging educational campaign in an effort to draw those distant from Torah back to it. If we look at the daily life of an average Jew (and even not such an average Jew) throughout the generations, we see that the majority of the time he devotes to *mitzvah* observance and serving God is connected with prayer. There even developed a term known as *a prayerbook Jew (a Siddur Yid)*, describing one who was not learned at all but who was nevertheless deeply rooted in Judaism because he was raised from his childhood on the prayer book. This

---

[32]*Mishneh Torah, Hilkhot Tefillah* 1:4–5.

was not always so. The Men of the Great Assembly placed great emphasis on prayer as a mass educational vehicle and formulated the prayers and the text of blessings by incorporating into them the essentials of the faith and basic Torah values.

Although our generation is much weaker than previous ones, we should still follow the same course plotted by the Men of the Great Assembly, and, if we do, Divine Providence will surely assist us. This route is education. As Rabbi Mizrahi writes: "And how will they return to the strength-giving source of the Torah if we do not inform them of the rationale of the Torah *(taamei ha-Torah)?*"[33]

All efforts must be focused on education, primarily of children, but also of adults. It is critical not to give up on anyone, not even those furthest from Torah. We must not be deceived by those who claim that whatever resources available to us are better devoted to educating those who are already observant, and that pursuing the nonobservant will necessarily come at the expense of the potentially greater gains than might be accomplished with the already committed. Isn't it preferable, they argue, to devote more effort and energy to the education of the elite few and forego the masses who are anyway so hard to attract to Torah?

Yet, historical precedent argues against this position. When the standardized prayers and blessings were first instituted, there were undoubtedly a few Jews who had previously been able to reach great heights in their private worship and who were now constrained by the newly imposed formal nature of the prayers and blessings made incumbent upon all Jews, rendering their personal prayers more routine and less inspired. Nevertheless, the benefit of the group at large was determinative, even at the expense of these elite few. The Talmud (*Sanhedrin* 111a) already addressed this idea by relating that Resh Lakish took the verse "and I will take you, one from a town and two from a family, and I will bring you to Zion" (Jeremiah 3:14) literally, implying that the others would be lost.

---

[33] *She'elot u-Teshuvot R. Eliyahu Mizrahi,* no. 57.

Rabbi Yohanan rebuked him, explaining the verse to mean that even "one from a town" can bring merit to an entire town, and two members of a family can bring merit to the entire group.

From a practical standpoint as well, the presence of children from nonobservant homes in a classroom contributes to an overall improvement in the level of the studies there. Rabbi Mizrahi attests to the fact that the presence of Karaite children in Rabbinite schools created a competitive spirit in the classroom which raised the level of learning there.[34]

Jewish day schools must make an effort to attract students from all backgrounds and cannot be content with classrooms composed exclusively of children from observant homes. Obviously, in every community, differing circumstances will determine whether to maintain one school for everyone, where all the children study together, to have different tracks within one school, or even to have different schools. What is critically important, though, is that the Torah education establishment compete effectively with all other factors influencing adults and children in today's world in order to be able to attract the public to Torah and *mitzvot*. This is what the Rambam meant when he wrote, "to draw them near through words of peace that they may return to the strength-giving source, the Torah."[35] Attracting them with words of peace is the first step.

It is worthwhile to cite here the instructive words of Rabbi Mizrahi, in his aforecited responsum, stating his strong opposition to the ban imposed by extremists against teaching Karaites:

> This ban was not instituted for the sake of Heaven, nor with the intention of improving the world *(tikun ha-olam)*. . . . But it was created out of a sense of jealousy and hatred which some

---

[34]Ibid. He added that "when we stopped teaching Karaites, the competitive spirit was gone and the level of Torah learning was diminished among us. There is no calamity greater than this."

[35]*Hilkhot Mamrim* 3:3; above, p. 185.

had against the teachers who were respected by Karaites, or against the Karaites themselves. . . . Were it not for the jealousy and anger which they had, they would never have been motivated to act this way.

There are indeed many problems, particularly with regard to the children of intermarriages; but these too can be solved if only there is the proper intention of "drawing them near through words of peace" and if the parents are prepared to commit themselves to having their children study in a Torah-observant school. Torah scholars in the last generation have already dealt with the criteria necessary to convert a child born of a Jewish father and non-Jewish mother, requiring that the father agree, with the mother's consent, both to circumcise his son and to have him (or his daughter) undergo a ritual immersion for the sake of conversion.[36] Their ruling applies even if he cannot guarantee that the children will study in a Torah-observant school, how much more so would it apply when such a guarantee could be forthcoming. Clearly, all factors must be carefully considered, especially whether the school is of the sort which can influence the child positively. Indeed, it was on the basis of such a positive consideration that Rabbi Yehiel Yaakov Weinberg permitted the acceptance of such a child to a Jewish school, provided that at the age of thirteen he convert halakhically.[37] One must also take into account the fact that if the children will not be converted at a young age but will nevertheless continue to live within a Jewish society and appear as Jews, then in

---

[36]See *She'elot u-Teshuvot Maharam Shik, Yoreh De'ah*, no. 248; R. David Tzevi Hoffman, *She'elot u-Teshuvot Melamed le-Ho'il, Yoreh De'ah*, nos. 82, 87; R. Abraham Isaac Hakohen Kook, *Daat Kohen*, nos. 147–49; *Iggerot Mosheh, Yoreh De'ah*, vol. 2, no. 128; vol. 3, no. 105; and R. Hayyim Ozer Grodzinski, *She'elot u-Teshuvot Ahi'ezer*, vol. 3, no. 28.

[37]See Rabbi Yehiel Yaakov Weinberg, *Seridei Esh*, vol. 2, no. 91. There is also the potentially negative influence on other students, which must be seriously considered as well. See *Iggerot Mosheh, Orah Hayyim*, vol. 2, no. 73.

all likelihood other Jews will inadvertently marry them, and there
is no greater tragedy than this. My colleague, Rabbi Gedaliah
Felder, also suggested that if both parents agree to raise the child as
a Jew and have him (or her) undergo a halakhic ritual conversion,
the child should be accepted, but it should be done while the child
is still young.[38]

It seems appropriate to summarize with a quote from Rabbi
Herzog: "If, in the Rabbi's assessment, there is a good chance that
the parents will observe Judaism, and there is a concern that they
may distance themselves further from Judaism if we do not accept
them, . . . then we may accept [the child into the school]."[39] This
concern that the Jewish parent may himself or herself also become
further alienated from Judaism if his or her child is rejected brings
us back once again to the issue of "putting a stumbling block before
the blind," particularly if we are talking about a person who
intermarried out of ignorance, without any rebellious intention, as
is so common today. It goes without saying that this is the case with
so many Russian immigrants either in Israel or America, but it is the
case even across America where many men marry women whom
they think are Jewish because one of her parents is Jewish, and they
have children whom they want to educate and be considered as
Jews.

However, in the final analysis, it is impossible to establish any
general rules in this area. Everything depends on the assessment of
those rabbis who are sensitive to all the issues concerned, who are
well versed in all the details of the *halakhah*, and whose intentions
are exclusively for the sake of Heaven.

"A JUST WEIGHT AND BALANCE"

We have seen that the notion of *arevut* vis-à-vis another Jew obtains
even in a case where the *mitzvah* of *tokhahah* does not apply, such as

---

[38]See Rabbi Gedaliah Felder, *Nahalat Tzevi* (New York, 1959), 132.
[39]See Rabbi Herzog, *Heikhal Yitzhak, Even ha-Ezer,* no. 21.

a Jew who sins but who is considered to be "a child taken captive." In such a case, direct rebuke is unlikely to succeed, but we are still obliged to expose our fellow Jews to Torah and Jewish observance through the medium of a coordinated educational effort.

Our Rabbis said:

> Moses and Samuel are deemed equivalent to one another, as it says, "Moses and Aaron among his priests, and Samuel among those who call His name" (Psalms 99:6). Now come and see the difference between them. Moses used to enter and come to God [in the Tent of Meeting] and hear God speak whereas, in the case of Samuel, God would come to speak to him, as it says, "And the Lord came, and stood" (1 Samuel 3:10). Why was this so? The Holy One, Blessed be He, said: I relate to a person in a just and equitable way. Moses would sit, and whoever had need of a judgement, would come to him and be judged. . . . But Samuel would make an effort to go to every region and judge, so that they needn't trouble to come to him. . . . Said the Holy One, Blessed be He: Moses would sit in one place and judge Israel—let him come to Me to the Tent of Meeting to hear the Word; but Samuel who traveled to the Jews in cities to judge them—I will go and speak to him, in fulfillment of what it says, "A just weight and balance are the Lord's" (Proverbs 16:11).[40]

Clearly, the rabbis did not come, God forbid, to find fault with Moses. Their aim was to point to the fact that in different situations, the demands are different. In the times of Moses, the entire Jewish people were concentrated in a small area, several miles square. Therefore, Moses could afford to stay in one place and have anyone seeking the word of God come to his tent. The situation was different in the times of Samuel, when Jews had settled in all parts of their land. In his generation, it was necessary for him to take the

---

[40]*Shemot Rabbah* 16:4.

trouble to travel to the farthest borders of the land in order to spread Torah. Had Samuel conducted himself as did Moses, he would not have discharged his obligation as leader. A leader must respond to situations he confronts not only by following the model of earlier generations, but also by assessing the special needs of his own generation.

In this way I would like to explain the following tale from the Talmud:

Rav Aha bar Rav Hanina said: The Holy One, Blessed be He, never retracted a beneficent decree to exchange it for a bad one except in this case, as it is written: "And the Lord said to him, Go through the midst of the city, through the midst of Jerusalem, and set a mark upon the foreheads of the men that sigh and that cry on account of all the abominations that are done in her midst . . ." (Ezekiel 9:4). The Holy One, Blessed be He, said to Gabriel, "Go and mark a *tav* of ink on the foreheads of the righteous so that the angels of destruction do not have control over them, and mark a *tav* of blood on the foreheads of the wicked so that the angels of destruction may have control over them." Justice pleaded before God: "Master of the Universe, in what way do the latter differ from the former?" God answered her, "The former are thoroughly righteous while the latter are thoroughly wicked." Justice said: "Master of the Universe, the former had the opportunity to protest the latter's conduct [to change them], but did not!" God said: "It is revealed and known to me that had they protested, it would have gone unheeded." Said Justice: "Master of the Universe, You may have known, but did they know that?" And this is what it says: ". . . and begin at My Sanctuary *(mikdashi)*." And it says "And they began [to slaughter] the old men who were before the House." Rav Yosef taught, "Do not read it 'my Sanctuary *(mikdashi)*,' but 'those sanctified to Me *(mekudashi)*' — these were the people who observed the entire Torah from A to Z." [*Shabbat* 55a]

There are many interpretations of this selection, and I will add my own to them. One cannot suggest that those considered by God to be thoroughly righteous, of whom it was said that they observed the entire Torah from A to Z, did not also fulfill the commandment of rebuking their neighbors. Rather, they wanted to do so in a direct fashion, making reference to specific sins, as rebukers had done in earlier generations. However, they immediately discovered that their reproof was ignored and they therefore thought that they were exempt from having to admonish any further. They did not take the trouble to recognize that their generation was different from earlier ones, and that now indirect paths had to be taken to draw nonobservant Jews of their time back to Torah and Jewish observance. It was inappropriate for them, at that time, to remain in the sanctuary but, rather, they should have travelled the length and breadth of the land in a serious attempt to influence their coreligionists. True, in the generation of the Temple's destruction, God was aware that such activity by the righteous would have been fruitless, but they themselves were not aware of this, since they had not even attempted to do it. As a result, they were punished, and all their merits did not protect them, for "all who have in their ability to protest and do not do so are held accountable for the sins of those whom they were able to prevent from sinning."

On the other hand, how great must be the reward awaiting those righteous like Samuel who know how to adapt their actions to their particular time and place. For the Divine Presence came to him, in fulfillment of the verse, "A just weight and balance are the Lord's" (Proverbs 16:11). The rabbis have already commanded us to love all Jews without distinction, and draw them near to Torah. This is the way of God Himself, as the Rambam explained in his *Letter to Yemen*:

> God informed and promised us that He will never hate us altogether, even though we might rebel against Him and violate His commandments. He has said: "Thus says the Lord, If heaven above can be measured, and the foundations of the

earth searched out beneath, then I will also cast off all the seed of Israel for all that they have done, says the Lord God" (Jeremiah 31:36). And it says, "And they who turn many to righteousness are like the stars, forever and ever" (Daniel 12:3).[41]

---

[41]A more elaborate version of this essay appeared in *Tehumin* 11 (1990): 41–72.

Ahavat Yisrael:
A Selected Bibliography

Nathaniel Helfgot

The following is a selected bibliography of books and articles, both in English and Hebrew, on the general topics of *ahavat Yisrael* (love of fellow Jews), *kiruv rehokim* (outreach to the unaffiliated), *tokhahah* (the obligation to rebuke), and the general relationship of the Orthodox community toward nonhalakhic Jews. These sources treat the topics both legally and conceptually.

I *AHAVAT YISRAEL*

1. "Ahavat Yisrael," in *Entziklopedia Talmudit*, 2nd ed., 1:211–15. Jerusalem, 1972.
2. *Ahavat Yisrael*. Jerusalem, 1967. A Hebrew pamphlet published by the Merkaz le-Hasbarah Datit be-Yisrael.
3. Bar Shaul, Elimelekh. "Ahavat Re'ah," in *Mitzvah va-Lev*, 167–77. Tel Aviv: Abraham Tzioni, 1957.

4. Bulka, Reuven, P. "Love Your Neighbor: Halakhic Parameters." *Journal of Halacha and Contemporary Society* 16 (1988): 44–55.

5. Cohen, Dov. *Ahavat Haverim.* 3rd ed. New York, 1989.

6. Cohen, She'ar Yashuv. "Yesodah shel Ahavat Yisrael," in *Ish bi-Gevurot: Mugashim li-Khevod ha-Rav Alexander Safran.* Jerusalem, 1990.

7. Epstein, Yosef. *Mitzvat ha-Shalom.* New York: The Institute for the Study and Spread of Halacha and Ethics, 1969.

8. Filber, Yaakov. "Ahavat Yisra'el." *Gevilin* 25 (1966): 103–09.

9. Gezundtheit, Binyamin. "Ve-Ahavta le-Re'akha ka-Mokha." *Alon Shvut* 120 (1988): 87–110.

10. Goren, Shlomo. "Ahavah ve-Sinat Hinam le-Or ha-Halakhah." *Hatzofeh* (March 30, 1984): 5.

11. Gutel, Neryah. "Ve-Ahavta le-Re'akha ka-Mokha — Perat u-Kelal," in *Tobias,* ed. Hayim Rosenberg, 203–15. Jerusalem: Keren Tobias/Ariel, 1984.

12. Hess, Yisrael. "Le-Mitzvat Ahavat Yisrael bi-Yamenu." *Morashah* 1 (1971): 43–53.

13. Kook, Avraham Yitzhak ha-Kohen. "Ahavat Yisrael," in *Orot,* 89–93. Jerusalem: Mossad ha-Rav Kook, 1982.

14. Lamm, Norman. "Loving and Hating Jews." *Tradition* 24:2 (1989): 98–122.

15. _____ . "Ahavat Yisrael ve-Sinat Resha'im," in *Halakhot ve-Halikhot,* 149–60. Jerusalem: Mossad ha-Rav Kook, 1990. This is an expanded Hebrew version of Dr. Lamm's article, "Loving and Hating Jews," cited in no. 14, above.

16. Leibowitz, Nehamah. "Lo Tisna et Ahikha bi-Levavekha," in *Iyunim Hadashim bi-Sefer Vayikra,* 282–92. Jerusalem: Torah Education Dept. — World Zionist Organization, 1983.

17. _____ . "Ve-Ahavta le-Re'akha ka-Mokha," ibid., 300–04.

18. Lichtenstein, Aharon. "Ve-Ahavta le-Re'akha ha-Mokha." *Alon Shvut-Kesher Tefuzot* 1 (1982): 10–20. A lecture by Rav Lichtenstein reconstructed and prepared for publication by Nathaniel Helfgot.

19. Neuman, Yaakov. "Ahavat Yisrael Mul Sinat Yisrael." *Shanah bi-Shanah* (1983): 283–89.

20. Perlow, Yaakov. "The Nature and Obligation of Ahavas Yisroel: Love for One's Fellow Jew." *The Jewish Observer* 18:2 (1985): 8–13.

21. Schochet, Immanuel J. "Let Sins be Consumed and Not Sinners." *Tradition* 16:4 (1977): 41–61.

22. Shaviv, Yehudah. "Iyunim bi-Mitzvat Ahavat Re'ah." *Alon Shvut—Kesher Tefuzot* 2 (1987): 36–47; reprinted in *idem, Avi'ezer,* 25–32, Alon Shvut: Tzomet, 1990.

23. Soloveichik, Ahron. "Jew and Jew, Jew and Non-Jew." *Jewish Life* 33:5 (1966): 6–22.

24. Spero, Shubert. "The Self and the Other," in *Morality, Halakha and the Jewish Tradition,* 201–23. New York: Ktav/Yeshiva University Press, 1983.

25. Tzuriel, Moshe. "Ha-Mitzvah shel Sinat Resha'im." *Ha-Maayan* 17:4 (1977): 1–4.

26. Unterman, Issar Yehudah. "Gidrei Ahavah ve-Sinah ba-Halakhah u-bi-Mussar ha-Yahadut." *Kol Torah* (1968), 3–9; reprinted in *Shevilin* 20 (1968): 10–17.

II *KIRUV REHOKIM*

1. Avihal, A. "Yahasenu la-Hofshiyim—mi-Mekor Torat ha-Rav Kook." *Bi-Sedei Hemed* 12:3 (1968): 140–45.

2. Brokher, Yaakov. "Ben Haradah le-Tikvah—Hashpaatenu al Tzivyon ha-Medinah ve-Tafkidenu bi-Kiruv Rehokim." *Ha-Maayan* 1 (1953): 25–30.

3. Broyde, Michael, and Hertzberg, David. "Enabling a Jew to Sin: The Parameters." *Journal of Halacha and Contemporary Society* 19 (1990): 7–34.

4. Goren, Shlomo. "Kol Yisrael Arevin Zeh ba-Zeh—le-Or ha-Halakhah." *Mahanayim* 49 (1960): 8–18.

5. Hartman, David. "Halakhah as a Ground for Creating a Shared Spiritual Language." *Tradition* 16:1 (1976): 7–40. This article generated a number of rejoinders and responses by Rabbis Solomon

J. Spiro and Tzvi Marx. See *Tradition* 16:3 (1977):. 50–57; 18:1 (1979): 99–110; 19:1 (1981): 35–41. It was translated in Hebrew as "Ha-Halakhah ke-Basis le-Hidabrut Ruhanit," *De'ot* 46 (1977): 21–29.

6. Karelitz, Yeshayahu. "Hashash Issur Lifnei Iver le-Umat Mitzvat ha-Hesed ve-ha-Shalom." *Ha-Maayan* 12:4 (1972): 73.

7. *Kiruv Levavot.* Tel Aviv, 1967. A Hebrew pamphlet published by the Kibbutz ha-Dati.

8. Levi, Leo. "Limud Torah le-Aherim ve-Kiruv Rehokim." *Ha-Maayan* 20:4 (1980): 3–15; reprinted in *idem, Shaarei Talmud Torah,* 35–54, Jerusalem: Feldheim, 1981.

9. Riskin, Shlomo. "Reaching Out to the Non-Committed." *Jewish Life* 39:4 (1972): 8–12.

10. Scheinberg, Hayyim Pinhas. *Sho'alim bi-Teshuvah.* New Jersey: Association for Jewish Outreach Professionals, 1991.

11. Tekhorsh, Katriel Fishel. "Horaat Torah le-Talmidim she-Enam Mekayimim Mitzvot." *Shemaatin* 9 (1966): 32–34; reprinted 24:90 (1987): 48–50.

12. Weinberg, Yaakov. "They and We are One (On the Obligation of Kiruv)." *Jewish Outreach* 1:1 (1989): 4.

13. Weinberger, Moshe. "Attitudes and Methods in Jewish Outreach." *The Journal of Halacha and Contemporary Society* 20 (1990): 77–110.

14. _____ . *Jewish Outreach: Halakhic Perspectives.* New York: Ktav, 1990.

15. Yisraeli, Shaul. "Be-Gidrei ha-Hovah le-Hahdarat ha-Torah bi-Yisrael." *Ha-Torah ve-ha-Medinah* 9–10 (1958–59): 160–79.

III *TOKHAHAH*

1. Ahituv, Yosef. "Halitehu le-Rasha ve-Yamut – Himanut me-Hatzalat Adam me-Het." *Tehumin* 9 (1989): 156–70.

2. Bar Shaul, Elimelekh. "Tokhahah ve-Ahavah." *Shanah bi-Shanah* (1960): 131–40.

3. Gershuni, Yehudah. "Birurim bi-Mitzvat Tokhahah le-Yahid u-le-Tzibbur." *Ha-Torah ve-ha-Medinah* 9–10 (1958–59): 558–63.

4. _____ . "Bi-Inyan Mitzvat Tokhahah ve-Arvut," in *Sefer ha-Yovel Mugash le-Khevod ha-Rav Dr. Yisrael Elfenbein*, 75–94. Jerusalem: Mossad ha-Rav Kook, 1963.

5. Henkin, Yehudah Hertzl. "Mutav she-Yihiyu Shogegim ve-Al Yihiyu Mezidin." *Tehumin* 2 (1981): 272–80.

6. Kahn, Paul. "Psychotherapy and the Commandment to Reprove." *Proceedings of the Associations of Orthodox Jewish Scientists* 7 (1983): 37–49.

7. Kahn, Yair. "Mitzvat Tokhahah." *Alon Shvut—Kesher Tefutzot* 16 (1989): 26–31; reprinted in *Daf Kesher* 2 (1990): 186–88.

8. Kook, Avraham Yitzhak ha-Kohen. "Arevut ve-Tokhahah." *Tehumin* 5 (1984): 283–84.

9. Kook, Simhah ha-Kohen. "Mitzvat ha-Tokhahah bi-Yahid u-bi-Tzibbur." *Tehumin* 7 (1986): 121–38.

10. Lamm, Norman. "Hokhe'ah Tokhiah et Amitekha." *Gesher* 9 (1985): 170–76; reprinted in *Halakhot ve-Halikhot*, op. cit., 168–75.

11. Levi, Leo. "Mahaah le-Mi she-Eno Rotzeh le-Kablah." *Ha-Maayan* 26:2 (1986): 3–10.

12. _____ . "Mahaah ve-Sinah la-Dat be-Yamenu." *Ha-Maayan* 26:3 (1986): 14–27.

13. Molkho, Moshe. "Hafganot ve-Hasimat Rehovot bi-Shabbat." *Tehumin* 7 (1986): 107–16.

14. _____ . "Hafganot ve-Tokhehot." *Tehumin* 8 (1987): 49–58.

15. Rozen, Yisrael. "Ha-Yesh Issur Lifnei Iver bi-Hafganot bi-Shabbat." *Tehumin* 7 (1986): 139–43.

16. Shlesinger, Eliyahu. "Mahaah al Hillul Shabbat." *Barkai* 4 (1987): 126–32.

17. Strikovsky, Aryeh. "Kiyyum Mitzvat ha-Tokhahah bi-Yamenu." *Siah Mesharim* 16 (1988): 7–8.

18. Zilberstein, Yitzhak. "Ha-Hovah le-Hafgin Neged Hillul Shabbat." *Tehumin* 7 (1986): 117–21.

IV RELATIONSHIP TO NONHALAKHIC JEWS

1. Amital, Yehudah. "Al Maamado shel ha-Yehudi ha-Hiloni bi-Yamenu ve-ha-Hityahasut Elav." *Amudim* 35:10 (498; 1987):

382–89; reprinted in *Alon Shvut – Kesher Tefutzot* 13 (1987): 1–18; *Mamlekhet Kohanim ve-Goy Kadosh*, ed. Yehudah Shaviv, 332–43, Jerusalem, 1988; *Shanah bi-Shanah* (1988): 337–49; translated into English as "A Torah Perspective on the Status of Secular Jews Today," *Tradition* 23:4 (1988): 1–13.

2.   Angel, Marc. "Religious Zionism and the Non-Orthodox," in *Religious Zionism*, ed. Shubert Spero and Yizhak Pessin, 108–20. Jerusalem: Messilot – World Movement of Mizrahi–HaPoel Ha-Mizrahi/Torah Education Dept. – World Zionist Organization, 1989.

3.   Ben-Salma, Zekharyah. "Sovlanut Kelapei ha-Porshim mi-Darkhei ha-Torah ad Hekhan?" *Mi-Safra le-Sefa* 25 (1986): 15–27.

4.   Efrati, Binyamin. *Ha-Senegoriyah bi-Mishnat ha-Rav Kook*. Jerusalem: Mossad ha-Rav Kook, 1959.

5.   Friedman, Natan Tzevi. "Yahasei Datiyim ve-Hiloniyim le-Or ha-Halakhah." *Shanah bi-Shanah* (1967): 110–20.

6.   Grunblatt, Joseph. "Confronting Disbelievers." *Tradition* 23:1 (1987): 33–9.

7.   Katz, Jacob. "Yisrael af al Pi she-Hata, Yisrael Hu." *Tarbiz* 27 (1958): 203–17; reprinted in *idem, Halakhah ve-Kabbalah*, 255–69, Jerusalem: Magnes Press, 1986.

8.   Kirschenbaum, Aaron. "Crisis Halachah and Heterodoxy Today." *Judaism* 14 (1965): 88–91.

9.   Kook, Avraham Yitzhak Ha-Kohen. "Al Bamotenu Hallalim." *Sinai* 17 (1945): 1–5; reprinted in *Zikkaron*, 5–9 Jerusalem: Mossad ha-Rav Kook, 1945; *Maamarei ha-Reiyah*, 89–93, Jerusalem: Keren Katz, 1984.

10.   _____ . *Iggerot ha-Reiyah* 1:58–59, 143–44, 170–72, 368–70; 2:33–35, 142–43, 184–90. Jerusalem: Mossad ha-Rav Kook, 1963.

11.   Moreh, Aharon. "Birur be-Gidrei Tinok she-Nishbah." *Kotlenu* 12 (1987): 52–4.

12.   Morrel, Samuel. "The Halachic Status of Non-Halachic Jews." *Judaism* 18:4 (1969): 448–57.

13.   Riskin, Shlomo. "Orthodoxy and Her Alleged Heretics." *Tradition* 15:4 (1976): 34–44.

14. _____ . "Conflicts Within the Family: Religious and Secular in the State of Israel." *L'Eylah* 24 (1987): 2–5.

15. Shenker, David. "Din ha-Minim ve-ha-Hofshiyim she-bi-Zmanenu." *Ha-Mesivta* (1985): 242–51.

16. Sherman, Avraham. "Yahas ha-Halakhah Kelapei Ahenu she-Parshu mi-Derekh ha-Torah ve-ha-Mitzvot." *Tehumin* 1 (1980): 311–18.

17. _____ . "Yahas ha-Halakhah Kelapei Ahenu she-Parshu mi-Derekh ha-Torah—Helek Sheni: Onaat Devarim." *Tehumin* 2 (1981): 267–71.

18. _____ . "Pikuah Nefesh bi-Shabbat Kelapei ha-Porshim mi-Derekh ha-Torah." *Tehumin* 3 (1982): 24–29.

19. _____ . "The Halachic Approach Towards Non-Observant Jews," in *Crossroads: Halacha and the Modern World*, 11–18. Jerusalem: Tzomet Institute, 1987.

20. "Sovlanut ba-Yahadut—Rav Siah," in *Shenaton ha-Tziyonut ha-Datit*, 64–73. Jerusalem: Messilot—World Movement of Mizrahi–HaPoel MaMizrahi, 1987.

21. Yaron, Tzevi. "Sovlanut," in *Mishnato shel ha-Rav Kook*, 323–71. Jerusalem: Torah Education Dept.—World Zionist Organization, 1974.

22. Zikhel, Meir. "Mehalel Shabbat bi-Farhesya." *Shemaatin* 100 (1990): 227–42.

Contributors

Rabbi Yehuda Amital is Rosh Yeshiva of Yeshivat Har Etzion in Israel.

Dr. Judith Bleich is an Associate Professor of Judaic Studies at Touro College in New York City.

Rabbi Nathaniel Helfgot is on the Judaic Studies faculty of the Frisch Yeshiva High School in Paramus, New Jersey, and is an instructor at the Columbia University Beit Midrash, the Drisha Institute, and the Joseph Shapiro Institute of Lincoln Square Synagogue, all in New York City. He is the author of articles that have appeared in *Tradition, Jewish Action,* and *Tehumin.*

Dr. Ephraim Kanarfogel is Chairman of the Rebecca Ivry Department of Jewish Studies and Assistant Professor of Jewish History at Stern College for Women in New York City. He is the author of

Jewish Education and Society in the High Middle Ages (Wayne State University Press, 1991), as well as numerous articles in the areas of medieval Jewish intellectual history and rabbinic literature.

Dr. Norman Lamm is Jakob and Erna Michael Professor of Jewish Philosophy and President of Yeshiva University in New York City. His latest books are *Torah Umadda: The Encounter of Religious Learning and Worldly Knowledge in the Jewish Tradition* and *Halakhot ve-Halikhot*.

Rabbi Nachum L. Rabinovitch is Rosh Yeshiva of Yeshivat Birkat Moshe in Maaleh Adumim, Israel. He is the author of *Yad Peshutah* on Maimonides' *Mishneh Torah*, of which five volumes have already been published, as well as many articles on halakhic subjects. He served as rabbi and educator in America and England before moving to Israel.

Dr. Jacob J. Schacter is Rabbi of The Jewish Center in New York City and editor of *The Torah u-Madda Journal*.

Index